ADMINISTRATION POSTALE DES NATIONS UNIES
GRAND PRIX DE L'ART PHILATÉLIQUE
GROTE PRIJS VOOR FILATELISCHE KUNST
7-8.12.74
brussel bruxelles

COCOS (KEELING) ISLANDS
FIRST DAY OF ISSUE

EXPOSITION PHILATELIQUE INTERNATIONALE
PHILEXFRANCE 82
11 AU 21 JUIN 1982
CNIT - PARIS LA DÉFENSE
LA ROCHELLE GARE   2-1-82
82
PHILEXFRANCE

17 LA ROCHELLE GARE
10H45
2-1
1982
CHARENTE MME

ADMINISTRATION POSTALE DES NATIONS UNIES
COLMAR
1-3.6.1974
EXPOSITION NATIONALE

JOHANNESBURG
15·3·1976

UNITED NATIONS, NY 10017
HUMAN ENVIRONMENT
MAR. 19. 1982 · FIRST DAY OF ISSUE

89058 SCILLA (RC)
30·3·1979
Giorno di emissione
Veduta panoramica

CINQUANTENAIRE TIMBRES CARITAS
5
12
74
LUXEMBOURG

Norsk Folkedans
Oslo · 25-2-1976

1211 GENÈVE
PREMIER JOUR
28.5.76
CONFÉRENCE DES NATIONS UNIES SUR LES ÉTABLISSEMENTS HUMAINS
ADMINISTRATION POSTALE DES NATIONS UNIES

KØBENHAVN V
28 MAJ   1970
POSTENS FILATELI
FRIMÆRKETS UDGIVELSESDAG

BERLIN 12
100 JAHRE BERLINER PHILHARMONISCHES ORCHESTER
1882-1982
15.04.1982
1000
ERSTAUSGABETAG

BRANDS HATCH
GRAND PRIX OF EUROPE
15 July 72
DARTFORD, KENT

WALVISBAAI BAY
1978·03·10

REYKJAVÍK
11. XI.   1975
DAGUR FRÍMERKISINS

BAILE ÁTHA CLIATH
4·XI
FOUR PENCE
AUSTRALIA   WESTERN
POSTAGE
1977
STAMPA '77

TVØROYRI
29.9.   1977
ÚTGÁVUDAGIN

XXII NYÁRI OLIMPIAI JÁTÉKOK
MOSZKVA
BUDAPEST 4. 1980. VI. 19.

3000 BERN
PRO JUVENTUTE · AUSGABETAG 29.11.74

4th CENTENARY CELEBRATIONS
हल्दीघाटी
HALDIGHATI
21-6-76

स्वतंत्रता के उज्ज्वल प्रतीक—महाराणा प्रताप
अनुपम वीरता का रण-स्थल — हल्दीघाटी

MAHARANA PRATAP—LUMINOUS SPIRIT OF FREEDOM
HALDIGHATI—BATTLE OF LEGENDRY CHIVALRY

ACU INTERNATIONAL T.T. RACES
5 JUN 1976
UNION MILLS   ISLE OF MAN

THE GUINNESS BOOK OF
STAMPS
FACTS & FEATS

James Mackay

GUINNESS BOOKS

Editor: Honor Head

Published in Great Britain by
Guinness Publishing Ltd, 33 London Road,
Enfield, Middlesex EN2 6DJ

British Library Cataloguing in Publication Data

Typeset by Crawley Composition Ltd in Bembo
Printed and bound in Yugoslavia by Mladinska Knjiga, Ljubljana

CONTENTS

ACKNOWLEDGEMENTS

I wish to thank the following individuals and organisations for their assistance in the compilation of this book: Ministry of Communications, Kabul, Afghanistan; the Head Postmaster, Aitutaki, Artimpex, Tirana, Albania; the Ministry of Communications, Buenos Aires, Argentina; the Philatelic Bureau, Melbourne, Victoria and the Director of Public Relations, Australian Post Office Headquarters, Melbourne, Australia; Österreichische Post und Briefmarkenversandstelle, Vienna, Austria; the Press Information Service, Ministry of Posts, Nassau, Bahamas; Service des Collectionneurs, Administration des Postes, Brussels, Belgium; Bangladesh Action Public Relations, London; the Bhutan Stamp Agency, Nassau, Bahamas; The Philatelic Bureau, GPO, Bahrain; Administracao Central, Empresa Brasileira de Correios e Telegrafos, Rio de Janeiro, Brazil; Filatelia, Sofia, Bulgaria; Agence Philatelique, Bujumbura, Burundi; the Canadian Philatelic Service, Ottawa, Canada; James Hu and the Philatelic Department of the Directorate General of Posts, Taipei, Republic of China; Direccion Nacional de Correos y Telecommunicaciones, Santiago, Chile; Philatelic Bureau, Ministry of Posts, Rarotonga, Cook Islands; Officina Filatelica, San Jose, Costa Rica; the Philatelic Division of the Ministry of Communications, Havana, Cuba; the Department of Posts, Ministry of Communications and Works, Nicosia, Cyprus; Artia Philatelic Department, Prague, Czechoslovakia; Postens Filateli, Copenhagen, Denmark; the Philatelic Office, Cairo, Egypt; the Philatelic Agency of Ethiopia, Rwanda and Tunisia, Brussels, Belgium; the General Direction of Posts and Telegraphs, Helsinki, Finland; Service Philatelique (France and Andorra), Paris; Agence Philatelique d'Outremer, Paris; Post-Zentrales Postverkehrsamt, Berlin, German Democratic Republic; Bundesministerium für das Post und Fernmeldewesen, Bonn, West Germany; Deutsche Bundespost Landespostdirektion, West Berlin; the Philatelic Service, Athens, Greece; Agence Philatelique, Conakry, Guinea; Philatelia Hungarica, Budapest, Hungary (Hungary and Mongolia); Frimerkjasalan, Reykjavik, Iceland; the Postal Service Philatelic Section, Bandung, Indonesia; Ufficio Filatelico Centrale, Amministrazione delle Poste e delle Telecomunicazioni, Rome, Italy; the Philatelic Services, Tel Aviv-Yafo, Israel; the Philatelic Information Service, Department of Post and Telegraphs, GPO Dublin, Republic of Ireland; the Office of the Director General, Posts and Telegraphs, New Delhi, India; the Philatelic Agency, Tokyo Central Post Office, Japan; Korean Publications Export and Import Company, Pyongyang, D P R Korea; the Philatelic Agency, Central Post Office, Seoul, South Korea; the Post Office Department, Monrovia, Liberia; Official Philatelic Service, Vaduz, Liechtenstein; Direction des Postes, Office des Timbres, Luxembourg; Oficina Filatélica Mexicana, Mexico City, Mexico; Office des Emissions de Timbres-Poste, Monaco; Filatelistische Dienst Netherlands; the Philatelic Bureau, Wanganui, New Zealand; the Philatelic Bureau, Willemstad, Curacao, Netherlands Antilles; Department of Posts and Telecommunications, Vila, Vanuatu; Oficina de Control de Especies Postales y Filatelia, Managua, Nicaragua; the Philatelic Bureau, Niue; Postens Filatelitjeneste, Oslo, Norway; the Head Postmaster, Penrhyn Island, Cook Islands; the Manager of the Philatelic Bureau, Port Moresby, Papua New Guinea; the Bureau of Posts, Stamps and Philatelic Division, Manila, Philippines; Export and Import Enterprise 'Ruch', Warsaw, Poland; Reparticao de Filatelia, Lisbon, Portugal; the Philatelic Bureau, Harare, Zimbabwe; Rompresfilatelia, Bucarest, Romania; Mezhdunarodnaya Kniga, Moscow, USSR; St Vincent Philatelic Services, St Vincent, West Indies; Philatelic Bureau, GPO Apia, Samoa; The Philatelic Section, GPO Freetown, Sierra Leone; the Philatelic Bureau, GPO Singapore; Ufficio Filatelico, San Marino; The Philatelic Bureau, Pretoria, Republic of South Africa; Direccion General de Correos y Telecomunicaciones, Madrid, Spain; the Philatelic Bureau, P & T Department, Colombo, Sri Lanka; Directorate of Posts Philatelic Office, Damascus, Syria; the Director General, Department of PTT, Khartoum, Sudan; the General Directorate of Posts, Stamps Division, Stockholm, Sweden; General Directorate of PTT, Philatelic Office, Berne, Switzerland; Philatelic Promotion Centre, Post & Telegraph Department, Bangkok, Thailand; Ministère des Transports et des Communications, Tunis; PTT Isletme Genel Mudurlugu, Posta Dairesi Baskanligi, Filateli Servisi, Ankara, Turkey; the Stamp Section, GPO Nuku'alofa, Tonga; UN Postal Administration, Palais des Nations, Geneva, Switzerland; US Post Office Department, Washington, DC, USA; Xunhasaba Philatelic Department, Hanoi, DR Vietnam; Ministerio de Comunicaciones, Oficina Filatelica Nacional, Caracas, Venezuela.

Special thanks are due to John Hayball and the staff of 'H' Division, the Crown Agents, Sutton; Mike Orbell and David Luke of the Jersey Postal Administration, St Helier, Jersey; J J Bonar and the staff of the British Philatelic Bureau, Edinburgh; Mrs Jean Farrugia, Mrs Celia Constantinides and the staff of Post Office Archives, London; Victor Kneale, George Christian and Peter Newbold of the Isle of Man Postal Authority; and Sam Malamud of the Inter-Governmental Philatelic Corporation, New York, NY, USA.

I am also indebted to Kathleen Wowk, Press Office of Stanley Gibbons, Michael C Goodman, Prince Dimitry Kandaouroff, the late Halley Grant of Edinburgh, IDC Construction of Stratford-upon-Avon, Herbert Wachtel and P. Spek.

The author and publishers wish to acknowledge the following sources of illustrations: Birmingham Evening Post 25; Bradbury Wilkinson & Co Ltd 192, 193; British Film Institute 218; Edinburgh City Libraries 47; Mrs Sheila Goldsmith 170; Arthur Guinness Son & Co Ltd 33; Harrison & Sons Ltd 93, 94, 195, 196, 202; Michael Holford 7; Illustrated London News 27, 32 (right and lower), 34, 73, 187, 209; Pitney-Bowes 65 (lower), 66 (lower); the Post Office 16, 17, 23, 29, 30, 35 (lower), 70, 95, 96, 177; Stanley Gibbons Limited 76, 214, 215, 216, 217; United States Postal Service 68, 69 (upper); Wiggins Teape (Mill Sales) Ltd 204 (lower right); Peter Wilson 178. They also wish to thank especially for help and assistance: Janet Adams of Action Lines Business Consultants; F R Coe and his colleagues of Bradbury Wilkinson & Co Ltd; John Goodhind and Alan Greene of Hale Paper Company; Derrick Howlett and Steve Green of Harrison & Sons Limited, Malcolm Hardstaff, Head of Biology Department, Marlborough College and Nigel Fitt of the Post Office.

PREFACE

Books about stamps generally fall into two categories. There are the catalogues which list and price stamps in chronological order of issue, and there are the books which range from beginners' manuals to learned treatises dealing with every aspect of a single stamp issue. This book is totally different, being concerned with the facts and feats of philately, the 'firsts', records, largest, smallest, rarest, the oddities and extravagances, the bizarre and the esoteric in stamps and the postal services of the world.

Many of the old orthodoxies have been examined, explored anew and rejected. Which country *really* issued the first commemorative? Who was the first stamp collector? Who, indeed, deserves the last word as the inventor of the adhesive postage stamp? Which is the world's smallest post office? These and many other facts have been carefully gone into, but whether I have succeeded in settling these controversies the reader alone must decide.

The scope of this book is rather broader than the title might suggest, since it encompasses the development of postal services over the past 5000 years. Though I endorse the philatelist's slogan 'The stamp's the thing', I have not neglected postal history – postal markings, the modes of mail transportation and aspects of postal administration.

Postage stamps are among the most familiar of everyday objects. Everyone handles and licks them and, I hope, spares them more than a passing glance. Many of us also collect them and quite a few study them in the greatest detail. This book is aimed at everyone, from the most advanced philatelist, who will discover many aspects of the subject beyond his own speciality, to the layman who has not hitherto stopped to think of these bits of coloured paper as a form of minuscule art, or appreciated the prodigious organisation involved in getting the mail to his letter-box from the ends of the earth.

This book has shown stamps and postal services in a new light. Inevitably, with a pioneering work of this kind, there will be errors of commission and omission. In a book which is concerned primarily with superlatives, every fact stated therein is open to debate, every record liable to be broken. The very nature of these facts is a challenge to readers to disprove them or go one better. After many years engaged in philatelic research I have come to the conclusion that the last word can never be written on this complex and fascinating subject. In particular, where I have provided lists (the world's rarest stamps, multilingual stamps, the most popular themes, the most prolific countries, the most industrious designers), readers will, I hope, be encouraged to compile further lists of their own.

The Postal Services

The oldest postal services in the world were established in China about 4000 BC and in Egypt and Assyria by 3000 BC. Like the Chinese, the Egyptian service, organised during the Third Dynasty, was used mainly by court officials, while that in Assyria was apparently open to the merchant classes as well as officers of state. There is strong evidence to suggest that a well-regulated service existed between Egypt and Syria (whose princes were vassals of the Pharaohs) and between the rulers of Assyria and Babylon. Correspondence has been preserved between the king of the Mitanni (in upper Syria) and Amenophis IV, King of Egypt, containing condolences on the death of the Pharaoh's father.

The earliest surviving letters consisted of clay tablets in cuneiform (wedge-shaped) script, baked and hardened, and inserted in clay envelopes. They were transmitted by the royal court, merchants and private individuals in Cappadocia (Asia Minor) and date from 3000 to 1500 BC. The largest hoard of these tablets, discovered by the Czech archaeologist Bedrich Hrozny in 1925, was found at Kültepe (Kanesh) near Kayseri, SE of Ankara in Turkey and contained examples dating back beyond 2000 BC.

The earliest references to postal services of any kind are to be found in the Old Testament. Nehemiah 2: 7–9, states: 'Moreover, I said unto the king. If it pleases the king, let letters be given me to the governors beyond the river, that they may convey me over till I come into Judah; And a letter unto Asaph the keeper of the king's forest . . . Then I came to the governors beyond the river, and gave them the king's letters.' This took place 'in the month Nisan in the twentieth year of Artaxerxes the king' (i.e., c 446 BC).

Esther 3: 12–15 states: 'Then were the king's scribes called on the thirteenth day of the first month, and there was written according to all that Haman had commanded unto the king's lieutenants, and to the governors that were over every province,

Cuneiform (wedge-shaped) writing on a
Sumerian clay tablet

and to the rulers of every people of every province according to the writing thereof, and to every people after their language; in the name of king Ahasuerus was it written, and sealed with the king's ring.

'And the letters were sent by posts into all the king's provinces to destroy, to kill and to cause to perish all Jews, both young and old, little children and women . . . The posts went out, being hastened by the king's commandment, and the decree was given in Shushan the palace.'

Further on, in Esther 8: 10–14, it is written: 'And he wrote in the king Ahasuerus' name, and sealed it with the king's ring, and letters were sent by mounted couriers riding on horses from the royal stables.

The oldest postal relay service in the world was organised by Cyrus the Great, ruler of the Persian Empire, in 539 BC. The Greek historian Herodotus (*c* 484–425 BC) gives a vivid description of this system in his *Histories*: 'Nothing is more expeditious than the method of transmitting messages, invented and used by the Persians. Along each route, at regular intervals equal to one day's journey, were relays of men and horses, housed in stations specially set up for the purpose. Snow, rain, cold or darkness could not prevent the messengers carrying on their work with the greatest speed. The first man to arrive passed the despatches to the second, who then passed them on to a third, and so on, until the despatches arrived at their destination . . . In the Persian language these relays were known as *angareion*.'

This was confirmed by the historian Xenophon (430–*c* 350 BC), in his *Cyropedia*, VIII, 6: 'Here is another invention of Cyrus, very helpful in the government of his vast empire, as it brought prompt information from every part of his dominions. Stables were set up at intervals equal to the distance which a horse could travel in a day without becoming exhausted; each stable had horses and grooms to look after them. He appointed to each station an intelligent man who would deliver to one courier the letters brought by another; who would provide rest and refreshment for the tired couriers and horses, and who would control the finances.

The Cursus Publicus, on an Italian stamp of 1976

Moreover, night did not hold back the progress of these messengers; a messenger who arrived by day would be replaced by another who would travel by night. They seemed faster than the flight of birds. It is no exaggeration to say that no other men could travel more rapidly across the earth.'

The largest postal network in classical times operated in China for the use of the imperial court and their civil servants. At the time of the visit of Marco Polo in the thirteenth century it operated from Peking to every corner of the empire, and had over 25,000 relay stations. The general public, however, were not permitted to use the service, under severe penalty, until 1879.

The longest postal route in classical times ran from Sardis to Susa, via Ancyra, Melitene, Arteba and Calonne, via oases across the Iranian desert. It was 1550 miles *2500 km* long, had 111 relay stations, and took a horse messenger 5 days or a foot mesenger 90 days to cover.

The oldest known illustration of a postal vehicle is a bas-relief *c* 250 BC from the Igel Column at Trier, in W Germany, and shows a two-wheeled vehicle of the Cursus Publicus (the Roman postal service), capable of carrying up to about 450 lb *200 kg* of mail.

The oldest postal guide is contained in the Goblets of Vicarello (*c* first century AD), otherwise known as the Apollinaire Vases – four silver goblets about 4 in *10 cm* high, discovered in 1852 in an old spa north of Rome. They bear engraved on their sides the names of the relay stations between Cadiz and Rome and their intervening distances.

The oldest postal map, known as the Peutinger Tables, dates from the late fourth century AD. A 13th century copy is preserved in the National Library of Vienna. Compiled by a monk at Colmar, it shows the Roman postal routes from the Indus Valley to Britain, with the *mansiones* (post stages) and *mutationes* (relay stations) clearly marked.

The earliest postal regulations date from the fourth century AD and concern the running of the Cursus Publicus, or Roman imperial postal system. Overall control was vested in the Prefect of the Praetorian Guard who was directly responsible to the Emperor himself. The *curiosi* (postal surveyors or inspectors) checked the smooth operation of the posts and ensured that the regulations were strictly adhered to. The day-to-day running of the service was the responsibility of the *praefectus vehiculorum* (transport chief) in each province. Each postal station was headed by the *stationarius* (postmaster) who administered the postillions, ostlers, blacksmiths and other staff and kept records of arrivals and departures. The *tabellarii* (messengers) carried the mails, varying both routes and working hours to suit themselves. The state was responsible for the upkeep of roads, and postal vehicles, and the salaries of the personnel, but each district was responsible for the maintenance of the relay stations. The Roman system fell into decay in the fifth century, although parts of it survived in the Visigothic kingdom of Spain (sixth century) and in the dominions of Charlemagne (eighth century).

The earliest writing materials consisted of baked clay (noted above), from 3000 BC till about 1000 BC. Papyrus, a form of translucent paper made from overlapping strips of pith from the stem of a reed, was used by the Egyptians from about 1200 BC. It was adopted by the Greeks and Romans and used by them till the sixth century AD. Wax tablets known as *codicilli*, were used by the Romans in the pre-Christian era, and thin shavings of wood were popularly used for letters in Roman imperial times. Animal skins were also used by the Greeks in pre-Christian times. Parchment, said to have been invented at Pergamum in Asia Minor, and consisting of specially tanned calf, goat, or sheep skin, was widely used in Europe from the sixth to the fifteenth centuries. Birchbark was used by the Russians in the eleventh and twelfth centuries, and has been used in more recent times in Canada.

Paper was first used as writing material by the Chinese in the second century BC. Its use spread overland to western Asia by the mid-eighth century AD and the Arabs are known to have manufactured paper by AD 751, using flax fibres and later cotton. From Asia Minor the use of paper spread to Greece and the Byzantine Empire in the late eleventh century. The Empress Irene is reputed to have used paper about that time, although the earliest extant Greek manuscript on paper dates from the mid-thirteenth century. It was first manufactured in Europe by the Moors of Spain in the twelfth century and came to Italy by way of Sicily during the Arab occupation. The oldest European document made of paper is a deed of King Roger of Sicily dated 1102. The earliest letter written on paper is dated *c* AD 1216 and is preserved in the Public Record Office, London. It was written by Raymond, Duke of Narbonne, to King Henry III of England. Paper was widely used for letters by the early fourteenth century, and rapidly superseded parchment.

Blotting paper is known from 1465, and was made of coarse, grey, unsized paper, yet sand continued to be popular as a drying agent until the eighteenth century. Brown paper for wrapping parcels is known from 1570.

The earliest envelopes were the clay outer shells which encapsulated the clay tablets of the Assyrians and Egyptians, 3000 BC. Letters written on animal skins and parchment were invariably rolled up and bound with narrow leather thongs (often strips from the same piece of skin) and sealed with wax. With the advent of paper, letters were folded so that the outer side could bear the address and any other superscription such as postal directions, the flaps being secured by sealing wax. This practice survived in Europe till the 1860s and even later in other parts of the world.

The first paper envelopes were hand-made and consisted of sheets cut and folded over the letter with four overlapping corners closed at the back with a blob of sealing wax. Machine-made envelopes were produced in France as far back as 1790, but were unpopular as their use effectively doubled the postal rate charged. Only from 1840 onwards, when the charging of postage according to the number of sheets was abolished, did envelopes gradually come into more general use. Nevertheless, the custom of sealing a letter by folding the outer portion of the sheet and securing it with a gummed wafer or sealing wax did not die out in Britain till the late 1850s. Postally-used envelopes before 1840 are rare and highly prized by collectors.

The earliest international posts of the Middle Ages were organised by trade guilds for their members. Among the first – if not *the* first – was the Metzger Post organised by the guild of butchers in Germany in the twelfth century. One of the conditions attached to the privilege of setting up as a butcher was the possession of a horse and undertaking to carry mail. To the butchers' guild is given the credit for having first used a curved horn to announce the arrival of the mails – the posthorn which features in many of the emblems of the postal services of the world to this day. The Metzger Post survived till 1637, when it was absorbed into the official service of the Holy Roman Empire. Thereafter it continued until the late 18th century.

Medieval royal couriers, on stamps of France (1962) and Belgium (1957)

By 1301 the Florentine merchants' guild, known as *Arte dei Mercanti di Calimala* (the drapers' society) had organised a postal service operating between Florence and the major trade fairs in France. Members of the guild paid a levy to their messenger, known as the *scarcelliere* (from the *scarcella* or saddle-bag containing the letters).

Monastic posts, operating between the monasteries, abbeys and convents of the great religious orders and their headquarters in Italy and France, were organised from the beginning of the twelfth century. The monastic messenger was known as a *rotularius* or *rotuliger*, from the roll (*rotula*) of parchment containing messages. These rolls contained letters and replies and consisted of numerous pieces of parchment sewn end to end, as the roll circulated from monastery to monastery. Such a roll might take several months to go the rounds and would be extremely bulky by the end of its journey. The roll announcing the death of the Abbess Matilda (daughter of William the Conqueror) in 1113 was over 65 ft *20 m* long and had been to 252 religious houses. Monastic rolls of this type continued till the mid-sixteenth century.

Postal services operating between the medieval universities were organised from the beginning of the thirteenth century. The students were grouped into 'nations', each of which had its messenger maintaining regular communications with the appropriate country. Thus the English nation at the Sorbonne despatched messengers to London, Oxford, Dublin, Glasgow, Edinburgh, Aberdeen, Bergen, Uppsala, Cracow, Hungary, Courland, Bohemia, Moravia, Pomerania, Silesia and the German principalities. The university posts differed from the other early systems in that they were usually permitted to carry private correspondence from the general public. The revenue derived from these posts defrayed the salaries of the teaching staff. These university posts survived in central Europe till the eighteenth century.

The world's oldest municipal post was organised

by the Hanseatic League in Bremen by the middle of the twelfth century. Bremen was eventually the centre of the Hanseatic network, from which routes went via Hamburg to Lübeck and via Rostock and Stettin (Szczecin) to Danzig (Gdansk).

The claim is sometimes made on behalf of Strasbourg, but the earliest reference to its civic messenger service (*Laufferboten*) only dates from 1322.

The longest surviving international service, dating from the Middle Ages to modern times, was operated by the Counts of Thurn and Taxis. This family, one of the oldest and noblest in Europe, traced its origins back to an ancestor who won the surname della Torre (of the tower) for his heroic defence of a tower during a siege of Milan in the late fourth century. This name was rendered in French *de la Tour* and in German *von Thurn*. The name Taxis was derived from another ancestor, Tacius, whose memory is perpetuated in the Monte degli Tassi near Bergamo, and rendered in French as Tassis. Count Roger I of Thurn and Taxis established a relay-service of posts linking northern Italy and the Tyrol and was knighted by the Emperor Frederick III for his services in 1450. Francis I was appointed 'Captain and Master of our Posts' by Philip I, Archduke of Austria, in 1501. Four years later Philip, now king of Spain, signed a postal treaty in Brussels establishing a courier service between Spain, the Low Countries, France and Germany. In 1506 a route linking Mechelin (Malines) in Belgium with Innsbruck in Austria was established. Later members of the family rose in power as their postal network expanded. Leonard I was appointed Chief Postmaster of the German Empire by Rudolf II. In 1574, when Prince Lamoral I was appointed Grand Master of the Posts, the service was thrown open to the general public and no longer restricted to state correspondence. The postal network of Thurn and Taxis continued to expand throughout the seventeenth and eighteenth centuries, despite such setbacks as the Thirty Years War (1618–48). At the height of their power the

Francis (1450-1517), Baptista (1476-1541) and Leonard I (1523-1612), Counts of Thurn and Taxis, on Belgian stamps of 1952

Thurn and Taxis family operated a service which stretched from the Baltic to the Adriatic and from Poland to the Straits of Gibraltar. By that time the service was yielding an annual profit of 4 000 000 livres. The family had 20 000 employees, thousands of horses and carriages and a considerable amount of property (including the palace in Frankfurt am Main housing the Diet of the German Confederation).

Their supranational power was broken by Napoleon who permitted the states of the Rhine Confederation to establish their own postal services. Although their privileges were restored by the Congress of Vienna they could not withstand the relentless march of national postal progress. By 1850 their operation had been reduced to three grand duchies, three duchies and a handful of petty principalities – Bremen, (till 1855), Camburg, Gotha, Hamburg (till 1859), Hesse-Kassel, Lippe-Detmold, Lübeck (till 1859), Reuss, Saxe-Weimar-Eisenach, Schaumburg-Lippe, Schwarzburg-Sondershausen, Coburg, Frankfurt, Hesse-Darmstadt, Hesse-Homburg, Hohenzollern-Hechingen, Hohenzollern-Sigmaringen, Nassau, Saxe-Meiningen and Schwarzburg-Rudolstadt. This medieval anachronism actually issued stamps for use

Stamps of Thurn and Taxis, 1865 rouletted series

in these areas, from 1852 till 1867. The princely family of Thurn and Taxis backed Austria in the Seven Weeks' War and paid the penalty by being forced by the victorious Prussia to sell its postal monopoly, in 1867, for 3 000 000 thalers. Prince Maximilian Charles, Count of Thurn and Taxis, was the last hereditary Grand Master of the Posts and died in 1871. The family postal service had lasted over 420 years.

The oldest state post of modern times, permitting the circulation of private correspondence, was founded by King Louis XI of France, by an edict of 19 June 1464.

In England, Sir Brian Tuke was appointed Master of the Posts in 1516, but private correspondence was not permitted till 1581. Ten years later the circulation of private correspondence going abroad by unofficial means was expressly forbidden.

In Portugal, Luis Homem was appointed Grand

Master of the Posts in 1520. The service was gradually extended to the general public throughout the sixteenth century, but did not become fully public until the government took over the service in 1798. In Italy the Duke of Savoy appointed Messer Scaramuccia as Postmaster General on 10 January

Fouquet de la Varane, who opened the French state posts to the general public about 1598

1561, later elevated to the title of General of the Posts and Admiral of the Po.

A state monopoly on the carriage of private mail destined for overseas, first hinted at in an ordinance of 1591, was fully instituted on 10 March 1604, in the reign of King James I. An inland service, under Thomas Witherings, was established in 1635.

Public postal services were established in other European countries in the seventeenth century: Denmark and Holland – 1624; Russia – 1630; Sweden – 1636; Finland – 1638; and Norway – 1647.

The first public postal service in America was established on 5 November 1639, when Richard Fairbanks of Boston was appointed Postmaster of the Massachusetts Bay Colony. Postal services were organised in the other English colonies: Virginia (1657), New York (1672), Connecticut (1674), Philadelphia (1683) and New Hampshire (1683). The postal service became a parliamentary monopoly on 17 February 1692. In the previous year Thomas Neale was appointed first Deputy Postmaster General (i.e., under the Postmaster General in London) and charged with the handling of all mails arriving from overseas and destined for the various European settlements in North America.

The first internal postal network in America was established in 1693 by the father and son, Duncan and John Campbell, who organised the service as an adjunct to their newspaper, *The Boston Newsletter*, which circulated widely in the American colonies. Every 15 days they despatched a courier from Boston bound for New York and another from New York to Boston, delivering mail *en route* and exchanging mailbags at Say Brook. Other services developed in the eighteenth century: Philadelphia to Newport, Virginia – 1737; Philadelphia to New York – 1742; Albany to Boston – 1760. By 1792 the four main routes (Boston–Albany, New York–Connecticut, Baltimore–Annapolis and Philadelphia–Pittsburgh) were being operated by concessionaires on 7-year leases.

The oldest public postal service in the British Commonwealth dates from 1487 and was organised by the Venetians in Cyprus for the use of the Knights Templar and the merchant classes. The service ceased in 1570 when Cyprus fell to the Turks.

The first attempts to facilitate the international handling of mail, whereby one country would accept the prepaid correspondence of another, were made by Canada and the United States on 1 June 1792. By the terms of a postal convention which came into effect on that date letters from Canada to addresses in the United States could be prepaid all the way. Hitherto postage could only be paid to the 'lines' (the frontier) and the amount of the American postage had to be recovered from the recipient. The Canadian Post Office acted as agent for the US Post Office and got a 20 per cent discount on the American postage it collected. The US Post Office, however, declined to act for Canada and therefore American mail destined for Canada could only be prepaid as far as the lines, as before. When the United States introduced stamps in 1847 the Canadian Post Office ceased to collect the American postage. Henceforward letters from Canada to the United States had to bear American stamps (covering the postage from the lines) and be prepaid in cash to cover the postage to the lines. This cumbersome and retrograde system was abolished in 1851 when Canada itself adopted stamps and a new convention between the United States, the United Kingdom and British North America was arranged, enabling postage to be prepaid in cash or stamps all the way from one country to the other.

Both Britain and France had extensive commercial interests in many overseas countries and solved the problem to some extent merely by establishing their own post offices and postal agencies in these countries (see below). The Anglo-French postal convention of 1843 governed the complex structure of mail transmission by British and French ships to many parts of the world. A series of accountancy marks was employed to distinguish letters originating overseas, addressed to France and transmitted via Britain, or some other combination of factors. The convention was modified in 1846 and 1855, the latter permitting the reciprocal acceptance of mail bearing adhesive stamps. Complex postal conventions and bilateral postal treaties continued to be negotiated between two or more countries until the formation of the General Postal Union in 1874.

The first international postal union was negotiated between Austria and a number of German states in 1850. It was subscribed to by Austria-Hungary, Baden, Bavaria, Brunswick, Hanover, Oldenburg, Prussia, Saxony, Thurn and Taxis and Württemberg, as well as the North Italian principalities of Modena, Parma and Tuscany which were then in the Austrian sphere of influence. As part of the agreement the stamps issued by these countries were more or less standardised as to colours for each rate. Baden, Thurn and Taxis and Württemberg actually referred to the German-Austrian Convention in the inscription of their stamps.

The postal union was severely disrupted by the Italian campaigns of 1859-60 and came to an end during the Seven Weeks' War between Austria and Prussia (1866). It was partially superseded by the North German Postal Confederation (1867). The experience gained in organising this Confederation, and the subsequent unification of the German postal services when the various states were absorbed into the new German Empire (1871–2) enabled Heinrich von Stephan, the Prussian Postmaster General, to

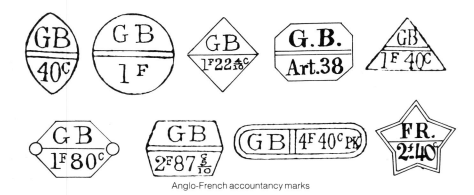

Anglo-French accountancy marks

put forward the proposals which led to the foundation of the General Postal Union in 1874, renamed the Universal Postal Union in 1878.

The first attempt at a world-wide postal union was made in 1863 when the Paris Postal Conference was convened under the chairmanship of Montgomery Blair, Postmaster General of the United States. It was attended by delegates from Austria, Belgium, Costa Rica, Denmark, Ecuador, France, Great Britain, Italy, the Netherlands, Portugal, Prussia, Spain, Switzerland, the United States, Hawaii and the Hanseatic League. The conference was held in the Hôtel des Postes, Paris from 11 May to 8 June 1863 and though it did not come to any practical conclusion it shed light on the problems of international mail handling. Many of the postal conventions and bilateral treaties made after 1863 were inspired by the resolutions of this conference. Montgomery Blair, pre-occupied by the problems of mail handling during the American Civil War, was unable to take the matter further and a decade elapsed before the idea was revived, early in 1873, by Heinrich von Stephan who drew up an agenda for a postal conference. This was duly convened at Berne, Switzerland on 15 September 1874 and attended by delegates from 22 countries. All of the countries involved in 1863 (except Costa Rica) took part, and in addition Egypt, Greece, Hungary, Luxembourg, Norway, Romania, Russia, Serbia, Sweden and Turkey sent delegates. An agreement was reached on 9 October, ratified at Berne on 5 May 1875. The terms of the union came into effect on 1 July 1875, except in France, where the matter, referred to the French parliament for deliberation, was delayed some 6 months.

The first country to join the General Postal Union after the founder members was British India, in July 1876, followed shortly by the French colonies, Brazil, the Spanish colonies and Dutch overseas possessions.

The name Universal Postal Union was adopted at the second conference, held in Paris in 1878 and attended by delegates from 38 countries. The Universal Postal Union now embraces virtually every country and postal administration in the world, and is the only international organisation to have continued to operate smoothly for over a century, despite two world wars and other major upheavals. At the Paris conference in 1947 it was decided that the UPU should become a specialised agency of the United Nations. Its permanent headquarters is located in Berne. The UPU has issued is own distinctive stamps, under the aegis of the Swiss PTT, since 1957.

Stamps of Baden and Württemberg, 1851, containing a reference to the German-Austrian Postal Convention in their inscription

Heinrich von Stephan, founder of the UPU (1831-97)

Montgomery Blair, proponent of the Paris Postal Conference of 1863

The Hotel des Postes, Paris, venue of the 1863 conference

The first international organisation to issue its own stamps was the League of Nations. Swiss stamps overprinted SOCIÉTÉ DES NATIONS were introduced in 1922 and used from the League's headquarters in Geneva.

The Swiss subsequently overprinted stamps for use by the International Labour Office (1923), the International Education Office (1944), the World Health Organisation (1948), the International Refugees Organisation (1950), the World Meteorological Organisation (1956), the Universal Postal Union (1957), and the International Telecommunications Union (1958).

Stamps for use at the United Nations European

The UPU Monument, Berne

Swiss 5fr stamp overprinted for use at the
League of Nations, Geneva

headquarters in Geneva were issued under the aegis of the Swiss PTT from 1950 to 1969. Since then stamps have been issued by the Geneva headquarters in its own right. Distinctive stamps have been issued by the United Nations in New York since 1951, and in similar designs by its Vienna office since 1979. In addition, the United Nations has issued stamps in Belgian currency, for use at the UN pavilion at the Brussels World Fair (1958), and in Canadian currency for use at the Montreal Expo (1967).

Special stamps have been issued by the Netherlands for the exclusive use of the Hague Court of Justice since 1934, and by France for the European Council at Strasbourg since 1958 and for the United Nations Educational, Scientific and Cultural Organisation (UNESCO) in Paris since 1961.

The only country to have had a dual system of stamps issued by two administrations in identical designs, but different languages, was the New Hebrides, under the terms of the Anglo-French Condominium established in 1906. The first issue, in 1908, consisted of Fijian stamps overprinted in English and stamps of New Caledonia overprinted in French. From 1911 till 1980 every stamp issued by the British postal administration (except the Coronation commemorative of 1953) was matched by a stamp issued by the French. In most cases identical designs were also used, differing only in the inscriptions and the position of the French and British national emblems. The denomination of these stamps was expressed in gold centimes and francs – the system used for international postal accounting. This practice continued with the earliest issues of Vanuatu, as the New Hebrides became known following the attainment of independence in 1980, but since 1981 stamps have merely been inscribed bilingually, in English and French.

The only country with two entirely separate postal administrations is Andorra, ruled jointly by France and Spain since 1288 (or more correctly, by the Count of Foix and the Bishop of Urgel

Stamps issued by the Netherlands for the International Court of Justice and by France for the Council of Europe and UNESCO

respectively). Today it has two titular heads of state – the President of the French Republic and the Bishop of Urgel. French and Spanish stamps are believed to have been first used in Andorra in 1877, but the UPU subsequently assigned responsibility for Andorra's external mail to Spain. France organised a courier service across the Pyrenees from Andorra between 1887 and 1931. The Spanish post office in Andorra la Vieja was established on 1 January 1928 and distinctive stamps introduced the following March. A rival French post office was opened in Andorra la Vella (same place) on 16 June 1931, similarly equipped with its own distinctive stamps. These stamps, inscribed in Spanish or French, and with values expressed in pesetas or francs respectively, are in use to this day, but confined to external mail.

The only countries to grant their citizens free postage have been Andorra (see above) and Greenland. To this day all local, internal mail in Andorra is transmitted free through the post. Prior to December 1938 both internal mail and letters from Greenland to Denmark were transmitted free of charge. Only parcels required to be prepaid, and for this purpose parcel stamps were issued by Greenland from 1905 till 1938. The vast majority of these stamps were cancelled on arrival in Copenhagen, and examples with Greenland postmarks are worth considerably more. Stamps with a numeral cancellation were, in fact, used as savings stamps.

The post offices of the world are listed in the three-volume *Nomenclature Internationale des Bureaux de Poste*, published by the Universal Postal Union, Berne. The post offices are listed alphabetically, from Aaback (Finland) to Zyznow (Poland).

The number of post offices in the world reached its peak of 437 168 in 1968. Since then retrenchment has considerably reduced this number. The greatest cutback has taken place in the United States, which had 76 688 post offices in 1900 (when the population stood at 76 million), dropping to a mere 32 626 in 1967 (when the population had risen to 200 million). Since then the number of post offices has gradually risen again to 39 486 (1979).

The largest post office in the world is the head post office in Chicago, Illinois which contains public counters, philatelic bureau, sorting offices and administrative offices of the USPO. It was opened in 1931.

King Edward Building, London, EC1, contains public counters, sorting offices, the National Postal Museum, philatelic centre and some administrative offices, but the bulk of the administration is housed in separate buildings nearby and in the vicinity of the Post Office Tower in Howland Street, WC1.

20c, 1963 series, of the New Hebrides, English and French versions

Stamps issued by the Spanish and French Post Offices in Andorra

The longest public post office counter in the United Kingdom is in the Trafalgar Square Branch Office, London, WC2. It is 185 ft (*56·4 m*) long, with 33 positions and is open 24 hours a day, 7 days a week, including public holidays. It was opened in 1962.

The largest sorting office in the United Kingdom is in Birmingham and occupies an area of 17½ acres (*7·1 ha*), and handles 3 500 000 items of mail every day.

The smallest post office in the world has been claimed by many places, the current contender being Ochopee, Florida, USA.

Previous American claimants were Bill's Place, Pennsylvania (7 ft 2 in × 4 ft 11 in *2·18 × 1·50 m*), closed in the 1950s, Cypress Gardens, Florida (opened in 1957), and Little Orleans, Maryland – dimensions unknown.

Australia has produced several contenders for the title. The post office at Locksley, New South Wales, was quoted in 1958 as being 8 ft 6 in × 7 ft 6 in *2·59 ×*

The largest combined parcel and sorting office in Europe is in
Birmingham. It covers 17½ acres of operational floor space, and
handles 160 million letters and 26½ million parcels in a year

The longest Post Office counter in
Britain at Trafalgar Square, London.
It is 185 ft *56.38 m* long and has
33 positions

Ochopee post office: smallest in the USA

2·29 m, but this record was beaten by Biggs Flat, South Australia, (7 ft × 5 ft 2·13 × 1·52 m). An earlier office, however, was probably the smallest of all time and measured a mere 6 ft × 4 ft 1·83 × 1·22 m. This was the post office at Lower Cape Bridgewater, Victoria, opened in 1863 and closed in 1953.

The smallest post office in the United Kingdom has likewise been the subject of considerable controversy. In 1934 a Sunday newspaper claimed that the post office at Garsdale Head, Sedbergh, Cumbria was the country's smallest and measured 9 ft × 6 ft 2·74 × 1·83 m. Great Oak, Gwent and Rose Ash, Devon both claimed the title in 1947, but measurements were not given in either case. In September 1952 a London newspaper claimed that the office at Twinstead, Sudbury, Suffolk was the smallest. Constructed of wood, it could only hold two people at a time. This record was beaten by the post office on the island of Foula, Shetland, according to a report in the *Scotsman* on 12 November 1960. This office is so small that it can accommodate only one customer at a time. Whether Foula is the smallest, it certainly is the remotest post office currently operating anywhere in the British Isles. Other Scottish post offices which might qualify as the smallest are located at Linicro, Isle of Skye (opened September 1955) and at Fountainhall, Stow, Borders. The former is in a cupboard under the stairs of the postmaster's house, while the latter consists entirely of a writing bureau standing in the hallway of the postmaster's house.

Postmarks of Ny Ålesund and North Cape, Norway and Haroldswick, Shetland

The most northerly post office in the British Isles at Haroldswick, on the island of Unst in the Shetlands. In the postmark, above, notice the misspelling of NORTHERNMOST

The highest permanent post office in the world is at Phari-Yong, Tibet, at an altitude of 15 000 ft *4575 m*. The highest in the United States is in the aptly named village of Climax, Colorado (11 320 ft, *3450 m*).

The highest post office in the British Isles is at Wanlockhead, Dumfries and Galloway (1500 ft, *451 m*). Between 1886 and 1904 an office existed on the summit of Ben Nevis (4406 ft, *1343 m*), but this handled telegrams only, in connection with the observatory.

The most northerly permanent post office in the world is situated at Ny Ålesund, Spitzbergen, Norway (78° 55′ 32″ N).

The post office in the town of North Pole, Alaska (pop. 600) is actually 14 miles *23 km* east of Fairbanks, 65° N, and not even within the Arctic Circle!

The most northerly on the European mainland is at the North Cape (Nordkapp), Norway. The most northerly in Asia is at Khatana, Siberia; the most northerly in America is at Barrow, Alaska. The most northerly post office in the British Isles is at Haroldswick, Unst, in the Shetlands.

The most southerly post office in the world is operated by the United States at the South Pole and serves (1981) some 1000 servicemen, scientists and naturalists engaged in geophysical research. Mail for this office is routed through Christchurch, New Zealand.

The most southerly post office in the British Isles is at Samarès, Jersey. The most southerly on the mainland of Britain is at The Lizard, Helston, Cornwall.

The most easterly post office in the British Isles is the North Lowestoft sub-office, High Street, Lowestoft, Norfolk.

The most easterly post office in the United States is Lubec, Maine (pop. 1600).

The most westerly post office in the British Isles was situated on Great Blasket island, Co. Kerry, 10° 30′ W (now closed). The most westerly is now the post office on Valentia Island, Co. Kerry. The most westerly post office in the United Kingdom, after the severance of the Irish Free State in 1922, was on the Hebridean island of St Kilda (pop. 37 at the time of its evacuation in 1930). The military garrison stationed on the island since 1958 use an unofficial cachet inscribed 'The furthest station west'. Temporary post offices have functioned on the island in recent years, mainly in connection with new issues of commemorative stamps. The most westerly permanent post office in the United Kingdom is at Garrison, Co. Fermanagh (8° 30′ W).

The oldest post office in the United Kingdom, still in its original building, is at Sanquhar, Dumfries and Galloway. The post office is unique in having occupied the same house since its inception in 1763, a fact which was officially recognised in a pictorial postmark, 1974. The Sanquhar post office is often, though inaccurately, claimed to be the oldest post office in Britain. The post office, as an abstract term, has existed in many towns and cities since the mid-seventeenth century.

Cachet used on military mail from St Kilda, Outer Hebrides

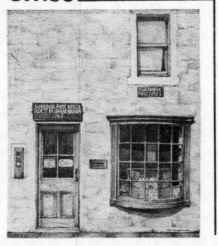

COMMEMORATIVE COVER • FIRST DAY OF SPECIAL CANCELLATION

The oldest post office in England is in the village of Shipton-under-Wychwood, Oxfordshire (since April 1845).

The post office serving the smallest population is that on Suwarrow, an atoll in the Cook Islands group. The island (800 m *2625 ft* long and 270 m *885 ft* broad) is 200 miles *320 km* from its nearest inhabited neighbour, and has only one inhabitant, New Zealander Tom Neale, who was appointed postmaster on 22 July 1969. Prior to that Mr Neale had served in an unofficial capacity as postmaster and coast-watcher. Mail from the island is known with an official datestamp and Tom Neale's own circular cachet.

The most sparsely populated area in the United Kingdom served by its own post office is the island of Canna in the Inner Hebrides (pop. 20). At one time, however, the neighbouring island of Rum, which has had a post office since 1 May 1891, had a population of only 12.

The world's only undersea post office was established on the sea-bed off the Bahamas on 16 August 1939 as part of the facilities of the Williamson Photosphere, operated by the American Field Museum. It consisted of a globular, glass-walled chamber, equipped for the observation of under-

Commemorative cover from Sanquhar, 'The Oldest Post Office in Britain'

water phenomena. The Photosphere and its post office were manned by Captain Charles Williamson. Mail bore a special oval postmark inscribed SEA FLOOR/BAHAMAS. This unique post office was depicted on the 5 shilling and 1 dollar definitive stamps issued by the Bahamas in 1965-71.

Every post office was forced to close down in the Indian principality of Bundi except the head office, in 1899 when famine swept the country and the economy virtually collapsed. The reconstruction of the postal services was not completed till 1914 when the offices were re-opened.

The greatest number of foreign post offices in any one town was eight which operated in Constantinople. Not all of them were in simultaneous operation: France (1799-1923), Britain (1832-1923), Austria (1863-1914), Russia (1863-1918), Germany (1884-1914), Italy (1908-23), Poland (1919-23) and Romania (1919-23).

The greatest number of foreign post offices open simultaneously was six, which functioned in Constantinople and the Chinese port of Shanghai at

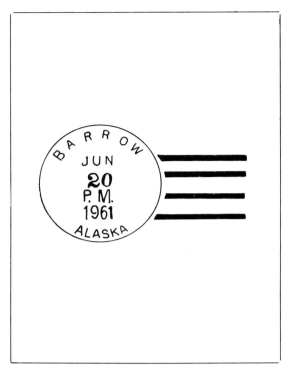

Postmark of Barrow, Alaska, where the most northerly post office in the US is situated

Postmark of Suwarrow, Cook Islands, 1969

Bahamas 5s stamp of 1965 showing the Undersea Post Office of 1939

the turn of the century. Separate post offices were operated by Britain, France, Germany, Japan, Russia and the United States. The number was almost increased to seven in 1908, when the Belgian government proposed opening its own post office, but this was vetoed by the Chinese Imperial Postmaster General (a Frenchman!). Belgian stamps overprinted CHINE were prepared, but never actually issued. In addition Shanghai had a Municipal Post, established in 1864, which eventually had branch offices in sixteen other Chinese cities and issued its own stamps from 1865 till 1898. From 1863 onwards the Chinese Imperial Customs operated a postal service which also had an office in Shanghai. In 1898 the municipal and imperial services were joined.

Five foreign post offices (British, French, German, Japanese and Russian) existed at one time in the treaty port of Chefoo, and five (British, French, German, Italian and Japanese) in Tientsin. The last of the foreign post offices in China, the French office in Kuang-Chou (Canton), remained in operation till the Japanese occupation in 1943.

The place which has had the greatest number of different postal administrations is the island of Kastellorizon, off the coast of Asia Minor. Until 1915 it used Turkish stamps, but was then occupied by the French navy and used stamps of the French Levant from then until 1920, when stamps overprinted CASTELLORIZO were briefly used. On 21 August 1920 the French withdrew, whereupon the island was occupied by the Italians to whom it had been awarded by the Treaty of Sevres. At first it was under naval administration but was transferred to the Italian civil administration of the Dodecanese and used stamps inscribed or overprinted CASTELROSSO. The island was captured by the British during the Second World War and British stamps overprinted for use by Middle East Forces were employed until 31 March 1947. From then until 15 September 1947 it was under Greek military administration and used Greek stamps overprinted s.d.d. (initials of 'Military Occupation, Dodecanese'). Since November 1947 ordinary Greek stamps have been used. Kastellorizon has thus been under Turkish, French, Italian, British and Greek administration – all in the space of 32 years.

The postal administrations with the most post offices
(UPU statistics, 1986):
India 144 396
USSR 93 076
China (People's Rep) 50 969
USA 39 270
Turkey 28 086
Japan 23 698
UK 21 211
This is the first edition with the statistics for the People's Republic of China which previously were unavailable.

The administration employing the most full-time staff
is China (People's Rep) which had (1986) 983 000 employees. The United States now employs 784 557.

Other figures are:
USSR 775 000
India 543 000
France 303 700
West Germany 272 781
UK 200 170

Postal administration with the fewest employees
Pitcairn Island, South Pacific – one part-timer.

The largest volume of mail in 1986
was handled by the United States Post Office with a grand total of 146 827 627 000 items.

In the same year the British Post Office handled 13 035 400 000 items.
The comparable total for the French Post Office was 16 774 900 000 items.
The other leading postal countries in 1986 were:
USSR 58 831 000 000
Japan 18 108 732 000
West Germany 15 291 212 000
India 12 193 669 000

The postal administration with the largest total receipts
in 1986 was the United States Post Office. The grand total, expressed in international gold francs, was 90 640 961 764.
The receipts of other leading countries were:

France	(1985) 23 767 735 157
West Germany	22 691 923 076
UK	13 730 259 258
USSR	9 863 945 578
Canada	5 400 101 817
Netherlands	4 429 847 230

The postal administration with the most motor vehicles
was the United States Post Office, which operated 137 446 vehicles in 1986.
The other leading countries, in descending order of mechanised mobility, are:
Japan 70 124
USSR 52 400
France 49 600
West Germany 42 802
UK 34 000
China (People's Rep) 27 115
By contrast India, which ranks among the largest postal administrations and serves a population of 685 184 692, has a mere 1450 motor vehicles.

The earliest posting-boxes
were the *tamburi* of Florence, established in the early years of the sixteenth century. These were closed wooden boxes with an aperture at the top, and were installed in the main churches so that anonymous letters of denunciation against wrong-doers and suspected enemies of the state could be 'posted'.

The first orthodox system of roadside posting-boxes
was established in Paris in 1653 by Renouard de Villayer, Master of the Petite Poste, to facilitate the interchange of correspondence in the French metropolis. These boxes were erected at the intersections of the main thoroughfares and were emptied thrice daily. Unfortunately, the boxes were vandalised and anti-social individuals had a nasty habit of depositing 'night soil' in them, so that the letters were polluted. There are also instances recorded of mice and other vermin inhabiting the boxes and making a meal of the letters. The service, which also

The new UPU headquarters, Berne, Switzerland

made use of some kind of stamps (see Chapter 3) was consequently short-lived.

Posting-boxes were revived at the beginning of the nineteenth century and both France and Prussia were using them about 1800. They spread to Belgium in 1836 but did not appear in the British Isles until 1852.

Posting apertures for unpaid letters were a feature of British post offices from the earliest times. The oldest post office posting-box of this kind still in existence is an iron box originally situated on the wall of the Wood Street post office, Wakefield in 1809. It remained *in situ* till 1964 but is now preserved in the local museum.

The first pillar boxes in the British Isles were erected on 23 November 1852 in St Helier, Jersey. They were constructed by a local blacksmith, John Vaudin, and cast at Le Feuvre's foundry, Bath Street, St Helier. The introduction of these boxes was due to Anthony Trollope, the novelist who was then employed by the Post Office as a surveyor (postal inspector). Trollope had seen similar posting-boxes in France and had recommended their adoption in Britain. The success of the experiment in the Channel Islands led to their introduction on the mainland in 1853.

The oldest pillar boxes still in use are those at Hauteville and Union Street, St Peter Port, Guernsey. Six pillar boxes were erected in and around St Peter Port on 8 February 1853 as part of Trollope's experiment. Controversy surrounds this record, since it was long considered that they could not possibly be the 1853 originals. Mrs Jean Farrugia, Archivist of the British Post Office and a recognised authority on posting-boxes, has proved conclusively that the two boxes at Hauteville and Union Street were never replaced. In design and construction they certainly conform to Vaudin's 1852-3 prototypes. The Guernsey postal administration has recognised this fact by depicting the Union Street box on a postage stamp of 1979.

The oldest pillar box on the British mainland, still in use, is at Barnes Cross, Holwell, Bishop's Caundle, Dorset and dates from late 1853.

The first wall-boxes were made by Smith and Hunter of Birmingham in 1857-8. Only one of the original batch is still in use, at The Mall, Newport, Isle of Wight.

Posting-boxes on public vehicles are believed to have been first used on tramcars in New York City in 1886. This practice spread to Paris in 1891 and was adopted in Britain in 1893. The tramcars of Huddersfield were equipped with posting-boxes for the first time on 20 March 1893. Stockport, Bradford

Medieval letter box, on an Italian stamp of 1976

The oldest pillar box still in use in the British Isles, on a Guernsey stamp of 1979

Bishop's Caundle pillar-box: oldest in England

and Portsmouth followed later in the same year, while Wakefield attached posting boxes to omnibuses. Mobile posting boxes of this type spread to Dundee (1894), Swansea (1895) and Halifax (1902). Most of these services were suspended during the First World War and the last services were withdrawn in September 1939. The practice was, however, re-introduced on the seafront tramcars of Blackpool in September 1981, a special postmark being provided to denote such posting.

The earliest automatic posting device for pre-paid letters was installed by the postmaster of Waltham Cross on his own initiative in 1844. The *Morning Post* (3 October 1844) reported: 'In the window of the office in the place of a square of glass, a sheet of zinc is inserted, in which two longitudinal holes are cut – one for the receipt of letters and the other for pence. In the centre of the plate is a revolving handle, which acts upon some simple machinery within. Above the handle are these words – "Put your letter in and turn the handle up; put your penny in, then turn the handle over". Here, then, is a simple means for posting and prepaying a letter – there is no waiting till the Postmaster is "rung" from any part of the premises he may happen to be in, to his own and the letter-sender's inconvenience – here is, in fact, a plan that is worth consideration by postmasters, and all those whom it may concern.'

The post office at Ware, Hertfordshire is believed to have used the same device. The Postmaster General decided against the general adoption of this device on the grounds that some posters might not understand its operation, or post letters unpaid. The result of the operation was that the penny fell upon the letter to which it belonged. The postmaster, on emptying the box, affixed an adhesive stamp to each letter thus posted.

The first stamp vending machine attached to a pillar box was in Cannon Street Railway Station, London in 1885. Postcard-vending machines were tried experimentally in Manchester, attached to pillar boxes, in 1886.

Pillar boxes, painted blue instead of the traditional red, were erected in the London area in 1930, and extended to the provinces the following year, for airmail. They were discontinued in 1938.

The postal administration with the greatest number of pillar, wall and other forms of posting boxes is the USSR which had 586 731 boxes in 1986, or one per 386 inhabitants. The other leading countries were:
India 495 143
USA 395 000
China (People's Rep) 176 843
France 159 800

Special tramcar postmark, Blackpool, 1981

Japan 150 380
West Germany 111 873
Jersey claims to have the most posting-boxes *per capita* in the world – but this does not stand up to close examination. Jersey has 169 boxes for a population of 74 500 – or a box for every 440 people (1980).

An automatic post office was erected experimentally in Bath in 1924. It consisted of a telephone kiosk (pay-phone) integrated with a posting-box and a stamp-vending machine. From this prototype was developed Telephone Kiosk No 4, introduced generally in England in 1929 and having stamp-vending machines built into the back of the kiosk.

The numbering of houses for postal purposes began in Paris in 1463-4, the Pont Notre Dame district being the first so numbered.

The highest street number in the United Kingdom is 2679 Stratford Road, Hockley Heath, West Midlands, owned since 1964 by Mr and Mrs Howard Hughes. The highest number in Scotland is 2629 London Road, Mt Vernon, Glasgow – part of the local police station.

The slowest delivery of mail is claimed by everyone at some time or another. Undoubtedly the record, however, must go to the Parisian postal service which recovered letters in 1882, 1910, 1920, 1942, 1951 and 1954 dredged from the bed of the Seine where they have lain since the Siege of 1870–1. During that period an attempt to get mail into the beleaguered city was made using zinc-coated steel spheres known as *boules de moulins*. The bundles of letters were wrapped in waterproof material and hermetically sealed in the spheres and then allowed to float downstream into the city. The experiment was unsuccessful since German marksmen took pot-shots at the *boules* and sank most of them. Amazingly, the Paris post office made every effort to deliver the salvaged letters to the addressees or their descendants. The most recent recovery of a *boule* occurred in 1968 at Rouen, well downstream from Paris, and contained several hundred letters dated January 1871. The French Post Office took charge of the *boule* and its contents but the Rouen Tribunal judged on 22 February 1972 that they should go to the finder, M. le Grevelle, who was ordered to retain the letters till 1998 in case the heirs of the addressees should turn up to claim any of them.

In 1986 the average number of postal items (letters, postcards and printed matter) posted per inhabitant of the leading countries was:
USA 648·11
Switzerland 636·96
France 297·03
West Germany 240·44
UK 222·25
Japan 147·74
India 17·05
China (mainland) 3·17 (1980)

BY LAND

Every item of mail is handled, at some stage or other, by a person on foot. The foot-post, post-runner, messenger, mailman, letter carrier or postman is literally the foot soldier of the world's postal services, no matter how sophisticated and mechanised the handling of mail.

The earliest reference to a foot-post in Britain occurs in the minutes of Aberdeen corporation, 1591 when provision was made for an allowance and a livery of blue cloth with the town's armorial bearings in silver on the sleeve, for Alexander Taylor, the 'town post'. When the General Letter Office was founded in 1660 its messengers were

The highest numbered house in Britain: No 2679 Stratford Road, Hockley Heath, West Midlands, owned by Mr and Mrs Howard Hughes

known as post-boys, even though they might be of advanced age. In the eighteenth century they became 'letter-carriers', a name which continued until August 1883 when, in consequence of the increase of duties to include the carriage of parcels, they were re-designated postmen. They were first equipped with uniforms in 1793.

The first town postmen in Britain were the messengers employed by William Dockwra in his London Penny Post (1680-2). By the beginning of the eighteenth century bellmen were employed in London; they patrolled the streets every hour, ringing a bell to call people out to collect their mail, or to entrust letters to them for onward transmission. Charles Povey, who organised a Halfpenny Post, using bellmen, was fined for infringing the Postmaster General's monopoly and several of his bellmen were similarly punished. Nevertheless, the Post Office absorbed the bellman system and this continued in London and most provincial towns until 1855, by which time the use of adhesive stamps and street posting boxes had done away with the need for them.

Mounted post-boys were used exclusively on the major post routes of Britain until 1784, when mail-coaches were introduced. Horse messengers, however, were retained in the remoter rural areas. The last horse-postmen in the British Isles were employed in the Outer Hebrides, between North Uist and the tidal islands of Baleshare and Grimsay. Their services were converted to mailvan working in September 1961 when the islands were linked by causeways.

The first horse-drawn mail-coaches since Roman times were employed by the Thurn and Taxis postal service in Europe by 1650. The word 'coach' is derived from the Hungarian town of Kocs where they first ran.

The first mail-coach in the British Isles ran between London and Bristol on 2 August 1784, the service being instigated by John Palmer, a theatre proprietor of Bath, who petitioned the Prime Minister, William Pitt, suggesting that stage-coaches on the now improved roads should carry the mails, with armed guards in attendance. The mail-coach system eventually covered the British Isles and the coaches ran at an average of 11 mph *18 km/h*. The death-knell of the mail-coach system was sounded on 17 December 1845 when the London-Louth mail-coach, having completed its 135-mile *217 km* run from the capital to Lincolnshire, was uncoupled from its team of horses and loaded on to a railway flat car at Peterborough for the return journey to London by rail. By 1860 the railways had virtually ousted the mail-coaches from all the main routes of the United Kingdom, but they survived in remoter areas for a further half century. The last horse-drawn mail-coach in regular service ran from Campbeltown to the Mull of Kintyre as late as 1914.

The longest route of a foot-post was that between Lhasa and Peking, via Nagchuka and Lanchou, a distance of 1,988 miles *3200 km* which took foot-messengers 189 days to cover.

The longest-lived system of mail delivery was the Dak or Dawk system of India which could trace its origins back in an unbroken line to the Roman system of relay runners. The dak runner carried letters in a cleft stick and was accompanied by a *mashalchi* (torch-bearer) to guide him through the night, and a tom-tom beater to ward off wild animals. By the seventeenth century the duties of torch-bearer and drummer were combined. The dak runners went from one relay station to the next, all round the clock, and another runner set off as soon as he arrived. The system reached its zenith in the reign of Akbar (1542-1602) when more than 4000 runners were employed. The system was taken over without change by the East India Company. Efficiency was improved by Warren Hastings who added *munshis*

An early foot post in the reign of Charles I, about 1613

Mounted postboys, depicted on stamps of Belgium (1962) and Sweden (1967)

(writers or postal inspectors) and *ghari-wallahs* (time-keepers) who ensured that the daks operated at the regulation 5 mph *8 km/h*. Dak runners are in use to this day.

Horse daks were introduced by Sher Ali Shah (1541) on the 2000-mile *3220-km* stretch of road between Bengal and Sind. Mail carts (dak tonga) were introduced in the eighteenth century.

The bush mailman, accompanied by an Aboriginal tracker, made the first overland mail run in Australia between Melbourne and Sydney, early in 1838. The first mailman was John Conway Burke who rode from Melbourne to the Murray River where a second rider carried the mails on to Yass and thence by mail-coach to Sydney.

The Pony Express was organised in 1859 to expedite mail between the eastern United States and California. Previously the journey between St Louis, Missouri and San Francisco took three weeks. The pony express used 190 relay stations with 500 horses and 80 first-class riders (including Buffalo Bill Cody who made a record run of 384 miles *618 km* without stops except to change horses). The scheduled time for the run from St Joseph, Missouri to Sacramento, California was ten days, but the pony express riders carried Lincoln's first inaugural address over the 2000-mile *3220-km* route in seven days seventeen hours, probably an all-time speed record for mail carried by horsemen. The completion of the tele-

A horse-drawn mail cart in India, 1867. Letters were conveyed any distance for less than one (old) penny. One horse is in the shafts, the other harnessed alongside and this arrangement frequently resulted in the vehicle's capsizing

Stamp and advertising card of the Coolgardie Cycle Express, 1893

graph to San Francisco on 22 October 1861 brought this service to an end.

Bicycles were first used for the transmission of mail in Britain in August 1883. Special cycles, with one large wheel and four small ones, were used. Officially called the Barstow Centrecycle, it was soon dubbed 'the hen and chickens' and was used for the carriage of parcels until about 1900.

In 1893 James A Healy organised the Coolgardie Cycle Express for mail packets containing gold dust during the Western Australia gold rush, and produced special stamps for the service. A similar service was the Lake Lefroy Goldfield Cycle Mail in Western Australia, 1897. Arthur C Banta organised a cycle mail between Fresno and San Francisco during a railway strike in July 1894. Following the collapse of the Imperial Austrian postal service in November 1918, the municipal authorities in Vaduz, Liechtenstein (then dependent on the Austrian service) organised a bicycle post to take mail across the frontier to Switzerland for onward transmission. Special stamps were issued to prepay the handling charge. Similarly a bicycle mail known as Coralit was established in Italy in 1944 and issued special stamps till June 1945 when the service was discon-

tinued. A local service known as the Moulins Post in Timaru, New Zealand, used boy cyclists to deliver mail, 1968-9.

Bullock mail was operated in India between 1846 and 1904, using bullock-drawn carts along the Grand Trunk Road between Allahabad and Delhi. It was expanded by 1855 to cover postal routes between Calcutta and Peshawar and throughout Bengal. The Calcutta Post Office had a separate counter for bullock mail and a distinctive handstamp for use on parcel receipts. The Bullock Train was transferred to private enterprise in May 1862 – the Indian Carrying Company – but reverted to the Post Office in 1868. Thereafter it was used to convey mail from the outlying hill-stations to the nearest railhead. By 1875, 41 government Bullock Train offices were operating in the North West Provinces and the Punjab, handling parcels and freight. As the railways developed in the 1870s the bullock routes were gradually closed down. The last line, from Ambala to Simla, closed in October 1904.

A similar service, known as the *Kuhpost* (cow post) operated between Rothenuffeln and Hille in Germany in 1878.

Camels have been extensively used for the carriage of mail, all over North Africa, the Middle East and Central Asia. Less well-known, however, are the postal services operated by camels in Western Australia and South Australia in the mid-nineteenth century, and in Texas, New Mexico and Arizona in the same period. One-humped camels or dromedaries were used in these services. In Soviet Central Asia, the two-humped or Bactrian camel was used for a service linking Dushanbe, capital of Tadjikistan, with the railhead at Guzar 200 miles *322 km* away. Pairs of camels were also used to haul mail-carts.

Reindeer were employed in the haulage of mail sledges in northern Scandinavia and Russia at the turn of the century. There is, however, no truth in the widely held belief that the caribou was similarly employed in Canada in the late nineteenth century. This myth gained currency because a local postal

India 2a 6p, 1937 showing the bullock mail

service in British Columbia and Vancouver was called Barnard's Cariboo Express.

Cats were used for a mail service in Liège, Belgium in 1879, some 37 cats being employed to carry bundles of letters to villages within a 30 km *18·6 mile* radius of Liège city centre. The experiment was short-lived as the cats proved to be thoroughly undisciplined.

Dogs were employed to haul mailcarts in the coastal towns of Sussex, England in the late nineteenth century. The service was terminated abruptly, following complaints from animal lovers that the dogs were being ill-used. A regular mail service using sledges drawn by dog teams operated from Fort Yukon, Alaska as late as the 1950s, but was discontinued about 1960 when a local air service was substituted. Occasional runs by Alaska Dog Team Post, however, continue to this day.

Mail was first carried unofficially by railway on 11 November 1830, on the Liverpool and Manchester route. The first mail conveyed by rail in America was by the *Best Friend* locomotive of the South Carolina Railroad on 15 January 1831 and by the Baltimore and Ohio Railroad in January 1832. The first official mail contract was awarded on 1 January 1838 by the US Post Office to the Baltimore and Ohio Railroad.

Mail was first carried by train on a semi-official basis on 4 July 1837, by the Grand Trunk Railway between Birmingham and Liverpool. On 10 December special trains (Up and Down Special) at a cost of £10 a trip were introduced. Frederick Karstadt, son of a Post Office surveyor, suggested sorting carriages, so that clerks could sort the mail en route.

The first experimental sorting carriage, a converted horse-box, ran between Birmingham and Liverpool on 24 January 1838. The first railway postmark, inscribed MISSENT TO RAILWAY POST OFFICE, was issued to the Mail Coach Officer on 27 January 1838. It is sometimes stated (erroneously) that this service commenced on 6 January 1838, but this is the date on a memorandum by George Louis to the Secretary of the Post Office, Colonel Maberly, proposing this experiment.

The first apparatus for picking up and putting down mailbags from a moving train was patented by Nathaniel Worsdell, superintendent of

An interior view of a travelling post office (TPO) showing mail being sorted

the Grand Junction coach-making works, on 4 January 1838, following successful experiments on the line near Winsford, Cheshire in December 1837. Worsdell offered his invention to the Post Office for £3500, but was offered only £500 which he refused. The Post Office then got one of its employees, John Ramsay, to 'revise' Worsdell's apparatus and this was tested at Boxmoor on 30 May and generally adopted on the London-Liverpool line in November 1838.

The first instance of mail carried by train being damaged in transit occurred on 3 March 1838 when mailbags sent forward by train from Manchester were fastened between the engine and mail-coach and were burned by cinders from the track.

The first all-mail train in the world was the London and Bristol Special Mail which commenced

The track-side mailbag exchanging equipment last used on 4 October 1971 enabled up to 40 lb *18 kg* of mail to be exchanged to and from a travelling post office at speed

on 1 February 1855 and consisted of two sorting carriages and a van hauled by a Fire Fly 7′ single locomotive. At Bristol it connected with the passenger train from Paddington to Exeter. The combined mail train was known as the London and Exeter Railway Post Office. The Special became a Limited Mail in June 1869 when a first class passenger carriage was added.

The oldest named mail train in the world is the Irish Mail which began running from London to Holyhead on 1 August 1848. Prior to the completion of the Britannia Tubular Bridge on 18 March 1850 passengers and mail were conveyed by horse-drawn coach over Telford's Menai Bridge from Bangor to Llanfair.

Travelling post offices and exchange apparatus in Britain were suspended from 22 September 1940 till 1 October 1945, due to the Second World War.

Apparatus for exchanging mailbags on British Railways was last used on 4 October 1971, just north of Penrith.

Parcel coaches, drawn by horses, were first used by the British Post Office in 1887 in a bid to cut operating costs. Since August 1883, the Post Office had had to pay 55 per cent of its parcel revenue to the Railway companies. By 1890 the night parcel coach service was operating from London to Oxford, Colchester, Watford and Chatham. The coachmen and mail guards were popularly known as 'the phantoms of the night'.

Horse-drawn mail carts, for parcel traffic, were introduced in Britain in August 1883, five contractors being appointed to operate services on behalf of the Post Office in the major towns and cities.

The first horseless mailvan was a steam-driven vehicle employed by the Post Office between London and Redhill, Surrey in 1897. Later the same year a petrol-driven van was used experimentally at the General Post Office, London. A Daimler van was used in 1898 between Reading and Newbury. Three motor vans were introduced in 1903 for the London, Liverpool and Manchester parcel service.

The US Post Office advertised for a motor vehicle service in Chicago in 1899 but received no replies. The first motor service was operated by the New York Electric Company on 15 April 1901, carrying mail to and from the Buffalo post office and the Pan American Exposition showground, a distance of 4½ miles 7 km.

The first motor postbus was run by the Bavarian Post Office who used a 29 hp Daimler bus between Bad Tolz and Longgries on 1 June 1905. The original postbus is preserved in the Nuremberg Transport Museum.

The first postbus in the British Isles was a J2 seven-seater operated by the Post Office between Llanidloes and Llangurig, Wales on 20 February 1967. The first postbus in Scotland ran between Dunbar and Spott on 4 June 1968. Prior to 1934 many bus services in Britain carried mail under Post Office contract, but the modern postbus system uses Post Office vehicles, with postmen-drivers, and carries passengers on a fare-paying basis.

The first Highway Post Office, using motor vehicles for the collection, sorting and distribution of mail, was operated by the US Post Office between Washington, DC, and Harrisburg, Virginia, in 1941.

Special postmarks with the abbreviation H.P.O. were used.

ON WATER

The earliest recorded instance of sea currents being used to transmit correspondence was about 300 BC when the Greek philosopher, Theophrastus, launched bottles containing messages and thereby demonstrated that the Mediterranean Sea derived most of its water from the Atlantic Ocean. Benjamin Franklin tested the currents of the Gulf Stream by despatching bottles containing messages for the finders. A Royal Uncorker of Bottles was appointed in 1560 for the express purpose of examining water-borne messages and this appointment existed as late as the reign of George III (1760-1820).

Lady Grange, marooned by her husband on the island of St Kilda (1734-42) 'devoted her whole time to weeping, and wrapping up letters round pieces of cork, bound up with yarn, to try if any favourable wave would waft them to some Christian, to inform some humane person where she resided.' A letter by Lady Grange, dated 20 January 1738, transmitted by this means, was not delivered to the recipient till 1740. This method relied on the North Atlantic Drift and the prevailing westerly winds.

In 1876 John Sands, marooned on St Kilda for seven months, used hollowed pieces of driftwood (St Kilda 'mailboats') to get messages to the outside world. His first mailboat, launched December 1876, was recovered at Sortlund, Norway in September 1877. Another, however, was found a few days after launching, at Poolewe, Highland. The St Kildans used this method regularly from 1885 till 1930 (when the island was evacuated), and from 1906 the Post Office made a payment of 2s 6d to finders of these mailboats. Since the re-occupation of St Kilda by military forces in 1956 tin-can mails have been despatched from time to time, marked with a special cachet.

Other instances of floating mail include:
1894 Scottish Fishery Board survey of ocean currents over 53 000 message bottles launched by 1955.
1899 Buoys with letters from Andree's balloon fight were cast overboard on 11 July 1897 and recovered 11 September 1897 and 14 May 1899.
1902-4 Scottish Antarctic Expedition message bottles recovered between 1907 (Victoria) and 1952 (New Zealand).
1903 German South Polar Expedition, Kerguelen Islands; recovered New Zealand 1955! The long-distance record is for a bottle from Kerguelen recovered at Bunbury, Western Australia six years later – a distance of 16 000 miles *25 750 km.*

1954 National Institute of Oceanography oil pollution survey. Several thousand cards in PVC with cork floats dropped by aircraft over the Western Approaches. Recovered between Arctic Russia and the River Tagus, Portugal as late as 1965, though most were found round the British Isles.

1959 Guinness Breweries bicentenary launch of bottles off the American coast; two recovered at St

St Kilda 'mailboat', 1898

The retrieval of a mailbag adrift from the wreck of the German steamship *Schiller* which sank in dense fog near the Bishop Rock at 10.30 p.m. on Friday 7 May 1875 with the loss of 312 lives

The severe storms and flooding in November 1875 posing difficulty for the postal services in Windsor

Kilda in May 1960. The bottles contained a certificate from King Neptune.

The Tonga Tin-Can Mail was begun by Stuart Ramsay at Niuafo'ou in 1921 after a native mail swimmer was killed by a shark while propelling a can of mail through the surf. The service was taken over in 1932 by Walt Quensell who applied up to 23 different colourful Tin Can Mail cachets to outgoing correspondence.

Floating barrels and biscuit tins were used to convey mail from ship to shore at the Cocos Keeling Islands and the Brazilian penal island of Fernando da Noronha. No special postal markings are known in either case.

The first carriage of mail by canal boat was in 1540 by *schippers post* (literally 'barge post'), a network covering the whole of Holland. Special stamps were issued for prepayment of postage on mail conveyed by the Suez Canal Company, 1869.

The first carriage of mail by river steamer took place on 23 January 1812 when mail was conveyed by the steamboat *New Orleans* up the Mississippi from New Orleans to Natchez. By the 1820s steamboats were carrying mail on the Missouri, Hudson, Delaware and St Lawrence river systems. The first river mail service in Europe was that operated by the Royal and Imperial Society for Navigation by Steamship on the Danube and its Tributaries, formed in 1839. The *Donau Dampfschiffahrt Gesellschaft* issued its own stamps (1866–80) for use on mail carried on the Danube, Drava, Sava and Tisza, between Bavaria and the Black Sea. The first in Asia was the Calcutta-Allahabad steamboat service (1828) along 787 miles of the River Ganges.

The first regular packet service was instituted in 1633, linking Dover and Calais. The service was a weekly one till 1654 when two trips a week were sanctioned. Until 1783 the British insisted that a British packet boat must be used and the transmission of mails in any other ships was expressly forbidden. A service between Dover and Nieuport was established by 1683. Falmouth became the base of the Post Office Packet Service to Spain in 1688 and over the ensuing 150 years developed as the world's leading international mail centre. By 1825 Falmouth was the centre for 39 packet routes, to Europe, Asia, Africa and America. In the 1830s, however, Southampton gradually supplanted Falmouth which ceased to be an official packet station in 1850.

Other international packet services include: Corunna to Havana four times a year (established 1767), the Baltic service between Germany and

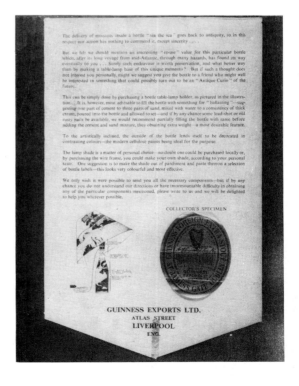

Floating mail 1959: the certificate from King Neptune to all labologists with guidance on making a table-lamp

Sweden (1824), France–United States (1783).

The first paddle steamship to carry mail was the *Rob Roy* which carried mail between Greenock and Belfast in 1818 and transferred to the Dover–Calais route in 1820.

The first screw steamship to carry mail was the French packet vessel *Napoleon*, on the Marseilles–Corsica route, 1836.

The first steamboat to convey mail across the Atlantic was the SS *Royal William*. Built in Quebec for the Quebec–Halifax route, she left Quebec for London via Pictou on 4 August 1833, taking 25 days to accomplish the crossing to Cowes, Isle of Wight. This was an unofficial mail, the first with official sanction being conveyed by the *Great Western*, from New York to Bristol, in 1838. Mail contracts were awarded to Samuel Cunard for the Britain–Canada and United States route (1840), the Peninsular and Orient Company from Britain to Iberia (1837) and from Southampton to India (1842), and the Royal Mail Steam Packet Company to the West Indies and South America (1842).

Mail was first sorted aboard ship on 1 October 1860, when the Holyhead and Kingstown Packet service was inaugurated. Four steamers, named after the provinces of Ireland, were used on this route. Each ship had two sorting rooms, one for letters and the other for newspapers and printed matter. Postmarks inscribed H. & K. PACKET were applied to

The Royal Mail Steam Packet Company's SS *Boyne*, 3318 tons gross built in Dumbarton, Scotland in 1871. She was wrecked on the French coast, near Brest on Friday 13 August 1875

mail in transit from 1860 onwards. Mail posted on board ship was also postmarked with special cancellations from 1919 till 1925 when the service was discontinued.

The first post offices aboard a ship, offering a full counter service to the passengers, were installed aboard the steamers *Columba* and *Iona* in July 1879. The ships were operated by David MacBrayne in Scotland on the Greenock–Ardrishaig route. The post offices were closed following the outbreak of the First World War but sorting and stamping of mail continued till 14 April 1917.

The first mail to be carried by hovercraft was on 20 July 1962, between Rhyl in N Wales and Wallasey, Merseyside. Pictorial postmarks were applied to mail carried in both directions by Saunders-Roe hovercraft.

IN THE AIR

The earliest records of the transmission of messages by air:
5th century BC. Messages by arrow, during the Siege of Potidaea.
AD 549 Letters flown by kite, recorded in China during a siege.

Cover from Clachan, Argyll to Lossiemouth, carried by the Greenock and Ardrishaig Packet, July 1879 – in the first month of the service

1575 Pigeon post used during the siege of Leiden in the Netherlands.
1784 Letters carried by balloon by Vincent Lunardi dropped overboard and recovered at Northaw Common, Hertfordshire, 15 September.
1807 Propaganda leaflets dropped over the French lines during the Peninsular campaign, at the instigation of Admiral Cochrane.
1850 Leaflets dropped by unmanned balloon over northern Canada during the search for Sir John Franklin's Arctic Expedition.

The first official carriage of mail by air took place on 17 August 1859, between La Fayette and Crawfordsville, Indiana, in the balloon *Jupiter* by John Wise. The transmission of mail was advertised in the local press and the letters endorsed PREPAID by Thomas Wood, postmaster of La Fayette. It is this that gives the *Jupiter* mail its official (albeit local) sanction. The USA issued a 7c airmail stamp in 1959 to celebrate the centenary of this flight.

The first government-operated air service took place during the siege of Metz (5 September–3 October 1870) when 31 unmanned balloons were launched, each carrying a bundle of 150–200 *papillons* (literally 'butterflies') or letter-flimsies. Larger bal-

Mail being loaded onto the hovercraft *Sea Hawk* under the watchful eye of her captain. The *Sea Hawk* plies between Southsea on the south coast of England and the Isle of Wight.

loons of the Goulier-Robinson type, with a payload of 30 000 flimsies were launched from 15 September till 3 October.

During the siege of Paris (1870-1) 65 balloons were flown out of the city. Customs officers, thrown out of work by the siege, were employed on the construction of the frames, and 25 seamstresses worked round the clock to stitch the fabric. Of the 65 balloons flown from Paris during the siege, 18 were manned by professional pilots, 17 by volunteers and 30 by marines. Six were captured by the enemy and two were blown out to sea and never seen again, but the other 57 made safe landings. The shortest flight was by the *General Ulrich* (22 miles *35·4 km* in 8 hours 45 minutes on 18 November) and the longest by the *Ville d'Orleans* (3142 km *1952 miles* in 14 hours, landing at Lifjeld in Norway – an average airspeed of 150 mph *241 kph* which was unbroken till 1915!).

The first mail actually flown by heavier-than-air machine was carried unofficially from Paris to St Nazaire, August 1908.

Mail was first flown unofficially in Britain on 3 August 1910 from Lytham Hall to Squires Gate, Blackpool by Claude Grahame White, as souvenirs of the Blackpool Aviation Meeting.

The first official airmail in the world was inaugurated on 18 February 1911 between Allahabad and Naini, India. L Pecquet flew a Humber-Sommer biplane carrying mail in connection with the United Provinces Exhibition and a pictorial postmark, showing the aeroplane, was used. India issued three

GB 5d stamp commemorating the 50th anniversary of the flight

A contemporary sketch showing a balloon being launched when Paris was besieged by the Prussians 1870-1

stamps in 1961 to celebrate the golden jubilee. The first official airmails in Britain, Denmark, Italy and the USA all took place in September 1911.

The first mail by heavier-than-air machine between two countries was *not* carried by Louis Bleriot on his Channel flight of 1909, but by Jorge Chavez the Peruvian aviator who died of injuries sustained when his aircraft crashed at Domodossola, Italy after crossing the Alps from Brig, Switzerland on 23 September 1910. A few cards carried on this epic and tragic flight were given a four-line cachet on arrival signifying 'Domodossola, first control station of the crossing of the Simplon by aeroplane'. Mail was carried by Agustin Parlá between Cape Sable, Florida and Havana, Cuba on 22 July 1913, between Cairo and Khartoum by Marc Pourpé on 4 January 1914, and between Buenos Aires and Montevideo by Teodoro Fels on 2 September 1917. Regular mail flights between London and Paris were inaugurated in June 1918.

The first non-stop mail-carrying flight over the Atlantic was successfully accomplished by John Alcock and Arthur Whitten-Brown in a converted Vickers Vimy bomber on 14 June 1919. The flight, from St John's, Newfoundland, to Clifden, Co Galway, took 16 hours 12 minutes. Newfoundland stamps specially overprinted and surcharged $1 were affixed to mail on this occasion. Previous Atlantic flights included one by American Navy flying boats (assisted by 27 destroyers at strategic intervals) only one of which completed the course in 12 days and carried no mail, and the mail-carrying flights by Raynham and Morgan, and Hawker and Grieve, both of which were abortive.

The most spectacular airmail of all time was that carried by the Balbo Mass Flight of 25 Savoia-Marchetti flying-boats from Rome to Chicago and return in July 1933. The squadron commanded by General Italo Balbo flew via Amsterdam, Londonderry, Iceland, Labrador, Shediac and Montreal and carried mail from Italy, the Netherlands, Iceland, Newfoundland and Canada. In connection with this flight Italy produced a commemorative label and Iceland a special airmail sticker. On the return flight both Iceland and Newfoundland issued special stamps. The most prolific issue was made by Italy which issued stamps in pairs of triptychs, the left-hand portion consisting of an undenominated registration stamp, the centre portion prepaying the ordinary postage and the right-hand portion prepaying the air postage as far as Iceland (19·75 lire) or the USA (44·75 lire). Each triptych was issued with an overprint comprising the abbreviated names of twenty of the pilots. As well as these 60 triptychs one was printed in different colours and overprinted SERVIZIO DI STATO for use on official letters to President Roosevelt and the Mayors of New York and Chicago. This triptych was also overprinted VOLO DI RITORNO (return flight), but never used.

The idea of microfilming messages to save weight in aerial transmission was first used in the Franco-German War, 1870–1. The technique was developed by the Parisian chemist Barreswil and used for messages transmitted by pigeon, sent from Tours to Paris. By means of photomicroscopy it was possible for a pigeon to carry up to 40 000 messages on 12–18 films measuring 38×60 mm rolled to a pin's thickness and inserted into goose or crow quills, through which a silk thread was passed to fasten it to the pigeon's tail coverts. On arrival in Paris the films were carefully removed, unrolled, mounted on glass slides and projected on a screen so that four telegraphists could transcribe the messages in longhand for onward transmission to the addresses by the city post.

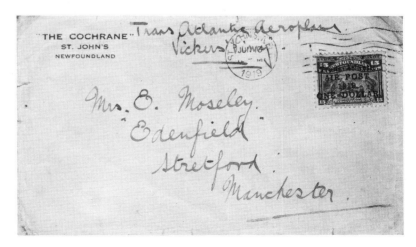

Cover flown by Alcock and Brown across the Atlantic, 1919

The idea was revived by Kodak in 1932 but rejected by the British Post Office who felt that the public would never agree to the use of form-filling or consent to their messages being exposed for all to see. In 1941, however, the scheme was brought into use, for the use of military personnel stationed in the Middle East. Kodak supplied equipment and technicians and established a processing station in Cairo. A standard form was devised and a charge of 3d per airgraph instituted. Completed forms were microfilmed and flown to England for processing at Kodak's Wealdstone plant near London. The prints were forwarded to London Postal Region, folded and placed in window envelopes marked 'Airgraph' and despatched to the addressees. The first airgraphs left Cairo on 21 April 1941 and reached England on 13 May. A service in the opposite direction was inaugurated in August 1941 and gradually extended to other war zones. The service ceased on 31 July 1945. In four years some 350 million airgraphs had been transmitted. The total weight of film used was no more than 50 tonnes – compared with an estimated minimum of 4500 tonnes which a similar number of ordinary letters would have weighed.

The first aerial stowaway was detected on the inaugural airmail flight from Rouyn to Three Rivers, Canada in January 1925 by the Laurentide Air Service.

The first airmail service by jet took place in May 1952 by Comet-1 of BOAC between London and Johannesburg.

Catapult mail was a method devised to speed up Trans-Atlantic mail. Light aircraft were carried aboard the liner *Ile de France* and catapulted into the air when near to the French coast, thereby saving a day in transit. Experiments were carried out on 8 and 12 August 1928 (without special markings) and then special stamps with a 10 franc surcharge were issued for use on mail carried on the flight of 23 August.

Although the French abandoned this idea it was taken up by the Germans who first used it from the *Bremen* on 22 July 1929 when a day's voyage from New York, and on 2 August on the return voyage to Bremen. Special cachets were applied to mail on both occasions but no special stamps were issued. Subsequently the *Bremen* used catapult mail at New York, Amsterdam, Cherbourg and Southampton. The system was extended in 1930 to the *Europa* and in the 1930-31 season also to the *Columbus*. It was discontinued in December 1931, temporarily resumed in the summer of 1932 and concluded on 5 July 1932 at Southampton (*Europa*). Catapult mail was also used on the South Atlantic service from the *Westfalen* and the *Schwabenland* stationed off the American and African coasts. In 1936 the *Ostmark*

was added to the service and specially designed for the purpose. These catapult services linked the Dornier-Wal flying-boats used on the main leg of the South Atlantic route by Lufthansa and Syndicato Condor. The service ended on the outbreak of the Second World War.

Glider mail was first carried in August 1923, at a gliding meeting at Gersfeld in the Rhineland, Germany. Obsolete stamps of the 1919 series were unofficially overprinted for the occasion. On 13 October 1923 Britain's only glider post took place. The *Daily Mail* offered a prize of £10 000 for the longest distance by motor-assisted glider (carrying only one gallon of fuel). Mail carried from Lympne to Hastingleigh bore special labels. A glider mail was flown from Wascherau bei Stockerau, Austria on 19 October 1923. The first international glider mail was flown from Graz, Austria, to Maribor, Yugoslavia in May 1933.

In 1930 a glider was towed across the United States from San Diego, California to New York. In 1934 a string of three gliders was towed from New York to Washington. One of the pilots associated with this Lustig Sky Train, Jack O'Mearay du Pont, organised a Glider Train from Havana to Miami in May 1935. Cuba issued a special 10c stamp for the occasion.

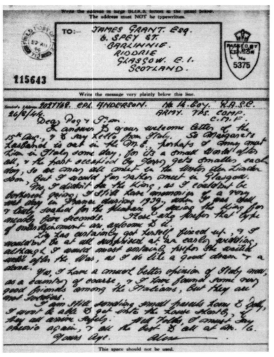

Service airgraph, 1944

Mail was first carried by autogiro in May 1934 in connection with the APEX airmail exhibition in London, from Hanworth to Windsor. In November 1934 souvenir mail was carried by the same autogiro between Melbourne and Portland, Australia during the Victoria Centenary celebrations. The first official autogiro service was operated in 1938 by Eastern Air Lines between Philadelphia Post Office and Camden airfield to expedite mails.

The first helicopter mail took place in July 1946 in Los Angeles and was operated by the Air Transport Command and Air Rescue Service of the USAAF. Mail bore a special cachet. The first in Europe was on 5 November 1947 between The Hague and Brussels, a special postmark being employed. The first in the UK took place in February 1947 when mail from the Royal Family was flown from HMS *Vanguard* to Plymouth, at the beginning of the Royal Tour to South Africa. A similar royal service took place between Dyce and Balmoral, Grampian in August 1947. An emergency service took mail to the keepers of the Wolf Rock Lighthouse in February 1948. Experimental flights in East Anglia led to the first public service on 1 June 1948, with fourteen termini.

The use of carrier pigeons is of the greatest antiquity. Indeed, the earliest example of this bird being used to convey a message to man would be the dove which brought the olive branch to Noah as a token of God's goodwill. The Greeks, Egyptians and Assyrians are all believed to have used carrier pigeons. Pliny tells how Brutus, besieged by Antony in Modena, used carrier pigeons to carry messages to the Roman consuls. Carrier pigeons were used at the siege of Leiden (1575), by the Rothschilds to get news of the victory at Waterloo (1815) three days before the news broke in London. In 1870-1 over 300 pigeons flew messages into Paris, first written by hand on tiny flimsies and later by microfilm *pellicule* (see above page 37). The pigeons were taken out of Paris aboard manned balloons.

The first commercial pigeon service was established in 1855 between Galle and Colombo, Ceylon (Sri Lanka) to expedite news of the Crimean War. It ceased in 1858.

In 1896 W Fricker experimented with carrier pigeons between the Great Barrier Islands and Auckland, New Zealand, and inaugurated a public service early in 1897. Special adhesive stamps were issued in November 1898. Two services operated till 1908 when extensions to the telegraph service rendered them superfluous.

Cover flown by autogiro, May 1934

Cover by first official
helicopter mail
operated by BEA in
East Anglia, 1948

Between 1931 and 1941 semi-official carrier pigeon services operated in India, using specially printed flimsies, often of a commemorative nature, and latterly raising funds for the war effort.

HM Naval Pigeon Service, formed in 1896 for use in naval emergencies, was used extensively in both world wars and also organised pigeongram flights for charities and fund-raising stunts in peacetime.

A pigeongram service operated between Guernsey and the island of Herm in 1949; special 1s stamps and flimsies were issued.

The only other instance of tame birds being used to carry mail was in the Gilbert Islands in the 1880s, when missionaries used frigate-birds to carry letters tightly rolled and inserted in a quill attached to their tail coverts.

Experiments with mail-carrying rockets had taken place in Austria since 1928 by Friedrich Schmiedl, but apart from personal messages no mail was carried till February 1931 when a V-7 rocket was successfully launched. The first rocket mail for the general public was the R-1 later the same year. Special (but unofficial) stamps, covers and cachets were used.

The first rocket mail in the UK was launched by the German, Gerhard Zucker, at Rottingdean,

Sussex in June 1934. An attempt to send mail by rocket from the island of Scarp to Harris in July failed when the rocket exploded.

The greatest number of mail rocket flights took place in India, 75 flights being launched by Dr Stephen Smith between September 1934 and December 1944.

The only stamp ever issued by a postal administration for a rocket post was the 10 centavos produced by Cuba on 15 October 1939 overprinted EXPERIMENTO DEL COHETE POSTAL AÑO DE 1939. Stamps and miniature sheets were issued in 1964 to commemorate the 25th anniversary of this rocket flight.

During the Apollo 11 moon flight in 1969 the astronauts took with them a die for a postage stamp actually showing them setting foot on the moon's surface. When the lunar module touched down on the moon the astronauts pulled an impression of this die on paper, thus creating the moon's first postage stamp. The die was returned to earth and then used in the production of the printing plate for America's 10c airmail stamp issued in September 1969. The astronauts also took to the moon an envelope franked with an imperforate coloured die proof of the stamp. This they cancelled on the moon with a special postmark inscribed MOON LANDING USA with the date JUL 20 1969 in the centre. The first lunar post office had the minimum amount of equipment – one rubber stamp and an ink-pad. All three astronauts laid hands on the rubber stamp and cancelled the envelope together.

Weird methods of transmitting messages included carved wooden sticks, known as *pilbud* or *härpil* (Sweden), which were used from the end of the ninth century, being carried by relays of messengers who stuck them in posts for the next man to pick up. Later, a more sophisticated form of carved wooden staves, known as *Budkavle* (Sweden) or *Budstika* (Norway), were used in the eighteenth and early nineteenth centuries, mainly for official notices.

Post Office Stones were large boulders with notices carved on them, urging the reader to look for letters hidden underneath. These stones were used at the Cape of Good Hope and St Helena by East Indiamen (both British and Dutch). Ships heading south would leave letters for ships on the return voyage to pick up and deliver in England or Holland. The Cape stones were used between 1602 and April 1632, while those at St Helena date around the middle of the century.

Post Office Shoes were old shoes and boots suspended from a large tree at Olifants Bay, South Africa, and used by East Indiamen as a form of post-box in the eighteenth century.

The Whalers' Tree at Stilla harbour near Cape Horn was used by the whaling ships of the Antarctic as a post-box. Ships on the homeward run to Nantucket, New Bedford and other whaling towns of New England would call here to pick up mail left among the tree's roots. Letters might take anything from 14 months to 4 years to be delivered.

HANDLING OF MAIL

Censorship of mail was practised in many countries in the seventeenth and eighteenth centuries but since this was wrapped in secrecy letters were not marked in any way to indicate that they had

been examined. The earliest instance recorded of mail endorsed, occurred during the Jacobite Rebellion of 1745-6. Letters delayed in transit between Scotland and England were subsequently marked OPENED BY THE REBELS – the endorsement being applied in manuscript by the Post Office. Unofficial examination of a similar nature occurred during the Irish troubles (1916-21) and covers are known with rubber stamps CENSORED BY THE I.R.A.

Official censorship of mail, involving the use of distinctive markings, began during the American Civil War. Various stamps, inscribed EXAMINED or APPROVED were used in the Federal prison camps on mail destined for the Confederate States. Letters from Union prisoners in Confederate camps were merely endorsed in manuscript EXAMINED. Postal censorship of mail from the combatants in forward areas applied to both sides in the Franco-German War (1870-1) and the Balkan Wars (1878-9). Both British and Boer authorities censored mail from armed forces and civilians in the combat zones during the South African War (1899-1902). Censorship was extended to mail to and from neutral countries contiguous to belligerent countries during the First World War, and in the Second World War this applied even to mail to and from civilians in restricted military areas.

Mail salvaged from shipwrecks and crashes is usually marked to indicate the cause of delay or damage. The first instance of shipwrecked mail being marked was in 1846 when letters saved from the wreck of the *Great Liverpool* were thus marked with a framed stamp.

Special labels affixed to mail salvaged from a train crash were first used in Canada in January 1873 on letters rescued from a crash on the Grand Trunk Railway near Grafton, Ontario. Rubber-stamped endorsement was applied to salvaged mail from the crash at Mattawan River, Ontario (June 1894), Grantham, Lincs (September 1906), train fires in France (1917, 1919 and 1924) and Capetown-Port Elizabeth Express, South Africa (May 1925). Letters salvaged from the Tay Bridge disaster (1879) were merely endorsed in manuscript.

The earliest example of handstruck marking on mail salvaged from an air crash occurred in July 1934. Partially charred mail salvaged from the explosion of the experimental mail-carrying rocket at Scarp, Harris was marked with a three-line rubber stamp by the Harris postmaster to explain the cause of damage. The first example of a mark applied to mail salvaged from an air-liner occurred in 1935, when letters from the *City of Khartoum*, which crashed off the coast of Alexandria, were thus treated. Subsequent examples include mail recovered

USA 10c airmail stamp, 1969 celebrating the first man on the moon

SALVED FROM
S.S. "LEINSTER".

DAMAGED BY
SEA WATER
IN AIRPLANE
ACCIDENT

GRANTHAM
RLY ACCIDENT

Special markings applied to mail salvaged from shipwreck, air crashes and train disasters

from *Scipio* (1936), *Boadicea* (1936), *Cygnus* (1937), *Calpurnia* (1938), *Centurion* (1939) and the Comet crashes off Singapore and at Prestwick (both 1954).

Disinfection of mail during time of plagues and epidemics was widely practised from the seventeenth century onwards. Strict regulations for the disinfection of incoming mail from plague-stricken countries were enforced in Britain by the Quarantine Act of 1710. Four methods of disinfection were used:
(*a*) opening the letter and exposure of contents to the air.
(*b*) fumigation over a brazier (scorch marks).
(*c*) splashing or dipping in vinegar (stains).
(*d*) piercing to let out the pestilential air (slits or cuts).
   Special marks were used in France, Italy, Malta and other maritime countries in the eighteenth and early nineteenth centuries.

Letter disinfected at the Malta Lazaret; note the slits to let out the pestilential air

Postmarks

The earliest postal markings of any kind are the red and blue markings on the letters of Egyptian court officials during the Third Dynasty (*c* 2778 BC), bearing the exhortation 'In the name of the living king, speed!' Examples are preserved in the Cairo Museum.

The earliest examples of a postmark in Europe consist of injunctions to the postal officials not to delay state correspondence. A formula used in Venice by the early fourteenth century was the Latin '*Cito, citissime, volantissime*' (quickly, very quickly, very fleetingly). By the sixteenth century the French were endorsing their mail '*en diligence*' (with speed and care), and it is from this endorsement that French mail-coaches came to be known as diligences. In Tudor England a common expression on the covers of letters was 'Haste, haste, for life, post haste' and this, in turn, has given the language an expression meaning with all speed.

Many of the more important state letters bore the signatures of the respective postmasters through whose hands they passed en route, together with the times of arrival and departure. Such express letters are of considerable interest to postal historians for the light they shed on medieval mail routes and the time it took to cover these routes.

Only when the state services were thrown open to the general public did a system of manuscript marking come into use to denote the amount of postage due from the recipient. Even after the introduction of handstruck postmarks, charges were often indicated in manuscript – black ink for postage due and red ink or crayon for prepaid letters.

The earliest record of manuscript postal charges comes from France in the mid-sixteenth century, when it became customary for senders to endorse the wrappers *Port quatre solz* or *Dte* (*décompte* ?) *pour le port cinq solz* to indicate that the letters had been prepaid, but these endorsements were quite unofficial and are not believed to have been applied by the post office. In 1588, however, the regulations for the Toulouse-Paris messengers stipulated that each letter had to be endorsed on the wrapper with the amount paid or due *à raison de huict soulz pour once poix de marc* (at the rate of eight sous per ounce weight). Charges were expressed simply as numerals in black or red ink. Examples before 1640, when the practice extended to the whole of France, are very rare.

The earliest letters of the general public in England were transmitted without charge markings. The service was severely disrupted during the Civil War (1642-9) and not resumed till 1652. From then onwards charges were indicated by simple numerals. Paid letters usually included a manuscript endorsement 'Post payd' or 'P Pd' but are relatively scarce. Manuscript was used to denote the amount of postage, with very few exceptions, until the advent of Uniform Fourpence Postage in December 1839 and the Penny Post the following January, but many offices continued to indicate charges in black ink. Even after the adoption of adhesive stamps in 1840 the British Post Office permitted the prepayment of letters in cash as late as the 1850s, the amount being indicated in red ink or crayon on the front of the letter. This concession was withdrawn in the provinces in 1852, but survived in the London area as late as 1855.

The earliest handstruck postmarks identifying the place of posting were in use in Milan at the

Diligence (mail-coach) on a French stamp of 1952

beginning of the fourteenth century and have been found on letters transmitted through the municipal post organised by the Visconti family. The first of these marks was embossed in colourless relief and bore the civic coat of arms and the Latin inscription *Sub pena furcarum* (under penalty of the forks) – a warning to messengers not to tamper with the mail, under pain of a particularly cruel instrument of torture. The last of the Viscontis, Filippo Maria, must have had trouble with his postmen in spite of this threat, for he introduced a postmark in 1425 inscribed *Sub pena mille furcarum* (under penalty of a thousand forks). Later marks incorporated tiny daggers and a star, thought to represent the medieval wheel-rack on which the limbs of wrong-doers were broken. The custom spread to other Italian city states, several of whom also used embossed albino stamps featuring their coats of arms.

The first postmark to incorporate an actual reference to the posts is recorded on a letter from Aleppo, Syria to Leonardo da Vinci at Amboise in 1519. The words POSTA CECA were struck on a wax seal. The meaning of this inscription has defied all attempts to unravel it!

The earliest postmark in Europe bearing the name of a town or place was inscribed D'JARSEY (21 × 3mm 0·83 × 0·12 in) and was applied at St Malo in 1683 on mail from Jersey; only two examples have so far been found. This pre-dates the general introduction of namestamps in France by twelve years. The earliest namestamp from Jersey itself (JERSEY in a curve) did not appear till 1794. France generally adopted namestamps in 1695, the name being preceded by the word DE (from) in most cases.

Ireland was using namestamps before any other part of the British Isles. The earliest example, dating from 1698, emanates from Strabane. Other towns from which namestamps have so far been recorded are Mullingar and Waterford (1699), Cork (1703), Lochrea (1703), Kinsale and Clonmel (both 1704). The earliest namestamps from England date from 1701, when Stone, Bolton and Coventry used such marks. A mark inscribed EXON is known on a letter from Exeter dated 1700, but its status has never been substantiated. Instructions to postmasters were issued in 1715 ordering them to provide their offices with namestamps but the practice did not become

STRABANE
Strabane, 1698: earliest namestamp in the British Isles

DUNS
Duns, 1731: earliest namestamp in Scotland

general till the 1730s. The earliest namestamps from Scotland were used at Duns (1731) and Dumfries (1732), both border towns which presumably copied the idea from their English neighbours.

The earliest marks identifying the origin of letters in the British Isles (other than datestamps – see below) were used at Dublin in 1667-8. The first type consisted of the letter W in a circle and is thought to identify Warburton, Deputy Postmaster General for Ireland at the time. A second type, with a D (Dowling?), has been recorded on letters of 1669. The earliest mark of origin of this type from England is the so-called 'hot-cross bun' mark, found on letters of 1681 from the Chichester, Farnham and Worplesdon area of Hampshire. The impression is said to resemble the rudimentary town plan of Chichester and it is thought that it was applied to mail to distinguish letters going to London on the Chichester road. It is known that Colonel Roger Whitley, manager of the postal services, wrote to Robert Tayer, postmaster of Chichester, in 1673 urging him to furnish himself with a stamp 'to distinguish yours from other letters . . .' and it seems likely that the hot-cross bun mark was the answer.

Letters carried by ships of the Dutch East India Company are known with the company's VOC monogram from 1665 – two years before the earliest postmark used in the Netherlands. Letters from Stockholm (1685) were impressed with a crowned oval incorporating a B (private mail) or F (official mail).

The world's first postal datestamp was devised by Colonel Henry Bishop, Postmaster General of Britain, who produced it as an answer to criticism that letters were often delayed in the post. An announcement in the April 1661 issue of the *Mercurius Publicus* stated: 'A stamp is invented that is putt upon every letter shewing the day of the moneth

D'JARSEY
Jersey arrival mark of 1683

DE LYON
Lyon postmark of 1695: earliest name-stamp in France

W receiver's mark, Dublin, used by Deputy PMG, Warburton, 1667

that every letter comes to the office, so that no Letter Carryer may dare detayne a letter from post to post, which before was usual.' The Bishop mark consisted of a small circle divided into two segments. One segment bore figures and the other a two-letter abbreviation for the month. Thus 18 MA would indicate 18 March and 21 IV meant 21 June. The stamp was made of wood and resembled two small rods with a semi-circular section, bound tightly together like the old-fashioned wooden clothes peg. At first Bishop marks were only used in London, but they spread to Dublin by 1670 and Edinburgh in 1693. They survived in London till 1787, in Dublin till 1795 and in Edinburgh till 1806. During the eighteenth century colonial versions were adopted in Albany (1773-87), Boston (1768-1800), Charlestown (1768-75), New York (1758-76), Quebec (1776-99), Philadelphia (1766-76) and Calcutta (1775-7). Though these stamps all followed the same basic pattern they can be identified by variations in shape, diameter, colour and the layout of inscriptions.

Exeter and Bristol were the first English provincial towns to use datestamps (1697), employing modified forms of the Bishop mark with the dates shown inside their initial letters. These Exeter and Bristol stamps were confined to Cross Post letters, mail intended for London continuing to go unstamped till the early eighteenth century.

The first handstamp showing the office name, to be used in North America, was a two-line type inscribed NEW/YORK, recorded in 1756. Other towns using postmarks in the colonial period were Annapolis, Hartford and Philadelphia (1766), Boston and Charlestown (1769), New Town and Williamsburg (1770), Newport (1771), Baltimore (1772), Albany (1773), Salem (1774) New Haven, Portsmouth, New London, Newbury, Norfolk and Suffolk (1775).

The first handstruck markings denoting postage due from the recipient were used at the Foreign Post Office in London from 1663 to 1667. They were rectangular, with a line across the centre and D (due) and the amount in figures. The stamps were suddenly discontinued and for almost two centuries the London foreign branch preferred to indicate charges in manuscript, a curiously retrograde step.

The first – and for almost a century, the only British provincial handstruck mark denoting postage to be paid by the recipient was used at Montrose, Scotland in 1742 and consisted of a tiny numeral '2' (twopence), applied by a wooden stamp. This mark is extremely rare, only three examples having so far been recorded.

Elaborate stamps incorporating the initials of towns from which letters came, together with the amount due in stuivers, were introduced at Amsterdam in 1667.

VOC mark of the Dutch East India Company

Swedish crowned B mark used on private mail

Bishop mark, 1661

NEW YORK

New York namestamp, 1756: first in America

The first postmarks to indicate distances were adopted in England in 1784. The numerals below or alongside the office name denoted the distance of the office from London, and assisted postal staff to compute the amount of postage due, based on the distance conveyed. These stamps were discontinued in 1795, when many of the mileages had been found to be inaccurate, but they were resumed in 1801. They were not introduced to Scotland and Ireland till 1808 (Dumfries, which had an English-style stamp in 1801, being the sole exception). The use of these mileage marks was terminated at the end of 1828, but a few offices in Scotland and Ireland were still using them as late as the mid-1850s, long after the computation of postage by distance had been abandoned.

The first handstruck postage stamps, indicating prepayment of postage, were invented by William Dockwra, a London merchant, who devised triangular stamps for a private service, the London Penny Post, which he established in 1680. Dockwra instituted a system of receiving-houses in London and Westminster. Letters handled by these offices were struck with distinctive double-lined triangular stamps inscribed PENNY POST PAID round the three sides. In the centre was a letter indicating the receiving-house – L (the head office in Lyme Street), W (Westminster), T (Temple) and P (St Paul's). Dockwra's post was strenuously opposed by messengers and porters whose livelihood was threatened. Titus Oates denounced it as 'a Popish contrivance' and alleged that the Jesuits were at the bottom of the scheme. In the main, however, Dockwra was opposed by the Post Office whose monopoly he infringed. Following a court action, the service was suppressed in November 1682, but shortly afterwards re-opened under Post Office control. Dockwra was eventually awarded a pension of £500 per annum and served as Controller of the Penny Post, 1696-1700. Somewhat similar triangular paid stamps were used by the government service till 1795.

The first stamps to show the time of posting were also invented by William Dockwra. Each letter transmitted by his London Penny Post was additionally marked with a small heart-shaped stamp indicating the hour of despatch. Stamps showing the hour were confined to the London and Edinburgh penny posts, but were discontinued in 1843 and 1838 respectively. Thereafter the time was indicated vaguely by means of code letters – M (morning), E (evening) or A (afternoon), and even this concession ceased about 1857. Gradually, however, the larger offices adopted a system of combined numeral and letter codes which identified the stamper and gave (to the Post Office if not the public) a rough idea of the time of stamping. Four-letter codes were inserted in datestamps in 1894 but time in clear was not restored and extended to the whole of the British Isles till 1895. Most European countries had adopted time stamps during the course of the nineteenth century and it seems strange that the country which invented them should have been so reluctant to use them, but the British Post Office had a very real aversion, frequently expressed, to letting the public know exactly when its mail was posted.

The first provincial penny post in the British Isles was established in Dublin in 1773. An Act of Parliament of 1765 had permitted towns to establish penny posts within their boundaries but none was willing to take up this responsibility. A private penny post was established in Edinburgh in 1774 and successfully operated by Peter Williamson. One of the most colourful characters ever associated with the posts, he was a native of Aberdeen who had been kidnapped at the age of ten and sold into slavery on the American plantations. As if this were not bad enough, he was later captured by Indians with whom he spent some years and earned the nickname 'Indian Peter'. He eventually returned to Scotland where he earned a living as a writer, publisher, printer and inn-keeper. He published the *Edinburgh City Direc-*

Rectangular charge mark (1663), Montrose '2' (1742) and Dutch 'stuiver' mark

R ISLE OF
WIGHT 97

MINEHEAD
180

Mileage marks of England, Scotland and Ireland, 1784-1828

Dockwra Penny Post mark, 1680

tory and advertised therein his local postal service which operated within a mile radius of Edinburgh Cross. He used paid and unpaid stamps, some incorporating the date, and his service ran for 19 years before it was absorbed into the government postal system. Williamson was granted a pension of £25 per annum in recognition of his service.

The oldest local post in the world, however, was the Paris Petite Poste founded by Renouard de Villayer in 1653. De Villayer, *Maître des Requêtes* (Master of Petitions) was authorised by a decree of 8 August 1653 to establish the post. The existence of the service is well documented in contemporary literature but it was short-lived and no example of any letter transmitted through it has been found. This service was not revived until 5 March 1758.

The earliest examples of franking privilege, permitting the free passage of official correspondence, cannot be ascertained since the oldest postal services in the world were established for this express purpose. Once the general public were permitted to use the postal services, however, and the question of payment arose, it became necessary to distinguish between mail on which there was a charge and that which was allowed to continue free of postage. The

Peter Williamson, 'Indian Peter' who operated a private penny post in Edinburgh in 1774.

Dockwra heart-shaped time stamp, 1680

Peter Williamson Penny Post, Edinburgh, 1774

first specific provision for such mail was made in a decree of the Council of State in 1652, during the Commonwealth, permitting letters to pass free through the post between Members of Parliament and certain government officials. Such letters were recognised by the impressions on their wax seals, but in 1653 it was decreed that all official letters had to be marked across the front 'These are for the Service of the Commonwealth'. French government correspondence of 1692-3 is known with the manuscript endorsement *'Pour les expresses affaires du Roy'*.

The earliest postmark associated with the franking privilege was a two line, unframed stamp inscribed AFFRANCHI/PAR ÉTAT (franked by state), struck in black or red on official correspondence from Paris in 1672. This stamp is all the more remarkable since it preceded any other handstruck postmark of France by 23 years. A considerable time elapsed before this was followed, in 1744, by a single line mark inscribed AFFAIRES DU ROY. During the Revolution, the use of franks proliferated rapidly, reflecting the turbulent nature of French politics at that time.

In Britain parliamentary and official mail was carried free of charge, the privilege being granted by Royal Warrant as the revenue of the Post Office went to the Crown. In 1764 postal revenues were surrendered by the Crown to Parliament in return for a Civil List. Thereafter the franking privilege had to be authorised by Act of Parliament. This necessitated the introduction of special stamps inscribed FREE in May 1764. At first these were undated but a date was incorporated in 1791. In 1799 a crown was also featured, and this was a characteristic of the English franks until they were abolished in 1840 as part of the package of postal reforms introduced by Rowland Hill. Only one type of 'free' handstamp was ever used at Edinburgh (1772-88) but

Dublin had a most elaborate system. Ireland, in fact, was using distinctive franks from 1706 onwards, the most attractive being the 'mermaids' – so-called from the female figure adorning their frame and probably derived from the figure on the heraldic harp.

The first postal marking denoting prepayment on newspapers and periodicals sent by post, was used by France in 1779. It consisted of a double circle inscribed PERIODIQUES, with the word FRANCS (franked = prepaid) and a crown and fleur de lis in the centre. The royalist emblems were removed in 1793 and by 1797 the Phrygian cap of Liberty, emblem of the Revolution, was substituted.

No special postal markings were used for this purpose in the British Isles, but since all newspapers bore a revenue stamp which, incidentally, allowed them to pass free through the post, this may be considered as a semi-postal stamp. These stamps, struck in red, were first adopted in 1712 when the tax was a halfpenny per newspaper. When the newspaper tax was abolished in 1855 the red stamp was allowed to remain on those papers sent by post and thus it is regarded from that date onwards purely as a postage stamp. The tax was repealed in 1870 and thereafter adhesive postage stamps or stamped wrappers had to be used instead.

Special Sunday postmarks were used in London and Dublin. It was a condition of the franking privilege that letters had to bear the date of posting, in the handwriting of the sender, and were not passed free of postage if posted on any other day. Since franked letters, if posted on a Sunday, were not stamped with the frank till the following day, a special Sunday mark was also impressed on them to explain the apparent difference between the handwritten date and the date in the frank. These marks were inscribed SUN or SUNDAY and, in the case of Dublin, were also applied to ordinary mail arriving in that city on a Sunday and not delivered until the following day. London also had special stamps instructing the postmen to deliver the letters before 10 am on Sunday morning. These Sunday marks survived the abolition of the franking privilege by several years.

The world's first cancellation, a form of postmark intended to cancel postage stamps and prevent their re-use, was the so-called Maltese Cross obliterator, supplied to every post town in the British Isles and used in conjunction with the adhesive stamps introduced in May 1840. Actually, the term 'Maltese Cross', coined by early philatelists, is inaccurate since the device was based on the Tudor rose and bears little resemblance to the eight-pointed cross of the Knights of Malta. The obliterators were made of

AFFRANCHI PAR ÉTAT

Franks used in France, England and Ireland

The earliest French and English newspaper stamps

brass in a uniform pattern so that it is not usually possible to identify the office at which cancellation took place. A few later replacement stamps, however, were sufficiently distinctive to be readily identifiable and these are much prized by collectors. Red ink was used at first, but from February 1841 onwards black was preferred (it had been used experimentally in London from late August 1840). Blue ink was used at Cheltenham, Preston and Truro, a rich shade of brown at Manchester, maroon (Epsom), pink (Ormskirk), yellow (Newnham-on-Severn), orange (Liverpool), vermilion (Bristol), magenta (Preston and Burton-on-Trent), and ruby (Aberdeen). A few instances of adhesives cancelled in both red and black Maltese Crosses are known. The office datestamp was applied to the back of the envelope or wrapper, in line with the practice obtaining before the adoption of adhesive stamps.

The Swiss canton of Zürich, which adopted adhesive stamps in March 1843, was clearly inspired by Britain's Maltese Cross in its choice of obliterator. This had the same outline as the Maltese Cross, but the Swiss cross was superimposed and circular ornaments inserted in the interstices. This obliterator is more accurately known as the Zürich Rosette. It

Sunday marks used in England and Ireland

Maltese Cross obliterator, 1840-44 and the Zürich rosette, 1843

was subsequently used also by Geneva (September 1843) and is known on the earliest federal stamps (1850). Black ink was favoured by Zürich and red by Geneva, but blue ink was also used.

Brazil, which issued its first adhesive stamps on 1 August 1843, did not provide special cancellers but made use of existing datestamps or undated name-stamps.

The first cancellers designed to enhance rather than deface the features of the reigning monarch were issued in Spain in 1850 and consisted of quatrefoils with lines extending outwards from the arches. They were intended to obliterate the stamp thoroughly while framing the somewhat homely features of Queen Isabella. A more elaborate obliterator, in the form of a baroque picture frame, was devised by Sicily in 1859 to cancel stamps portraying King Ferdinand (known affectionately as 'Bomba' from his habit of ordering the naval bombardment of his unruly subjects). The only other instance of a deferential cancellation may be found on stamps from the Indian state of Bhor in 1901. These stamps are not known to have been used postally and the fancy framework cancellation was only applied by favour.

The most thorough obliterators were devised in the mid-nineteenth century by postal administrations paranoid at the prospect of dishonest people washing off the cancelling ink and re-using the stamps. Examples of obliterators designed to cover the stamp with a pattern of lines which would defeat even the most resolute cleaning, include the oval grill (Buenos Aires, 1858-9), barred diamond (Toronto, 1858), the CGH triangular arrangement of close parallel lines (Cape of Good Hope, 1853-63), the oval pattern of parallel lines (Ceylon, 1855-67), the diamond pattern

of dots inscribed FRANCA (Ecuador, 1866), the diamond pattern of criss-cross lines or points (France, 1849-50), diamond pattern grill or parallel lines (Switzerland, 1851), the oval barred pattern (New South Wales, 1850), the circular pattern of parallel lines (Norway, 1855), the four-ring 'target' cancellation (Austria, 1850), the rectangular pattern of diamonds (Tuscany, 1851), the eleven-bar 'stummer stempel' of Lecco (Austria, 1851) or the heavy circular grids (United States, 1847-50). Even Spain soon abandoned its deferential cancellations and applied heavy oval bars to the stamps, regardless of the *lese majeste* involved. This was not quite as ruthless as a measure proposed by Dr Thebussem (*nom de plume* of the Spanish postal reformer, M P de Figueroa) who advocated the use of corrosive ink and even suggested an ingenious method of impregnating the paper with gunpowder, so that the stamp would literally explode when struck with the canceller!

Cancellation by tearing the stamp is not as heretical as it might first appear, and the practice is quite widespread in the cancellation of tickets. Mercifully for philately, however, it has only occurred in two instances. David Bryce, owner of the coastal steamship *Lady McLeod* which plied between Port of Spain and San Fernando, Trinidad, cancelled the stamps which he provided for the letters carried by his ship by lifting one corner of the stamp off the envelope and thinning the back with his finger nail. Later, however, he decided that cancellation in pen and ink was much quicker and more efficacious.

The first stamps of Afghanistan, the famous 'Tigers' of 1870-81, were customarily cancelled by the postmasters lifting a corner and tearing out a

Deferential cancellation,
Sicily, 1859

sizable chunk. It is therefore virtually impossible to find postally used examples of these stamps in perfect condition.

The first numeral obliterators were introduced by the British Post Office in May 1844. Although the office datestamp was applied to the reverse of letters it was felt that the obliterator should also identify the office at which it was applied. Separate sets of numbered obliterators were used in the London Chief Office (Inland Section), the London District Post, the provincial offices of England, Wales, the Channel Islands and the Isle of Man, and in Scotland and Ireland. Each series had a distinctive design – English (oval), Scottish (rectangular) and Irish (diamond-shaped), with the numbers in the centre. Each post town and many of the more important sub-offices were allocated a number. In the original series the English provincial numbers ran from 1 (Abergavenny) to 936 (Whitwell, Yorkshire), the Scottish numbers ran from 1 (Aberdeen) to 342 (Wishaw) while the Irish series ran from 1 (Abbeyleix) to 450 (Youghal). The Scottish and Irish lists were eventually extended to 755 (Isle of Canna) and 564 (Mount Charles), while the English series, having run out of three-figure combinations, then adopted letter prefixes and numbers from 1 to 99. The highest number in the English series was L05 (the Norwich Sorting Carriage). These numbers were subsequently used in other cancellers, date-stamps and charge and explanatory markings. The highest numbers actually recorded in 1844-style

obliterators were K95 (Shipton-under-Wychwood), 651 (Ancrum) and possibly 493 (Irish TPO).

These obliterators became obsolescent in the 1850s but quite a few survived into the early years of the twentieth century and both Aberdeen (1) and Southampton (723) continued to use these ancient obliterators well into the 1950s to cancel stamps which had been missed by machine cancellation.

Numeral obliterators were also adopted by many British colonies and quite a number of foreign countries in the 1850s. Below are listed the principal countries and a brief description of the pattern of numeral obliterator used.

Baden	five concentric circles (1851–67)
Bavaria	'mill-wheel' stamp (1850) concentric dashes (1856)
Brunswick	Irish-style diamond (1856)
Prussia	four concentric circles (1850–9)
Saxony	double circle with criss-cross pattern (1852–66)
Schleswig-Holstein	circular pattern of horizontal bars (1850)
Thurn and Taxis	four concentric circles (1852–67)
Belgium	rectangle within horizontal lines in a circular format (1850)
Canada	four concentric circles (1851) two concentric circles (1858)
New Brunswick	oval grid of parallel lines (1851–67)
Denmark	three concentric circles (1851)
France	lozenge pattern of dots (1852)
Greece	lozenge pattern of dots (1861)
India	various patterns of bars in a diamond format (1854–73)
Mauritius	three concentric circles (1849) two concentric circles (1850–68)
Norway	three concentric circles (1856–68)
Poland	six concentric squares (1860) four concentric circles (1860–3)
Queensland	sun burst (1860)
Portugal	upright oval of horizontal bars (1855)

Numeral obliterators of the British Isles, 1844

South Australia	London-style barred oval (1855–60)
Tasmania	English-style oval of bars (1853–61)
Victoria	'butterfly' pattern (1849–51) upright barred oval (1851–6)
Western Australia	horizontal barred oval (1859)

The first duplex cancellers, combining the date-stamp and the obliterator in a single instrument, were used in the London District Post in June 1853, for stamping 'too late' letters. This stamp had a rectangular datestamp and an oval barred obliterator. A stamp for use on ordinary letters, with a circular datestamp, was issued shortly afterwards. These and later London stamps are, more properly, double stamps, since the datestamp and obliterator were separate units. True duplex stamps, in which the obliterating element and the datestamp were inte-grated, were provided for a number of provincial offices in England at the end of May 1854. These duplex stamps were unusual in design and two of them at least were unique – the Reading 'biscuit' (1854) and the Rugby 'shoe' (1857). The true duplexes were experimental, and by 1858 had been superseded by standard patterns of double stamps. Though obsolescent from 1880 onwards, many survived till the twentieth century, the last survivor of this type being used at Barmouth in June 1932.

After a period of highly distinctive experimental stamps Scotland also settled on a series of double stamps which had rectangular obliterators. These were obsolescent from 1883, but one was still in use at Longniddry as late as 9 August 1923.

Double stamps were subsequently adopted by many British colonies and foreign countries. The only country regularly using them to this day is the United States, though the obliterating element is not numbered in any sequence.

Combined stamps, consisting of datestamps which also embodied an obliterating element as an integral part of the design were first used in Austria, 1850. Isolated cases of stamps combining obliterating elements with the name and date exist from then till the 1860s, such as the elaborate 'cogwheel' type of Gfoehl, the fancy oval type of Kaposvar and the barred oval type of Aussee Maehren, but these were more or less unique examples. Double-circle date-stamps with curvilinear ornament at the foot of the inner arc also existed from the 1850s and these were extensively used all over the Habsburg empire from 1850 onwards.

The first combined stamps in England and Wales were the so-called squared circles, first used at Leeds in September 1879. They were widely employed in the late nineteenth century, but a few survived into the twentieth century, the last recorded survivor being used at Cardiff on 21 September 1937. The first combined stamps in Scotland consisted of double circles, with the office number at the foot, flanked by twin obliterating bars. This type was first used at Edinburgh in March 1883. Though obsol-escent from 1906 a few survived the Second World War and the island of Colonsay was still using its stamp (issued in September 1899) in August 1955.

The squared circle type was also used in Italy, Canada, South Africa and New Zealand at the turn of the century. The German answer to this was the bridge datestamp, in which the date appeared in a single line 'bridge' between twin vertical groups of obliterating bars. First used in 1884, it was widely used in Germany till the 1920s, but modified versions were also employed in Austria, Hungary, Switzerland and the Scandinavian countries, surviv-ing in the last-named instance as late as the 1950s. This type was also used experimentally in England (1905), France (1913) and Ireland (1922), but all of these examples are very rare.

First London duplex and other experimental cancellations, 1853-7

The first office to use a combined stamp with a solid black bar between the circles was East Dulwich, London in April 1894. This type is consequently known to collectors as the Dulwich pattern. Oddly enough, it was preceded by some fourteen days by a somewhat similar stamp used at Sunderland, with much thinner bars at the foot. The Sunderland stamp was clearly an experimental type which was not subsequently adopted generally. The Dulwich type was later used all over the British Isles and spread to many overseas countries, mainly in the Commonwealth. Though obsolete since 1949 (when the current thin-arc stamps were introduced) many examples of the Dulwich type are still used forty years after the last of them were manufactured.

The earliest attempt at mechanised cancellation was a machine devised by Pearson Hill, son of Sir Rowland Hill, who began work on the problem in 1853 and by 1857 had constructed a machine which was given extended trials in London in September that year and also in February 1858. The Pearson Hill machine was operated by steam or a foot treadle and produced a distinctive double impression with the date inside sets of vertical lines. A later version had the name LONDON round the foot. Both types of cancellation are exceedingly rare. In 1858-9 a new Hill machine, known as the Parallel Motion, was tested. This produced an impression similar to the contemporary double stamps. Experiments in Edinburgh with these machines produced the famous Brunswick Star postmarks of 1863-5. Parallel Motion machines were widely used in the British Isles till the turn of the century. Other (less successful) machines tested in the late 1850s were invented by Charles Rideout and G H Creswell, both senior surveyors in the Post Office. All of these machines were hand operated, and purists tend to regard them as mechanically assisted handstamps.

The first high-speed stamping machine was invented by Johann Naas and Carl Fischer of Germany in 1865. It was introduced to England by J C Azemar, and tested by the Post Office in April-June 1869, with subsequent trials from mid-1872 till January 1873. It produced an impression with a circular datestamp and patterns of heavy horizontal bars. The trials were deemed unsuccessful.

Another German, Albert Höster, modified the Wirth model and produced cancelling machines operated by foot treadle. Höster machines were given a trial in 1882-3 and were subsequently employed in the London area till 1893. The Höster machines produced an impression with a large datestamp and a pattern of diagonal bars. The percentage of misses was too high, and the Post Office withdrew the machines when better models became available.

The first cancelling machine to be fully automated was invented by Thomas and Martin Leavitt of Boston, Massachusetts *c*1880. The Leavitt Brothers failed to develop their machine, however, and sold their patents in 1885 to Frank and Martin van Buren Ethridge of Boston who formed the American Postal Machine Company. The first Ethridge steam-driven machine was installed in Boston in 1886 and a similar machine was tested in London between September 1886 and April 1887. Steam- and later electrically-driven machines were adopted in Canada (1895), France (1898) and had spread to most countries in western Europe by 1900.

The first slogan postmark was used in London in 1661. It was applied by hand to letters destined for addresses along the Kent road and comprised a large circle containing a nine-line inscription: THE POST FOR ALL KENT GOES EVERY NIGHT FROM THE ROVND HOVSE IN LOVE LANE & COMES EVERY MOR(NING). Two types of handstamp were used until 1663. A similar slogan was used on mail going on the Essex road in 1674-5 and read: ESSEX POST GOES AND COMS EVERY DAY. Again two types are known to have been used. All of these seventeenth-century handstruck slogans are extremely rare. A rare variant of the latter slogan, with S.X. for Essex, is only

Dulwich datestamp, 1894

Squared circles: the earliest combined date and cancelling stamps

Pearson Hill Parallel Motion stamp, on an Italian stamp of 1976

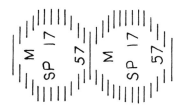

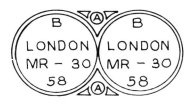

Experimental machine cancellations: Pearson Hill (1857), Rideout and Creswell (both 1858)

Cancellation by the experimental Azemar (1867) machines

known on letters preserved in the Public Record Office, London. This interesting flirtation with postal advertising was not revived in Britain for almost 250 years.

The first machine cancellation to incorporate a device in the obliterating lines was used to advertise the Columbian Exposition, Chicago in 1893. From 1894 many American post offices used machine cancellations incorporating the Stars and Stripes. The seven wavy lines of this flag were later adopted as the obliterating element in many machines used all over the world. Flag cancellations, supplied with American-made machines, were used in many other countries at the turn of the century: Canada (1897-1900), France (1898-1900), New Zealand (1899). Italy and Germany all had cancellations incorporating their national flags. A die was supplied to England in 1897 showing the Union Jack and inscribed 1837 VICTORIA 1897 to celebrate the Queen's Diamond Jubilee but it was never regularly employed. An American flag cancellation was used at the United States pavilion during the French International Exhibition in Paris, 1900. Slogans publicising contemporary events in the early years of this century include Canada's National Exposition, Toronto (1901), the St Louis World Fair (US, 1902-3) and the Jamestown Tercentenary celebrations (US, 1907), the Oberammergau Passion Play (Bavaria, 1910), the Brussels Fair (Belgium, 1910) and the Auckland Exhibition (NZ, 1912).

The first machine slogans used in Britain appeared in December 1917 and were inscribed BUY NATIONAL WAR BONDS NOW, BUY NATIONAL WAR BONDS and FEED THE GUNS WITH WAR BONDS.

The earliest suggestion for a machine slogan was made in 1878 by Robert Vaile who submitted a proposal to the British Post Office for a cancelling machine which included a slogan die. The Vaile machine, however, was never given a trial. In 1910 the manufacturers of Pears Soap suggested slogan advertising to the Post Office. In 1912 the town of Newport, Gwent petitioned the Post Office to be allowed to advertise its docks with the slogan THE WORLD'S LONGEST DOCK. Gordon Selfridge, proprietor of the world-famous department store in

Cancellation by the Höster (1882-3) machines

London, offered £20 000 to the Post Office in 1917 for the franchise to advertise his goods in machine cancellations. Though Selfridge was turned down, it was his suggestion which led the Post Office to advertise patriotic slogans.

Commercial slogans advertising branded goods have never been permitted by the British Post Office, but have slipped past official scrutiny on several occasions. The name of commercial firms is not permitted in slogan dies, but an exception was made for the stamp dealer Stanley Gibbons and the auction house Christie's in 1965 and 1967 respectively, when they celebrated their anniversaries with exhibitions which could legitimately be advertised in this way. Nevertheless, the use of the Stanley Gibbons slogan in a number of London machines allegedly upset some of Gibbons' rivals who insisted on their mail being hand-cancelled.

In February 1968 Newport, Gwent (see above), began advertising itself as THE HOME OF THE MOLE WRENCH. This created considerable interest and even inspired Patrick Campbell to write at length in the *Sunday Times* speculating that the mole wrench might be 'an obscenely Welsh ceremony, carried out at dead of night on the far side of some bestial slag heap'. A year elapsed before the Post Office tumbled to the fact that the slogan referred to a handy spanner invented by the firm of Mole and Son, and insisted that the name be replaced by a descriptive caption SELF-GRIP WRENCH.

Commercial advertising in the form of slogan postmarks has only been permitted in two countries. In 1923 a slogan postmark began appearing in the mail from the major Italian cities inscribed 'SPACE RESERVED FOR PUBLICITY – APPLY TO . . .' followed by the address and telephone number of the postal

advertising department. The following year the fruits of this advertising campaign could be seen for the first time. Readers of *Il Corriere Italiano* were urged to read Guido da Verona's new novel *Mata Hari* (the slogan was even embellished with a bust of the voluptuous Javanese spy), a clothing store advertised its sales and, inevitably, the tobacco companies were well to the fore. Smokers in Tuscany – according to one slogan – preferred Roma cigarettes, while Venetians were exhorted to ask for Savoia-Eva cigarettes – THE BEST AND MOST CONVENIENT. In the postwar years products advertised by slogan postmarks ranged from Motta bread to White Orchid perfume, from Rilsan synthetic fabric to Allonlit pistons and the Fiat Nuova 500. The last of these commercial slogans seem to have been phased out about 1960.

France soon followed Italy's example and advertised the medals from the Mint (1924). More commercial advertising, however, seems to have been confined to the tobacco companies who publicised Gitanes and Celtiques cigarettes and Nouveau Diplomate cigars in the 1930s.

The British Post Office actually considered doing likewise and an announcement was made in 1926 that it was proposed to carry commercial advertising in the obliterating die. This was strenuously opposed by several large companies on the grounds that their mail might inadvertently carry the slogan of their competitors. The Yorkshire confectioners, John Mackintosh and Sons even used specially printed envelopes with a broad black band at the top in order to render any slogan unreadable, and printed along-

Kent Post slogan, 1661: the world's first slogan postmark

Boston machine, 1885-7

Flag cancellations celebrating Queen Victoria's Diamond Jubilee, 1897

Early slogan postmarks, 1893-1913

British War Bonds slogan, 1917

side the message NEVER MIND THE POSTMARK – THIS IS THE RIGHT TIME TO BUY MACKINTOSH'S TOFFEE DE LUXE. The company was ordered to withdraw the envelopes, but they counteracted by querying the right of the Post Office to deface their mail with advertisements of rival products. The matter was raised in Parliament and the Post Office proposal was discreetly dropped.

The first local publicity slogan, advertising the amenities of holiday resorts, was used at Calais in 1921, extolling LE PORT, LA PLAGE, LES DENTELLES. This idea spread to other holiday resorts, Boulogne-sur-Mer using a slogan advertising CURE D'AIR and its casino by 1924. Other early instances of local publicity slogans have been recorded from Hyeres, St Lunaire, Dinard, Dijon and Carcassonne (1925) and Cluses, St Claude and Avignon (1926). Even industrial and commercial centres recognised the value of such publicity, and slogans were in use at Le Havre and Lille by 1926. These slogans consisted

entirely of words. The first French *flammes illustrees* (pictorial 'flames' – from the banners of medieval knights) did not appear until 1950, even though the concept of pictorial slogans was well established long before that date. The first local publicity slogan used elsewhere was VISIT THE DUNES, MICHIGAN CITY, authorised by Act of Congress, 5 October 1921.

The first pictorial slogans for local publicity were used in Berne and Geneva, Switzerland in 1942. Both slogans featured the municipal coats of arms.

The first local publicity slogan in the British Isles was used at Salthill, Co. Galway in the Irish Free State, in the summer of 1935 and stated briefly SALTHILL GALWAY FOR HOLIDAYS.

The first local publicity slogan in the United Kingdom was used by Hastings, Sussex on 1 April 1963. Depicting 'Happy Harold' it stated WE'RE READY FOR YOUR INVASION AT HASTINGS – an allusion to the Norman landing in 1066. Ironically it

Stanley Gibbons Centenary slogan, 1965

Christie's Bicentenary slogan, 1967

Controversial 'Mole Wrench' and 'Self-Grip' slogans of Newport, Gwent

was the Mayor of Bath, the late Major Adrian Hopkins (a noted philatelist) who had pressed the Post Office for years to allow local advertising but in the end Bath was narrowly beaten into first place by Hastings. Bath's first local slogan did not appear until 1 July 1963, this being the first to appear with the datestamp and slogan transposed, so that the message would be clear of the stamp.

Unfortunate slogans have been used on several occasions, their message defeated either by the stamps they cancelled, or the mail on which they were impressed. The most common instances are summonses for traffic violations despatched to holidaymakers and bearing tourist publicity slogans. A British national slogan ARE YOU FULLY INSURED? gave great offence when it was used to cancel notifications of impending hospital operations sent to would-be patients. A common American slogan of the late 1950s REPORT OBSCENE MAIL TO YOUR POSTMASTER is said to have been abruptly withdrawn, after it was used to frank invitations to the wedding of a senator's daughter.

These unfortunate juxtapositions could hardly have been avoided by the post offices concerned. More reprehensible, however, have been the slogans which did not take due consideration of the stamps they would be likely to cancel. The worst case was probably the Canadian slogan CONSERVE CANADA'S

Italian commercial publicity slogans, 1923-60

WILDLIFE which, in 1957, frequently cancelled a set of stamps devoted to hunting, shooting and fishing. An Italian road safety slogan was used in 1968 to cancel stamps commemorating the World Road Cycling Championship. An anti-drink slogan used in Southern Rhodesia seemed innocuous enough – ONE FOR THE ROAD MEANS ONE FOR THE GRAVE – but failed to take into account the fact that the current definitive stamp prepaying the inland letter rate depicted the grave of Cecil Rhodes in the Matopo Hills. In 1960 Dame Laura Knight designed a slogan cancellation for the World Refugee Year campaign and this showed a hand upraised in supplication. Unfortunately the thumb tended to be in line with the Queen's nose on the Wilding definitive stamps. The slogan was withdrawn on this account, but prior to that the postmaster of Halifax had the hand erased from the slogan used at his office. Examples of the defaced Halifax slogans are now scarce. Equally unfortunate was the use of a slogan in the United States ALIENS MUST REPORT THEIR ADDRESSES DURING JANUARY, which went all over the world cancelling the airmail stamp showing the Statue of Liberty and the caption 'Liberty for All'.

The first postmark provided in connection with a special event was a double-circle datestamp inscribed EXPOSITION UNIVERSELLE/POSTES which was produced by the French Post Office for use at a temporary office in the Universal Exhibition, Paris in 1855. Previously it was believed that a single-circle datestamp had been used at the Great Exhibition, London in 1851, but as this shows the London district letter W (not allocated till 1857) it must have been faked from a genuine handstamp provided for the 1862 Exhibition. Nevertheless, as postal facilities *did* exist at the 1851 Exhibition, the provision of a handstamp cannot be ruled out. A cover was found in 1979 bearing a straight-line mark in lower case lettering 'Great Exhibition', but even if this should prove to be authentic it is most unlikely to have been an official postal mark. More probably it was a private cachet of the Exhibition organisers.

The first postmarks actually known to have been used at a special event in Britain were the single-circle, double stamp and separate obliterator provided for the International Exhibition held in London from May till November 1862. Both ordinary and registered letters are known with these postmarks although they are rare. The double stamp and obliter-

Calais local publicity slogan, 1921

ator were applied in black and the single datestamp in red, on the back of mail arriving at the Exhibition.

The first postmark of this type used in Scotland appeared in 1888 for the Glasgow Exhibition, Kelvingrove. The first in Ireland was used at the International Exhibition, Cork in 1902.

The first special event postmark used outside the British Isles was at the Exposition Universelle in Paris in 1855.

The first time a postmark was used for commemorative purposes, without the facilities of a temporary post office, occurred in January 1959 when the British Post Office permitted devotees of the poet Robert Burns to post covers and cards at his birthplace to celebrate the bicentenary of his birth. Alloway, being a town sub-office, was not normally allowed to cancel mail, but an exception was made on this occasion. Although the ordinary office datestamp was employed, many thousands of souvenir covers were handled. Exceptionally the office was permitted to open on a Sunday, the bicentenary date being 25 January.

This precedent passed off without comment and was not immediately followed up, but in 1963 the Post Office celebrated the tercentenary of the Dover packet service with a pictorial postmark, two handstamps being used at the Dover sorting office for this purpose. This was the first time that a special

Salthill, Galway local publicity slogan, 1935

Hastings local publicity slogan, 1963

Bath transposed local publicity slogan, 1963

handstamp had been used without a temporary post office, merely to exploit a historic anniversary. Again, this was not immediately followed up, but in 1966 a lengthy series of special datestamps was produced to cancel souvenir covers and cards of the various matches at the World Cup Football Championship. From then onwards the number of temporary post offices declined as the number of special handstamps escalated. Mail for re-posting with these special postmarks may be sent to the post office supervising the use of the handstamps. As a rule, a special posting box is also provided but no post office facilities as such.

The first pictorial postmarks were the heraldic types used by the Italian city states from the early fifteenth century onwards. Pictorial elements were not uncommon in the earliest postmarks of many countries. Other early examples were the provincial paid stamps of France, with the fleur de lis (c 1700), Leon, Spain (c 1750) with a lion and armorial stamps of Amsterdam/Rotterdam. The earliest examples from the British Isles were the Perth lamb (1750), the Fort William thistle (1769) and the Birmingham chandelier (1772). The 'mermaid' postmarks of Dublin were used from 1808 till 1814; Belfast and Limerick had datestamps featuring shamrocks (1818–29).

Fancy cancellations were introduced experimentally by the British Post Office in November 1985, to test the use of Reiner self-inking datestamps at two sub post offices – Pathhead (Kirkcaldy) and Fairway (Port Talbot). In place of the conventional circle was a chain-link frame and this, together with lower case lettering and an unusual layout of the date, gave the postmarks a highly distinctive appearance. Similar stamps. but having capital lettering, were subsequently adopted on a permanent basis at the new Hemel Hempstead branch office in September 1987.

The greatest use of pictorialism in cancellations was made by the United States between 1850 and 1880. In this period it was left to the discretion (and initiative) of individual postmasters to provide themselves with obliterators. The majority of these were cut from cork or close-grained boxwood, but a few are known to have been made of brass, and latterly rubber was also used. Many of these were

produced by a Mr Klinkner of Oakland, California, and among his better known confections was the so-called 'kicking mule' which is known to have been used in Forbestown, Goleta, Port Townsend and Susanville. John W Hill (1836-1921), a clerk in the post office at Waterbury, Connecticut, was responsible for a number of unusual obliterators, in the form of a running chicken, an eagle, and an elephant. When he overstepped the mark by using a heart on St Valentine's Day and a clown's head on April Fool's Day, the USPO reprimanded him, but Hill's postmarks, used between 1865 and 1869, are now much sought after.

Pictorial obliterators were used by several hundred American post offices, attaining their zenith during the Civil War when many of them took on a patriotic flavour – the Stars and Stripes and the slogan UNION were particularly popular. These obliterators consist of silhouette profiles of all kinds from the recognisable (George Washington) to the whimsical (the pipe-smoker – another Waterbury mark). Stars, sun-bursts and masonic emblems were also popular. Among the most elaborate was the picture of a locomotive used at South Hanson, Massachusetts (1875). Fancy cancels (as they are known to collectors) were used to a lesser extent in Canada, the Maple Leaf emblem being especially popular there. They were used in Canada from about 1868 till 1900.

The oddest use of a fancy cancellation occurred in 1895 at Ste Genevieve de Batiscan in Quebec province, where an obliterator showing the Nicaraguan national coat of arms in great detail was used.

The first special event handstamps with a pictorial motif were used in London, 1890 at the Penny Post Jubilee Exhibition, South Kensington. Seven different handstamps were employed, all with motifs based on the crown. Four of them were in fancy shapes and all are known to have been struck in unusual colours – blue, red or violet. They were not used as cancellations but were applied to souvenir cards and covers on payment of a small fee. Two of them are of particular interest on account of their dates – 1790 (used at the replica of an eighteenth century post office) and 1990 (at the office of the future). The first pictorial cancellation in Britain was used in 1891 at the Royal Naval Exhibition. Struck in blue or rarely in violet, it depicted a fouled anchor.

The world's cheapest postmark was produced from a potato cut in half and crudely engraved with the fleur-de-lis emblem of the Scout movement. It was used on mail despatched by the Scout Post (*Poczta Harczerska*) during the Warsaw Uprising of 1944. Five later postmarks were cut from pieces of rubber from the soles of shoes and were rather more elaborate.

Double stamp of the London International Exhibition, 1862

The most expensive datestamps were those with ivory handles and tops of sterling silver, used at Croydon (1931-4) and Southampton (1937) at the launch of new airmail services. Only a handful of letters in each instance, despatched in silk mailbags, received these postmarks.

Coloured postmarks are not as unusual as one might suppose. Although black ink is most commonly used nowadays every colour in the spectrum has been employed at some time or another. Standardisation of colour was adopted by Britain in 1857, but occasionally other colours may be found to this day, especially in conjunction with rubber datestamps.

Datestamp of the Exposition Universelle, 1855

The first multicoloured postmarks were used by Czechoslovakia on 28 October 1935, red and blue postmarks being used on Independence Day souvenir mail in Prague. Three-colour postmarks were used at Pardubice on 25-27 September 1936, and at various other offices on twelve occasions thereafter, the last being used at Pardubice on 16 September 1940. Red, blue and other colours used individually were employed on the special handstamps of the German occupation, and also by Czech forces in exile in Britain during the Second World War.

Provincial paid stamp, France, c 1700

A self-inking roller with three components was used experimentally at the Wiltshire Philatelic Convention in April 1964 to strike special postmarks in black, red and green. Three-colour postmarks were not used again in Britain till the international philatelic exhibition Philympia, 1970. Different postmarks were used on each day of the exhibition and each was executed in three-colour combinations. This was claimed by the Post Office at the time as a 'first', the Wiltshire experiment having been forgotten. Again, however, nothing was done to follow it up and multicoloured postmarks have apparently sunk into oblivion.

Perth Lamb (1750), Fort William Thistle (1769) and Birmingham Chandelier (1772)

The largest handstruck datestamp in the United Kingdom measured 117 × 35 mm and was used on 27 October 1978 at Milton Keynes, when Volkswagen celebrated the opening of their new headquarters with a special event parcel datestamp. Although parcel stamps (generally measuring 80 × 38 mm) had been used at some of the old-style temporary post offices in showgrounds and exhibitions, this was the first time that a parcel stamp had been provided for a

Fancy cancels of the United States

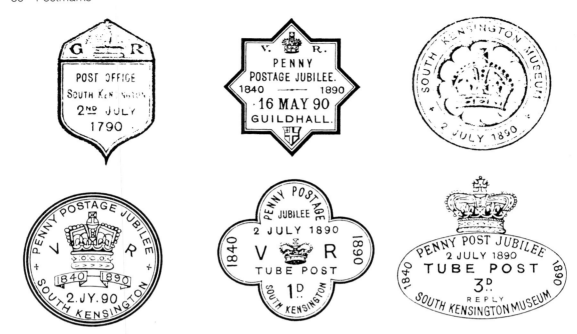

Pictorial postmarks of the Penny Post Jubilee, 1890

one-day event for which a temporary office was not provided. The datestamp consisted of the conventional pattern, with an extended portion on the left featuring the logotype of IDC, sponsor of the stamp, who had built the headquarters. A parcel stamp was required for a mailing of 1000 commemorative medals, struck by the Pobjoy Mint of Sutton, Surrey, marking the occasion and sent to Volkswagen agents and dealers in a box with a commemorative wrapper. The Post Office realised the implication of this too late and have since ruled firmly that special handstamps must be confined to those used on ordinary mail (letters and postcards). Collectors were understandably aggrieved at not having the opportunity to acquire this mark since it was not announced in the *Postmark Bulletin* published by the Post Office and was confined to the relatively small numbers of parcels despatched. It is thus unique among parcel stamps and undoubtedly the rarest of the modern special event stamps.

The smallest handstruck datestamp in the United Kingdom was used at Manchester on re-directed mail in the 1890s and measured only 15 mm in diameter. A single-arc datestamp used at Glasgow in the 1840s to denote late posting of letters measured 15·5 mm in diameter. The Creswell experimental datestamps, used in the rotary canceller of the late 1850s, in London and Exeter, measured 16 mm in diameter.

Datestamps with the longest place name in the world have been used at Llanfairpwllgwyngyllgogerychwyrndrobwllllantysiliogogogoch in Anglesey, Wales on two occasions since 1973 for one-day special events. The datestamps in everyday use, however, generally render the name in an abbreviated form – Llanfairpwll or Llanfair P. G. The name, meaning 'St Mary's Church in a hollow of white hazel, close to a rapid whirlpool and St Tysilio's Church', is said to have been coined by a local tailor in the nineteenth century as a tourist attraction.

The longest postmark name in the United States is Kleinfeltersville, Pennsylvania.

The longest inscription in a postal datestamp is probably FIELD BRANCH, BUREAU OF SUPPLIES AND ACCOUNTS, NAVY 10020 STA., CLEVELAND, OHIO, used in the 1960s. The longest in the United Kingdom was BARRINGTON COLLIERY, BEDLINGTON, NORTHUMBERLAND (42 letters), now closed.

The datestamp with the shortest name in the United Kingdom is that used at Ae near Dumfries, Scotland, the only two-letter place-name with a post office. Other two-letter postal names are: Au (Austria, Germany, Switzerland); Ba (Fiji, Ghana); Go (Japan); Ii (Finland); Is (USSR); Ko (Japan); Li (Norway, Thailand); Lo (Belgium); Lu (Switzerland); Mo (Norway); Na (Norway); Oi (eight

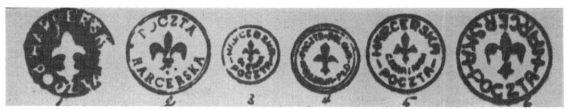

Polish Scout Post, 1944, using stamps made from a potato or rubber sole

different offices in Japan!); Ro (Denmark, Italy, Sweden); Sa (Portugal, Thailand); Ut (USSR); Va (Norway, Sweden); Ye (Burma); Yi (Uruguay).

In addition, four American post offices have had two initials or numerals for a name: A1 (Ohio), O.K. (Kentucky), T.B. (Maryland) and U.Z. (Kentucky) – all now closed.

Two one-letter names are both in Norway, but since they have the same name they invariably include the name of their districts to avoid confusion: Å in Åfjord and Å in Lofoten.

Postmarks featured prominently in a murder trial. To this day collectors name the experimental duplex stamps used in Glasgow, 1856-7 after Madeleine Smith who stood trial for the murder of her lover, Emile l'Angelier. The basis for the prosecution rested mainly on a series of letters from Miss Smith to l'Angelier. As the letters were undated the postmarks on the wrappers were of crucial importance and the failure of the prosecution to secure a verdict of Guilty was due in no small measure to the fact that the standard of postmarking was erratic – a fact commented on adversely by the judge in his summing-up. The offending postmark had, in fact, been withdrawn from use before the trial commenced so it is untrue to say that it was withdrawn because of the judge's comments. Furthermore, despite the poor quality of the postmarks on the Smith correspondence, the Madeleine Smith postmark is usually very clearly struck and poorly struck examples are relatively scarce! The verdict, incidentally, was Not Proven, that neat Scottish compromise which implies 'We know you did it, but cannot prove it. Off you go and don't do it again.' Even the extremely rare experimental type which immediately preceded this postmark is known as the pre-Madeleine Smith postmark.

Postmarks were used in a murder hunt in England in 1979-80. During the massive police hunt for the infamous Yorkshire Ripper, responsible for the murder and mutilation of a number of young women in Yorkshire and the north-east of England, a slogan without a town die was used on mail. The West Yorkshire Constabulary hit upon the slogan as a method of getting across the message that they

Southampton Airport silver and ivory datestamp, 1937

Czech three-coloured postmark, 1935

needed the co-operation of the populace, but rejected the conventional method as too expensive. The cancellation of all letter mail from Leeds alone would have entailed slogan dies for 24 machines and this would have been far too costly. A method of getting by with a single slogan die, however, was to apply a mark to all bills sent out by the North Eastern Gas Board's Leeds office, thereby reaching a high proportion of the public and producing the greatest impact for an economic outlay. The Post Office exceptionally agreed to this proposal and the North Eastern Gas Board also agreed to co-operate. The slogan was applied in black ink to NEGAS envelopes already bearing a post paid impression (Leeds Serial No. 18). The first batch of envelopes treated in this

Volkswagen commemorative postmark, Milton Keynes, 1978: largest used in Britain

manner went out on 27 October 1979 and the last was processed during the week beginning 21 January 1980. The use of a slogan to hunt down a major criminal in this way is without parallel in any country.

It is very unlikely to be used again, since it failed to achieve the desired result. The Ripper, Peter Sutcliffe, was ultimately caught in the routine fashion by two patrolling policemen.

Precancellation was first employed on 1 October 1870 by *The Times*, one of the few newspapers in Britain to have continued using the newspaper tax stamps after this 'tax on knowledge' was repealed in 1855. Thereafter these stamps, printed in black on the upper right-hand corner of the front page, served to denote the postage on copies transmitted by post. All stamp duties on newspapers were abolished on 1 October 1870 and, at the same time, the ancient privilege of transmission and retransmission which had permitted a newspaper to be sent several times through the post, was withdrawn. As the stamp could now only be used once it became necessary for

it to be cancelled. The Post Office allowed *The Times* to do the cancelling direct, as part of the printing process. The precancel took the form of an upright oval obliterator with the numerals '70', indicating the office of despatch, St Martin's-le-Grand. The only other newspaper to make use of this facility was the *Stamford Mercury* which used a printed obliteration with '742' (the number assigned to Stamford in the list of 1844). The *Stamford Mercury* last used this printed stamp and precancelled obliterator on 21 November 1878. Since then a highly distinctive hooded mark incorporating the old 742 number and the name 'Stamford' has been used on stamped newspaper wrappers. *The Times* ceased using precancelled printed stamps of its own design on 21 October 1911.

W H Smith were allowed to precancel stamped newspapers in August 1876 and other stationers soon followed suit.

The first adhesive stamps authorised for precancellation were the Canadian 'small cents' definitive series in 1889, following several months of unofficial usage. At first a minimum quantity of 25 000 items had to be transmitted but in 1906 this was reduced to $25 worth and since 1922 no minimum value has been fixed. Precancelled stamps, for use on printed

Rectangular datestamp of Llanfairpwll, showing the name in full

Circular datestamp of 1871 showing name as Llanfair-pwllgwyngyll

Manchester, 1896: Britain's smallest datestamp

Barrington Colliery postmark, 1919

Ae, Dumfries: shortest postal name in Britain, 1972

Madeleine Smith postmark, Glasgow, 1856-7

matter, were introduced by France in 1893. Other countries which adopted precancels were Algeria, Austria, Belgium, Hungary, Luxembourg, Monaco, the Netherlands, the Canal Zone, Tunisia and the United States. American precancels are particularly interesting because they indicate the town of posting. Canadian precancels also bore the town of posting until 1931, but since then serial numbers (corresponding to the numbers assigned under the Money Order system) have been used.

All Canadian precancels since 1889 have been printed at Ottawa under supervision of the Post Office Department. In the United States stamps precancelled at the time of printing were first provided by the US Bureau of Engraving and Printing, Washington in January 1923 to the postmaster of New York. Other precancels, however, were produced by outside contractors, and even handstruck precancels are known.

The rarest precancellation is the so-called Orangeburg Coil, issued by the US Post Office for use by the Bell Chemical Company of Orangeburg. Only one coil of 500 stamps was produced and very few examples are known to have survived.

The postal administration with the most cancelling machines is the USSR which claims to have over 12 243. Runners up are: France (8490), Italy (5245), Japan (2967), UK (2060) and Canada (1214).

The country with the fewest cancelling machines per capita, other than those very small

places (e.g., Pitcairn, Tristan da Cunha) which have no cancelling machines at all, is India. In 1980 a mere 410 cancelling machines were in use – or one for every 1 587 761 inhabitants!

Permit mailing, by which the Post Office grants permits to private firms to print their own franks on bulk postings, usually of printed matter, was first authorised by the US Post Office on 28 April 1904. These marks had to show the name of the town, the permit number, the word PAID and the value. The permit mailing system spread to Canada and New Zealand, still to this day the largest users of this method of mail handling.

The origins of a similar system in Britain are obscure. It is clear (from actual envelopes) that the Bank of England was allowed in 1932 to send out mail in envelopes bearing a circular printed device showing the amount of postage paid. These envelopes did not require to be cancelled by the normal postal machine and were obviously intended to save time on bulk postings. About 1937 the *Reader's Digest* was permitted to use a duplicated impression AYLESBURY BUCKS POSTAGE PAID on bulk postings, and during the Second World War newspapers posted in bulk to places abroad received a mark inscribed LONDON/POSTAGE PAID, either handstruck or printed directly on to the newspaper.

These early arrangements appear to have been made on a one-off basis, since it was not until 1966 that the British Post Office introduced Postage Paid Impressions (PPIs). PPIs were offered to bulk users despatching a minimum of 20 000 inland first or second class letters, 5000 bulky packets or 500 parcels of the same size, weight and shape. Each user was given a serial number and this, following the town name, had to appear in the impression printed or

Å – Norway's one-letter postal name, 1973

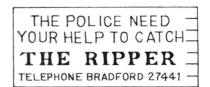

Yorkshire Ripper murder hunt slogan, 1979-80

Precancels used by *The Times* (1870) and *Stamford Mercury* (1911)

handstruck on the wrapper. Subsequently arrangements were made for mailings made simultaneously from more than one office to have a PHQ (Postal Headquarters) serial.

The first machine for impressing and registering stamps, the forerunner of postage meters, was invented by Carl Bushe of Paris in 1884, but he was unable to find a backer to develop it.

The first automatic franking machine in practical use was invented by Christian A Kahrs and installed in the foyer of the head post office in Christiania (Oslo) between 24 August and 14 September 1900. The machine was coin-operated, the insertion of 5- or 10-øre coins producing green or red franks, covering the inland printed matter and letter rates respectively. After posting, the postal authorities affixed adhesive stamps over the impressions and cancelled them in the usual manner, apparently regarding the impressions merely as receipts for postage paid. It is doubtful whether they could be regarded as meter marks in the true sense.

The first meter franking machines in the true sense were used in New Zealand in 1904. Experiments with coin-operated automatic stamping machines had taken place in Australia and New Zealand in 1903 but they were regarded as impractical on security grounds. Ernest Moss of Christchurch, however, made the breakthrough by inventing a postage enumerator or meter. The coin principle was retained at first, since the enumerator had to be activated by a gold sovereign which enabled the machine to frank 240 items before locking automatically. The Moss franking machines were marketed as a means of preventing theft of petty cash and stamps in offices rather than as a convenient method of speeding up the handling of mail. Subsequently a token was substituted for the gold coin, and later a totalisator device, a principle inherent in all postage meters since then.

A curious feature of the New Zealand meter franks was that mail had to be postmarked by the post office – a practice which continues to this day. Though metered mail was at first confined to New Zealand, arrangements were made with the British Post Office to allow metered mail from New Zealand to circulate in Britain at no further charge.

The first meter machines to incorporate a dated postmark were invented by Arthur H Pitney (who contributed the postage meter) and Walter H Bowes (who developed the cancelling element). Their Model A machine was first used at Stamford, Connecticut on 10 December 1920, following the sanction of postage meter machines for use on first class mail on 28 April 1920. Earlier American machines, used for third and fourth class permit mail, did not require a postmarking element.

The use of postage meters was sanctioned internationally by the Postal Union Congress in Madrid, 1920, to come into effect on 1 January 1922. The first firms to take advantage of this ruling were the Universal Automatic Machine Company of New Zealand and the Pitney-Bowes Postage Meter Company of the United States who, between them, produced most of the machines used in the 1920s.

The first postage meter used in Britain was made by Pitney-Bowes, authorised on 13 May and licensed on 16 August 1922. It was first used by the Prudential Assurance Company on 5 September 1922. Machines were installed shortly afterwards by two Kensington department stores (Barker's and Derry & Toms) and the London bookmaker, Joe Lee. The first NZ Universal machine was in use by Universal Postal Frankers Ltd from 18 October 1922.

The greatest number of postage meters licensed is in the United States, with 880 000. Other leading countries are France (140 785), UK (119 904), India (25 036), Switzerland (18 810), USSR (11 389), Japan (2690) and West Germany (1105).

Automatic facing and stamping of mail was pioneered by Britain. Experiments with the mechanical segregation and automatic facing of letters (i.e. stacking them right way up for cancellation), began

Precancelled stamps of USA (1903), Luxembourg (1903), France (1926), Belgium (1925) and USA (1980)

The original Pitney-Bowes Model A postage meter of 1922

First meter mark of New Zealand, 1904

Early meter mark of Norway, 1900-3

Early Pitney-Bowes meter mark of England, 1923

Three examples of postage meters produced by Pitney-Bowes in the past 60 years. From right to left, the Midget, the Simplex and a modern 5000 series meter

at the Post Office Research Station, Dollis Hill, London in 1934, using an optical scanning system. The first segregator was constructed the same year but results were poor. In 1938 an automatic letter facing machine was built, using a simple photocell as the detector, scanning the lower leading edge four times while the items rotated in a drum. When a stamp was detected the item was diverted to a stacker. The machine was unsuccessful because of practical problems in turning over the letters and the poor performance of the photocell for stamp detection. A second machine was built in 1949-50 using a photomultiplier at a fixed wavelength and two output stacks to avoid the old problem of turning over the letters. It had a manual feed since the problem of automatic segregation had not at that time been solved electronically. From this prototype was developed the automatic letter facing machine installed at Southampton in 1957. Electric scanners were used at first, followed by an ultraviolet optical scanner. The prototype Automatic Letter Facer (ALF) was first used on 19 December 1957. Subsequently experimental machines were tested at London, Liverpool and Glasgow in 1961-3 and a more advanced model at Norwich in 1965. Mechanised mail handling and cancelling became widespread in Britain in 1969-70.

Mechanised mail handling was first employed outside the United Kingdom in May 1963, when SEFACAN (Segregating, Facing and Cancelling) equipment was installed in Winnipeg, Canada. The electronic facing, sorting and stamping of mail is now carried out in 42 countries (1981). Special cancellations are used in most cases.

The first attempts at mechanical sorting of mail before delivery took place in the Netherlands. A machine for sorting incoming mail for street delivery was invented by J J M L Marchand and constructed by Professor J C Andriessen of Delft Technical College. It was called a Transorma (from *Trans*portation and *Sorting* of mail by *M*archand and *A*ndriessen) and was first demonstrated at the International Aero-Postal Conference at the Hague in 1927. It was installed at the Rotterdam head post office in 1930 and later machines were used in other Dutch post offices. The Transorma machine was first used outside Holland in September 1935 when two machines were installed in the Brighton and Hove sorting office. Each machine had five keyboards and was capable of sorting 24 000 letters per hour. Mail sorted by these machines received a mark consisting of a letter of the alphabet or numerals from 2 to 35. These machines were never used elsewhere. They were withdrawn in July 1968 on the grounds that they were inefficient, but their withdrawal meant that an additional fifteen manual sorters had to be employed!

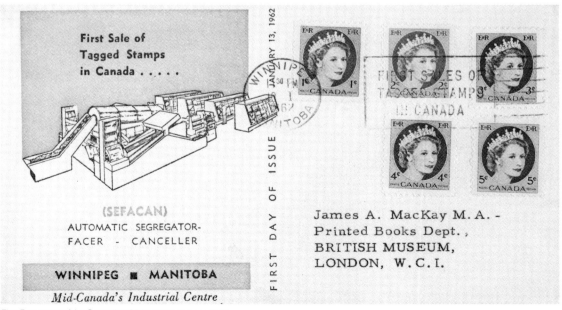

First Day cover of the Canadian SEFACAN stamps, 1962

Mail handlers, unloading sacks on a culling line, in a large
American sorting office. This is the first step in sorting mail before
the stamps are cancelled

This American letter sorting machine can route ZIP coded letters to as many as 267 destinations at a rate of one letter per second

Postcode publicity stamps from Japan, USA, Italy and the Netherlands

The electronic letter sorting and indicating equipment (ELSIE) can sort up to 3000 letters per hour to 144 different destinations as directed by the postman at the keyboard.

The automatic letter facer (ALF) can arrange up to 20 000 letters per hour so that they face the same way and the correct way up, separates first and second class mail and cancels the stamp

Electronic sorting of inward mail was first used at the Bath sorting office in October 1955, using ELSIE (Electronic Letter Sorting Indicator Equipment). Like the Transorma machines, this equipment produced impressions of letters of the alphabet. Later machines were modified for postcode working and this produced a pattern of phosphor dots, first used at Luton in 1960.

The first country to adopt postcodes was Germany, in 1942. This was a rudimentary system, using the two-digit numbers of the *oberpostdirektion* (postal area). Four-figure codes were introduced on 3 November 1961. Other countries adopting a four-figure system included Austria (1 January 1966), Australia (1 July 1967), Belgium (15 December 1969), Denmark (20 September 1967), German Democratic Republic (1 January 1965), Norway (18 March 1968) and Switzerland (26 June 1964). Countries using a five-figure system include Finland (1 January 1971), France (October 1965), Italy (1 July 1967), Sweden (19 March 1968), USA (1 July 1963) and Yugoslavia (1 January 1971). Japan has a variable system using from three to five digits (1 July 1968).

Several countries have an alphanumeric system which is capable of coding the actual street of the addressee, whereas the four- and five-digit systems merely code the town. The United Kingdom pioneered alphanumeric codes, Norwich having an experimental code in 1959. Postcodes were not generally adopted till 1966. Croydon being the first town to be fully coded. The system was not, however, fully implemented until 1973. The Philippines adopted an alphanumeric system on 1 January 1968, using a letter from A to O, representing the country's ten regions, and three digits. The gradual introduction of postcodes in Canada began in Ottawa on 1 April 1971 and was not completed till 1974. It consists of six letters and numerals in two groups of three, as in the British system (five to seven units).

Apart from the postmarks, which (with the exception of Britain) include the postcodes, every country using them has also issued stamps, labels, leaflets and slogan postmarks publicising their coding systems.

Adhesive stamps

What is believed to have been the world's first adhesive postage stamp was issued in Paris on 8 April 1653, in connection with the *Petite Poste* organised by Renouard de Villayer (see p.22 Chapter 1). The idea of producing stamps to indicate postal prepayment seems to have originated with Anne Genevieve, Duchesse de Longueville and mistress Fouquet, of the Surintendant des Finances. She is said to have suggested small slips of paper affixed with a solution of isinglass, and known as *billets de port payé*. These labels were inscribed 'Port payé . . . le . . . jour de l'an 1653' (postage paid on the . . . day . . . of the year 1653). They were sold for a sou in monasteries, mining offices, courthouses, colleges and prisons. The sender filled in the date in manuscript, affixed the stamp to the letter and posted it in one of the street corner posting-boxes provided for the purpose. The service came to an abrupt end, partly because the boxes were vandalised and the letters often damaged, but mainly because of the downfall of Fouquet. Although well documented in contemporary literature no example of these stamps has ever been discovered.

Postage stamps in the modern sense have many origins. Handstruck postage stamps denoting the prepayment of charges on letters had existed since Dockwra's penny post in 1680. Adhesive labels had been used since 1802 by the Board of Customs and Excise in Britain to prepay the taxes on hats, patent medicines and other dutiable articles. Stamped wrappers or letter sheets on which the device showing prepayment was printed or impressed *before* the letter was written, also existed long before 1840 (see Chapter 6).

One unsubstantiated statement (by Gustav Schenk in *The Romance of the Postage Stamp*, 1962) claims that a Scottish shipping company was using adhesive stamps for its private postal service in 1811. No details were given and no evidence in support of this claim can be found. Scotland claims to have been the birthplace of adhesive postage stamps. The Dundee

Stamp booklet of 1982 honouring James Chalmers; the inside front cover shows his prototype 'stamps' of 1837

bookseller James Chalmers (1782-1853) was actively involved in postal reform from 1825 onwards, suggesting various improvements in the mail service between Dundee and London. It is probable that he studied the problem of postal reform following the agitation in Parliament of Robert Wallace, MP for Greenock (who, significantly, was Rowland Hill's inspiration also). In the Treasury Competition (see p.74) of 1839 Chalmers submitted essays which were rejected as unsuitable. On 1 October 1839 he wrote to Rowland Hill 'If slips (i.e., stamps) are to be used I flatter myself that I have a claim to priority in the suggestion, it being nearly two years since I first made it public and submitted it in a communication to Mr Wallace MP.' This would place the first publication of Chalmers' scheme no earlier than the end of 1837. This is confirmed in other correspondence where Chalmers gives the date at which he *first* published his plan as November 1837. The italics are his.

In his pamphlet advocating postal reform, published on 22 February 1837, Rowland Hill wrote, 'Perhaps this difficulty (of using stamped envelopes in certain cases) might be obviated by using a bit of paper just large enough to bear the stamp and covered at the back with a glutinous wash, which the bringer might, by the application of a little moisture,

Sir Rowland Hill KCB, 1795-1879

attach to the back of the letter, so as to avoid the necessity of re-directing it.'

Quite clearly Rowland Hill had published his plan of reform, including the concept of the adhesive postage stamp, some nine months before Chalmers. The latter undoubtedly arrived at the same conclusion independently of Hill; his letter of October 1839 shows that he was until then ignorant of Hill's earlier publication. When he realised this he wrote again to Hill candidly withdrawing his own claim. In a letter of 18 May 1840 he wrote to Hill, 'My reason for not replying sooner proceeded from a wish to see the stamps in operation . . . I conceive it only an act of justice to myself to state to you what induced me to become a competitor; for in that capacity I never would have appeared if I had known that anyone, particularly you, had suggested anything like the same scheme . . . I have only to regret that, through my ignorance, I was led to put others and myself to trouble in the matter . . .'

Thus James Chalmers, in his own lifetime, acknowledged that Sir Rowland Hill had prior claim. Not till 1879, shortly after Sir Rowland's death, did Chalmers' son Patrick dare to challenge Hill's claims. In the *Dundee Advertiser* (of which he was the proprietor) he challenged Sir Rowland's reputation and charged him with having deliberately concealed

his father's plan. This sparked off a vendetta of pamphleteering between Patrick Chalmers and Pearson Hill (no fewer than 35 Chalmers pamphlets on the subject followed over the years!) and Pearson Hill gave as good as he got. Between 1884 and 1889, when the controversy was at its height, Judge John Tiffany took it upon himself to investigate the matter impartially and came to the conclusion that Sir Rowland's claim was upheld.

This unseemly squabble was carried into the third generation with Patrick's daughter, Miss Leah Chalmers, and Rowland's grandson, Colonel H W Hill, CMG, DSO taking up the verbal cudgels as late as 1940 when the centenary of the stamps was being celebrated. Patrick's case rests almost entirely on sworn testimonies by several of his father's old employees that they could remember him printing stamp essays in 1834. Unfortunately one of these men overstated his case in the *American Philatelic Journal* (September 1887) by saying that he was employed by Chalmers in 1834 and remembered his 'setting to work to draw up a plan of adhesive stamps when it had been settled that the Penny Postage system was to be adopted.' In 1834 the Penny Postage system had not even been heard of, let alone settled, so the evidence of Mr Whitelaw, relying on his memory of events in his teens, fifty years earlier, was highly suspect.

The year 1834 also figures in the only claim made against Sir Rowland Hill in his own lifetime. Dr John Gray of the British Museum challenged him, in the correspondence columns of *The Times*, after he had been knighted in 1864. Gray claimed to have pioneered postal reforms, including the adoption of adhesive stamps, as early as 1834. Gray's bibliogra-

Rowland Hill, on a Portuguese stamp of 1940

phy lists almost 1200 articles and pamphlets by him between 1819 and 1874 on all manner of subjects from entomology to municipal sewerage, but there is not a single reference to postal reform among them. Gray is best remembered as a pioneer writer on philately and as one of the earliest stamp collectors (see Chapter 8).

Other claimants to the title of father of the adhesive postage stamp include: Samuel Forrester (a Scottish tax official); Charles Whiting (a London stationer) who claims to have suggested 'go frees' in 1834; Samuel Roberts of Llanbrynmair, Powys (claim dating from 1827); Francis Worrell Stevens (a fellow schoolmaster of Hill's at Loughton, Essex in 1833, the date of *his* claim); Ferdinand Egarter of Spittal, Austria; Laurence Kosir or Koschier of Laibach (Ljubljana), who proposed postal reforms on 11 May 1836, including stamps, but was ignored by his superiors in the Austrian civil service; and Curry Gabriel Treffenberg (1791-1875) who devised a scheme for stamped stationery, known as *carta sigillata*, in Sweden as early as 1823.

No claim was made by Egarter himself, but in 1938 a letter was discovered in a family bible at Millstattin, Carinthia. Dated 20 February 1839, from Spittal to Klagenfurt, it bore a 1 kreuzer stamp printed in brown. It was examined by a panel of Austrian philatelists in 1952 but opinion as to the authenticity of the letter and its stamp was divided.

The Penny Black of May 1840, the world's first adhesive postage stamp

The letters O.P. on the stamp may have meant *Orts Post* (local post). In the 1830s it was customary to give postmen a tip of one kreuzer for delivering the mail and it may have been intended for that purpose. A second cover bearing one of these stamps was subsequently found, but is considered a forgery.

Treffenberg's *carta sigillata* was not such a new idea as stamped paper of this sort had been used for legal documents in Sweden since 1660. Though not used for postage, similar sheets were introduced in 1824 for newspaper wrappers, but represented a tax on newspapers rather than an indication of postal prepayment. These *tidnings stämplarna*, like their British counterparts, however, did allow free transmission by post. They survived as late as 1872.

Another possible forerunner of adhesive postage stamps was a 40 lepta label used in Greece in 1831 in connection with the poll tax, raising money for refugees from the Cretan insurrection of that year. Examples of these labels have been found on letters from Athens to Piraeus, seeming to suggest that they performed some kind of postal duty. The use of the *tesserakonta lepta* label on correspondence was, however, an isolated occurrence and it was not until 1861 that Greece adopted adhesive postage stamps.

The world's first adhesive postage stamp was the Penny Black of Great Britain, which went on sale on 1 May 1840 and became valid for postage on 6 May. For years it was assumed that its companion, the Twopence Blue, was issued simultaneously, a statement to be found in most catalogues and handbooks, but it has now been proved, from an examination of the files of the Post Office and the Board of Inland Revenue, that due to production difficulties the first consignment of 2d stamps was not delivered by the printers till the afternoon of 8 May.

The issue of the first adhesive postage stamps arose from the reforms instituted in Britain in 1839-40, first the introduction of Uniform Fourpenny Postage (5 December 1839) and then the reduction of the minimum rate to one penny on 9 January 1840. A competition sponsored by the Treasury was held in 1839 to find designs suitable for the proposed stamps. More than 2600 suggestions were submitted, but only 49 related to adhesive stamps. Awards were made to Benjamin Cheverton, Henry Cole, Charles Whiting, James Bogardus and Francis Coffin, but none of their designs was considered suitable. In addition essays for stamps were published independently by several people, including James Chalmers, whose designs were produced between 10 February 1838 and 30 September 1839.

In the end it was Rowland Hill's own suggestion which was developed into the finished design. He felt that a profile of Queen Victoria was not only the most suitable motif but would also deter counterfeiting, since the public would instantly detect any variation in the likeness – a shrewd psychological observation. Sketches of rough outlines for the Penny Black exist in Hill's own hand.

On 2 December 1839 Henry Cole, acting on Hill's behalf, approached the printing firm of Perkins, Bacon and Petch to enquire about printing the stamps. The firm agreed on 13 December. Hill ordered a die on 16 December, the profile of the Queen to be drawn from the medal commemorating Queen Victoria's visit to the Guildhall on 9 November 1837. The profile of the young queen was originally sculpted by William Wyon and adapted for stamp production by Henry Corbould. The die of the head was engraved by Charles Heath and his son Frederick, while the lettering and engine-turned background (another anti-forgery device) were engraved by Perkins, Bacon and Petch using the rose engine devised by Jacob Perkins. Various preliminary dies and progressive stages were produced before the final die was selected. The plate of 240 subjects was prepared in March 1840 and printing of the first consignment took place in April.

The size and upright format of the first stamps was based on adhesive labels which had been in use for two centuries at the Board of Inland Revenue. Embossed tax stamps on stout paper were affixed to parchment documents by lead staples, secured on the reverse by small adhesive labels pasted over them. These labels featured the cipher of the reigning sovereign. The check letters in the corners of the first postage stamps were likewise a security feature borrowed from these tax labels.

The engine-turning in the background was a feature derived from contemporary banknotes. The rose engine was developed by Jacob Perkins in 1819, originally for printing patterns on calico.

The earliest example of an adhesive stamp used on cover was the Penny Black, used at Bath on 2 May 1840. The postmaster of Bath appears to have misread his instructions and permitted postal use before the due date. Several other examples of Penny Blacks have been recorded with postmarks before 6 May.

The first stamp issued outside the United Kingdom was issued by the New York City Despatch Post on 1 February 1842. The idea of using stamps was conceived by Henry Thomas Windsor, an Englishman living in Hoboken, New Jersey. He formed a partnership with Alexander Greig to operate a local postal service in Manhattan, following the demise of the city's penny post. In the circular announcing this service Windsor and Greig stated: 'Letters which the writers desire to send free, must have a free stamp affixed to them. An

The New York City Despatch Post, 1842

ornamental stamp has been prepared for this purpose . . . 36 cnts per dozen or 2 dolls. 50c. per hundred.'

The stamps, of 3 cents denomination, were recess-printed in black (like the British stamps of 1840) and bore a full face portrait of George Washington, first President of the United States. A later issue incorporated the words UNITED STATES in the inscription, though the stamps had local validity only. The example of Windsor and Greig was soon followed by other operators of local services which flourished in the two decades until 1863 when the US Post Office assumed responsibility for house to house delivery in the towns and cities.

The first government issue of stamps outside the United Kingdom appeared in Switzerland on 1 March 1843 when the canton of Zürich issued 4 and 6 rappen stamps. They were the world's first stamps produced by the lithographic process and also the world's first bi-coloured stamps, since they were printed in black on paper which already had a background of horizontal red lines as a security feature. The stamps were produced by Orell, Füssli & Co. of Zürich and remained in use until 1850 when they were superseded by stamps of the federal postal administration. These stamps were valid only within the canton.

The first stamps, outside the United Kingdom, to be valid for postage throughout an entire country were issued by Brazil on 1 August 1843. By a decree of 30 November 1842 the Brazilian government was authorised to reform the postal service and introduce adhesive stamps. The idea had come from J D Sturz, formerly Brazilian consul in Prussia, who had seen stamps used in England and enlisted the help of the British chargé d'affaires in Rio de Janeiro in promoting the scheme. Using an engraving machine confiscated from Pedro Ludwig by the Brazilian Customs, and a transferring machine and other equipment purchased from Eduardo Lemerick in December 1842, Clementino Geraldo de Gonvea and Florentino Rodrigues Prado printed the stamps from dies engraved by Carlos Custodio de Azevedo and Guintino José de Faria. The stamps, in denominations of 30, 60 and 90 reis, featured the numerals of value on an engine-turned background. The circular motifs, devoid of inscription, were nicknamed the Bull's Eyes by collectors. In the same vein successive issues were nicknamed the Snake's Eyes (1844-6), the Goat's Eyes (1850) and the Cat's Eyes (1854-61).

Zürich cantonal stamp, 1843

The first stamp from any British overseas colony was the 5 cent blue issued by David Bryce on 16 April 1847 for use on mail carried by his steamship *Lady McLeod* between San Fernando and Port of Spain, Trinidad. The stamps were lithographed locally and bore a picture of the steamer above the monogram L McL. The stamp was a private issue with a limited validity and appears to have been used until 1849. The government of Trinidad did not issue its own stamps until 1851.

The first stamps authorised by a British colonial government were the 1d and 2d 'Post Office' stamps of Mauritius, issued on 21 September 1847. Uniform postal rates were adopted on 1 January 1847 and the production of stamps was entrusted to James Barnard of Port Louis, a jeweller, watch-maker and engraver. The stamps were based on the contemporary British 1d red and 2d blue stamps and portrayed Queen Victoria, the vertical side panels being inscribed POST OFFICE and MAURITIUS. The inscription on the left was later altered to POST PAID. These first stamps were unique in the sense that Barnard engraved one die for each stamp, side by side on a small copper plate which had previously been used for a lady's visiting card (and still had her details on the other side). Barnard then laboriously printed the stamps one by one, and pairs or other multiples are therefore impossible, though the American millionaire collector, Arthur Hind, once boasted to King George V that he had a pair of the 'Post Office' stamps.

Brazil 'Bull's eye', 1843

It has been stated that the inscription POST OFFICE was an error on Barnard's part. He had been instructed verbally but promptly forgot the exact wording of the inscription, till apparently reminded

Lady McLeod steamship stamp, Trinidad, 1847

of it by seeing the façade of the post office on his way home. On the other hand, 'Post Office Mauritius' was the usual inscription on the handstruck postal markings which preceded adhesive stamps. The status of the Mauritius 'Post Office' stamps as the world's first stamp errors is therefore open to question.

Only 500 of each denomination were produced. Since 1864, when their existence first came to the notice of collectors, only fourteen of the 1d (two unused) and twelve of the 2d (four unused) have been discovered.

The first stamps from the Australian continent were issued by New South Wales on 1 January 1850. Although this colony had used embossed letter sheets since 1838 (see Chapter 6) no proposals for adhesive stamps were made until December 1848 as part of a package of postal reform which came into effect in 1850. The stamps, in denominations of 1d, 2d and 3d, were each engraved by different craftsmen and recess-printed in Sydney. The frames of the stamps were copied from the contemporary British stamps, with POSTAGE at the top and the value at the foot, and an attempt at trellis-work in the vertical side panels. The central motif, however, was the great seal of the colony, showing settlers and convicts arriving at Botany Bay and was derived from a rack-plate by the Staffordshire firm of Josiah Wedgwood, which explains the curious motto at the foot – SIC FORTIS ETRURIA CREVIT 'Thus did Etruria (the Wedgwood factory) grow in strength'. The name of the colony was referred to indirectly in the band around the motif SIGILLUM NOV. CAMB. AUST. (Latin for the seal of New South Wales).

The neighbouring colony of Victoria should have issued stamps at the same time, but New Year's Day was a public holiday and, in fact, it was not until 3 January that the stamps went on sale. The 1d, 2d and 3d stamps were likewise based on the contemporary British stamps, with a profile of Queen Victoria. The name of the colony was also inscribed in the top and side panels.

The first stamps in Asia were issued in the Indian district of Scinde (Sind) on 1 July 1852. Considerable mystery still surrounds the manner and place of their production. The area was conquered in 1843 by Lord Ellen (famous for his telegram *Peccavi* – I have sinned) and placed under the governorship of Sir Bartle Frere who acted on his own initiative in arranging the production and distribution of half anna stamps. In his memoirs he stated that he obtained the stamps from De La Rue. No mention of this can be found in the firm's archives and it was not until 1854 that De La Rue became involved in the printing of Indian stamps. If Frere's memory was not faulty this would have been the first stamps

'Post Office' Mauritius, 1847

New South Wales 'Sydney View', 1850

Scinde 'Dawk', 1852, on a stamp of Pakistan, 1952

produced by this company. It must be said, however, that the possibility of De La Rue having been involved is exceedingly remote, since the stamps were unlike anything they ever produced.

The first stamps were embossed on circular red wafers, of the type then in vogue for sealing envelopes and wrappers, and bore the talismanic device of the Honourable East India Company, with the inscription SCINDE DISTRICT DAWK round the circumference, 'Dawk' or 'Dak' being Hindi for post. These stamps were unique (until the 1960s) in being struck singly in a circular format. They were superseded by similar stamps embossed in blue or albino in a more orthodox sheet format. They were withdrawn in October 1854 on the introduction of the general series throughout British India.

The first African stamps were the Cape of Good Hope triangulars, issued on 1 September 1853. The prepayment of postage by means of adhesive stamps was authorised as early as 1846 and two years later Perkins Bacon were asked to prepare dies and plates for 1d and 2d stamps. This order was counter-

manded soon afterwards and a further four years passed before the subject was raised again. In August 1852 the Cape government again approached Perkins Bacon and commissioned 1d and 4d stamps in a triangular shape. Sketches in triangular and pentagonal designs were forwarded to London by Charles Bell, the Surveyor-General of the colony, who believed that the use of abnormal shapes would facilitate the sorting of mail by the semi-literate native employees of the post office. William Humphrys engraved Bell's triangular design, showing the seated figure of Hope, and the stamps were recessprinted by Perkins Bacon and shipped to the Cape.

The most different stamps in the shortest time were issued during the Romanian occupation of Debrecen in eastern Hungary. Between 14 November 1919 and 4 June 1920, when Romanian forces evacuated the town under the terms of the Treaty of Trianon, some 124 different Hungarian postage, war charity, postage due, newspaper, express letter, savings bank and fiscal stamps were overprinted to signify the Romanian occupation.

The Turkish island of Cheustan (Makronisi or Long Island) in the Gulf of Smyrna, occupied by British naval units during the First World War, had at least 32 different stamps (not counting minor varieties) issued between 7 and 26 May 1916.

The world's longest-running stamps, without any technical changes were the Irish definitives ('e' watermark), in use for 28 years (1940-68).

The world's longest-running definitive set has been issued by Norway whose posthorn and numeral design has been in continuous use for the lower denominations since 1871. In a period spanning more than a century the series has undergone a number of technical changes. The original series was letterpressprinted with values in skilling. Since 1877 the

Cape of Good Hope 'Triangular', 1853

currency has been expressed in øre, from 1882 to 1893 the posthorn was unshaded, from 1893 to 1908 the name NORGE was rendered in seriffed lettering, the design was redrawn in 1909, photogravure was used in 1940-9 and 1950-7, and since then intaglio has been the printing process. Norway even issued two stamps, somewhat belatedly on 6 May 1972, to celebrate the centenary of the world's oldest design in current use.

Other examples of philatelic longevity are:

UK postage due labels (1914-71)	57 years
Tonga pictorial definitives (1897-1953)	56 years
Ireland definitives (1922-69)	47 years

The Sudan used the same design for its definitives from 1898 till 1941 and from 1948 till September 1951 – a period of 53 years, but with a seven-year gap. The design is of interest for several reasons. It was produced by E A Stanton, then a *bimbashi* (captain) in the Egyptian army but later a colonel in the British forces and one of Britain's foremost philatelists. The vignette showed an Arab postman mounted on a racing camel, the model being the Sheik of the Howawir tribe whom Stanton persuaded to dress for the part and to trot around with four straw-filled sacks representing mailbags, while a sketch was made. Optimistically, Stanton inscribed two of the mailbags KHARTOUM and BERBERA – towns which were still in the hands of the Mahdi at the time. These inscriptions duly appeared on the stamps, printed by De La Rue in 1898 – and continued to appear on the stamps for more than half a century – long after their significance had vanished. The Camel Postman designed by an Englishman in the service of the Khedive, ultimately became the national symbol of the Sudan, and appeared on commemoratives of 1948 and 1954 celebrating the opening of the legislative assembly and the attainment of self-government. Since then the Camel Postman has even become the motif on the obverse of Sudanese coins.

The stamp with the longest period of sale was the 1 öre definitive of Sweden, issued in March 1912 and still on sale at main post offices in 1970, if not later.

The oldest stamps still valid for postage are the United States definitive series issued on 17 August 1861. The issues of 1847 and 1851, valid until that time, were demonetised following the outbreak of the Civil War, to render worthless stocks held by the Confederacy. The acceptance in prepayment of postage was ordered to be discontinued in the north-eastern states on 1 November 1861 and in the remoter states and federal territories by 1 January 1862. All US stamps since August 1861 are still valid for postage. Anyone using the original 1861 series for postage would be most unwise; it has a face value of $1.75 (less than £1) but is catalogued by Stanley Gibbons (1988) at £10 400!

The longest definitive series to appear in the same year was the American Presidential series of 1938, released between 25 April and 8 December. It comprised 32 denominations, from ½ cent to 5 dollars. The cent and dollar values portrayed each of the 29 presidents from George Washington to Calvin Coolidge, those still living being omitted under the Act of Congress of April 1866 forbidding the portrayal of living persons. The half-cent values (½, 1½ and 4½) depicted Benjamin Franklin, Martha Washington and the White House respectively. Up to and including the 22 cents denomination each value corresponded with the number of the president – a useful aid in teaching Americans their political history.

Norway 'Posthorns' (1875 and 1978), Tonga 5s (1897-1953), Brunei 4c (1907-52), GB postage due (1914-71) and Ireland 2d (1922-69)

Sudan 'Camel Postman' (1898)

USA Presidential series, 1938

The longest definitive series ever issued was produced by Venezuela between 1951 and 1954 and consisted of sets of sixteen (seven ordinary and nine airmail) featuring the arms of each of the 23 states, with appropriate pictorial vignettes – a total of 368 stamps. Additionally, Venezuela issued a series depicting Caracas General Post Office, comprising eleven ordinary and fourteen airmail stamps in 1953, re-issued the following year with an amended inscription.

Portugal's Ceres definitive issue, launched in 1912, eventually ran to 86 stamps (ignoring minor shade and printing variations). In addition, 35 provisional surcharges and six revalidated overprints in 1928–9 brought the Ceres total to 127. This was the longest series with a single design.

Venezuela definitive series, 1951-4

Other lengthy definitive sets with uniform designs; on a simplified basis ignoring watermark, perforation or shade variations:

UK Machin series (1967-82)	74 stamps
France 'La Semeuse' (1903-38)	73 stamps
Norway 'posthorn and numerals' (1871-)	76 stamps
Finland 'arms' (1930-42)	58 stamps
Italy 'La Siracusa' (1953-77)	48 stamps

Saudi Arabia produced definitive sets in the 1960s which rank among the longest on record: 1960 – 47, 1964 – 82, and 1966 – 79.

The most prolific country of all time was the Arab sheikdom of Ajman, which awarded contracts to several overseas agencies in the late 1960s. These entrepreneurs produced a vast array of stamps, considerably in excess of real postal need. Output reached its peak in 1972, following the establishment of the United Arab Emirates and the imminent termination of all the stamp contracts. At least two rival contractors appear to have been active simultaneously and several contradictory statements were made as to the validity of some of the issues of 1967-72. Consequently the majority are listed only in an abbreviated form in appendices to the stamp catalogues, and a substantial number is ignored altogether. In 1971 alone Ajman issued at least 57 *sets*, totalling 440 stamps (excluding miniature sheets and imperforate versions). Many other issues were produced after 1 September 1971 but their authenticity was repudiated by the Ajman Postmaster General.

The least-prolific stamp-issuing country in recent years was the Canal Zone, which had only issued two stamps since 1968 – 13 and 15c definitives in 1976 and 1978 – and no commemorative since 1963. It ceased its postal service in September 1979.

Other examples of philatelic conservatism were Nauru – no new stamps between 1937 and 1954; Maldive Islands – no new stamps between 1933 and 1950; Nepal – no new stamps between 1907 and 1949. Various printings, distinguished by philatelists, were, however, produced in the intervening years.

Portugal 'Ceres' (1912-29), France 'La Semeuse' (1903-38), Finland 'Arms' (1930-42), Italy 'La Siracusa' (1953-77) and UK 'Machin' (1967-)

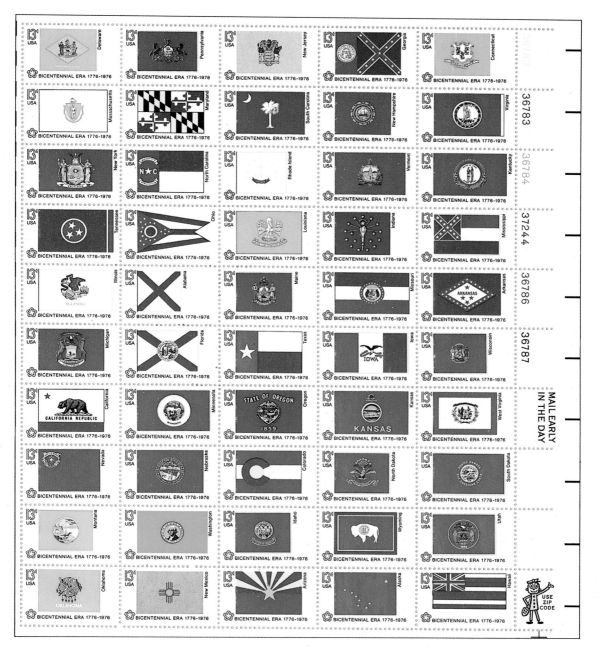

This sheet containing the flags of all 50 American States was issued at the time of the Bicentennial celebrations. It was available only as a complete sheet and this probably militated against its popularity with the general public and so commercially used examples of these stamps tend to be elusive

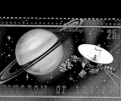
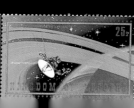
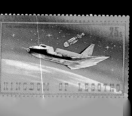

Mythological, religious and Christmas stamps

The arts on stamps

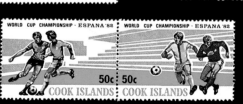

VIỆT NAM
BƯU CHÍNH
MACACA SPECIOSA
KHỈ CỘC
12 c

MALAWI 20c
AFRICAN BUFFALO
Syncerus caffer

BAHAMAS 50c

NR BULGARIA
Daxou
13 st

SILVER JUBILEE
1924–1949
BAHAWALPUR
SAHIWAL BULL
ANNA 1

ZAMBIA
CATTLE HERDING
42n

ANDORRA
CORREO URGENTE
25 CENTS

RUANDA
URUNDI
GORILLA
10c

POSTAGE AND REVENUE
RUHUNA
NATIONAL PARK
CEYLON
2c

Sperm Whale
Physeter catodon
NORFOLK ISLAND 24c

YOUNG FARMERS
CLUBS
1938–1953
AUSTRALIA 3½d

SUDAN

KENYA 50c

50 POSTAGE
PEOPLES DEMOCRATIC REPUBLIC OF YEMEN

AUSTRALIA POSTAGE
5c 5c

TANGANYIKA 5

6d Posgela Postage
Suid-Afrika South Africa

BARBADOS
BLACK BELLY SHEEP
40c

ZAMBIA
BACONI BULL
4d

RÉPUBLIQUE FRANÇAISE
POSTE 1c
MOYEN CONGO

BUFFALO
1d POSTAGE RHODESIA

FALKLAND ISLANDS
DEPENDENCIES
E R
13

WATERFOWL
CONSERVATION
6c
UNITED STATES

UGANDA 50c

POSTAGE AUSTRALIA
WESTERN
ONE PENNY

UNION OF BURMA
3P

Adelie Penguins
Ross Dependency 5c

SVERIGE 1 KR

26p C. Darwin

CORREOS DEL PERU
2 CTS
RIQUEZA DEL GUANO
WATERLOW & SONS LIMITED, LONDRES

AUSTRALIAN
ANTARCTIC TERRITORY
2c

SAINT HELENA
1/6d
FAIRY TERN

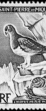

SAINT-PIERRE et MIQUELON
POSTES
1F
RF

5 CENTS
BLACK
PARROT
SEYCHELLES

50c
Ostrich (Mbuni)
Struthio camelus
TANZANIA

40c
Columba squamosa
Barbados

House Wren
Troglodytes aedon
½ C
E R
St.VINCENT

TURKS &
CAICOS
ISLANDS
E R
SOOTY TERN
¼

CORREO AEREO
140 c
TIJERETA
URUGUAY

Malaconotus
Telophorus
Prengyete
Bokmakierie
5s
LESOTHO

Gyrinochelus aymonieri

VIÊT NAM 30¢ BƯU CHÍNH

NEWFOUNDLAND POSTAGE
CODFISH NEWFOUNDLAND CURRENCY
1 ONE CENT 1

5 भारत INDIA

Trinidad & Tobago 45¢
Fish for Food
Bigeye Priacanthus arenatus

Hong Kong 香港
20c Epinephelus akaara

60 CENTS
SEA COW JAMAICA

CERNIA BRUNA
SAN MARINO L.1

TOXOTES JACULATOR
6 CENTS SINGAPORE

Falkland Islands EIIR SHELF FISHES
Merluccius hubbsi
Patagonian Hake 15p

CUNNING FISH
St. HELENA 1d

35P Hammerhead Shark Sphyrna zidea
Tristan da Cunha

BARBADOS 15 cents

SAINT-PIERRE ET MIQUELON
POSTES RF

CHAETODON AURIGA
CHRISTMAS ISLAND $1
INDIAN OCEAN GEORGE HARRAY

DEUTSCHE BUNDESPOST UMWELTSCHUTZ
60 Muster

10p EIIR
CYPRAEA SPINCA SANCTAEHELENAE
ST. HELENA

Priganana Bubble Apiotrum nilignenud
20¢ SINGAPORE

½d
TRISTAN CRAWFISH
TRISTAN DA CUNHA

30c
DIOPSIS FUMIPENNIS
REPUBLIQUE RWANDAISE
JENS VAN NOTEN

BERMUDA EIIR
SPINY LOBSTER 10c Panulirus argus

½c
CYPRAEA CHAIN
DOMINICA

$05 CORREIOS
Rutelina Imbricata
GUINÉ PORTUGUESA

REPUBLIQUE RWANDAISE 50c
BITIS

DEUTSCHE BUNDESPOST
20

STT.
13
Anisoplia austria
NR BULGARIA

LEPIDODACTYLUS LISTERI
CHRISTMAS ISLAND 40c
INDIAN OCEAN

SRI LANKA .50
Cethosia nietneri nietneri

HEMIARGUS HANNO EIIR
U.S.Cy
BRITISH VIRGIN ISLANDS 75c

SMALL TORTOISESHELL EIIR
22p
BAILIWICK of GUERNSEY

PRO JUVENTUTE 1967
40+10 HELVETIA

perlis
malaysia 20c

Doleschallia bisaltide
Solomon Islands 10c

紅蛺蝶
REPUBLIC OF CHINA

Swaziland 10c

18p
Large Blue

10c SINGAPORE
THE CLIPPER

BRITISH HONDURAS
HURRICANE HATTIE
BLUE BUTTERFLY
POSTAGE & REVENUE 25 CENTS

Colour plate of items referred to in the text.

Inverted and upright background, Dag Hammarskjold commemorative, USA, 1961

Switzerland 1fr printed in gold ink, 1867

Heligoland, 1867 and 1875 issues

First government-issued four-coloured stamps, El Salvador, 1897

Photogravure colour separations shown on a miniature sheet of Barbados, 1980

Intaglio colour separations on a French Postal Museum souvenir, 1966

Pour le MUSÉE POSTAL

impression taille-douce report   impression taille-douce   impression définitive

Phases d'impression du Timbre-poste
"Le Nouveau Né" de Georges de la Tour

5 Francs   IMPRIMERIE DES TIMBRES-POSTE · PARIS

Superlatives on Stamps *(on previous page)*
World's highest mountain (India, 1953), world's largest
monolith (Australia, 1976), world's remotest inhabited island
(Tristan da Cunha, 1969), largest gold-mine (South Africa,
1936), largest dam (USA, 1952), largest man-made object
(China, 1932), largest domed church (Italy, 1950), largest
amphitheatre (Tunisia, 1926), tallest obelisk (Turkey, 1914),
tallest wooden building (British Guiana, 1966), tallest tree
(USA, 1978), largest living creature (British Antarctic
Territory, 1981), fastest creature on land (Kenya, 1966),
world's largest earwig (St Helena, 1982), world's most
valuable stamp (Guyana, 1967), oldest parliament (Iceland,
1930), largest passenger liner (Tristan da Cunha, 1978),
fastest air liner (GB, 1969), oldest human remains (Kenya,
1982), highest-paid operatic singer (Italy, 1973), winner of the
most Oscars (USA, 1968), oldest reigning monarch
(Swaziland, 1967), most beautiful girl (Jamaica, 1963), first
all-aluminium ship (Guyana, 1969), first motor car (Mongolia,
1980), first space rocket (USSR, 1958), first woman in space
(Bulgaria, 1963), first book from movable type (USA, 1952),
first trans-Atlantic steamship (USA, 1944), first steam
locomotive (GB, 1975), first men on the moon (Belgium, 1969)

An attractive example of a miniature
sheet, a 3 dollar stamp from the
Commonwealth of Dominica

The unique stamp created and
printed especially for Carol Tully
through the good offices of Jimmy
Savile and Harrison and Sons

HENRY VIII/MARY ROSE

ADMIRAL BLAKE/TRIUMPH

LORD NELSON/HMS VICTORY

The five stamps of the British Maritime issue printed by intaglio and by photogravure in six colours by Harrisons of High Wycombe exemplify the stamp printer's art and skill

The 15½p shows Henry VIII and the pride of his navy the *Mary Rose*, built in 1510 and sunk in 1545

The 19½p shows Admiral Blake and his fleet flagship the *Triumph*, built in 1623

Britain's most famous sailor, Vice-Admiral Lord Nelson, is pictured on the 24p with his flagship HMS *Victory*, laid down in 1759

LORD FISHER/HMS DREADNOUGHT

VISCOUNT CUNNINGHAM/HMS WARSPITE

Admiral Fisher is shown on the 26p with his controversial innovation HMS *Dreadnought* a 17 900 ton battleship built at Portsmouth and launched by Edward VII in 1906

Admiral Cunningham, the outstanding British Naval Commander of World War II is shown on the 29p with HMS *Warspite*, completed in 1915

The Jumelle press at Harrisons of High Wycombe used for printing stamps

The Mulready envelope

This contemporary print shows an escaped lioness attacking the Exeter Mail Coach near Salisbury on the night of Sunday 20 October 1816

The Bristol Royal Mail in King Street, Bristol, *circa* 1830. Built in Temple Street, Bristol, this coach carried the Royal Mail between Bristol, Bath and London

The Avon Mercury Trimobile, built in Keynsham, leaves Small Street Post Office loaded with mail *circa* 1905

Concorde, the world's first supersonic airliner to enter regular airline service, is loaded with Datapost for New York, 1980. Datapost is carried to the USA in Concorde at twice the speed of sound

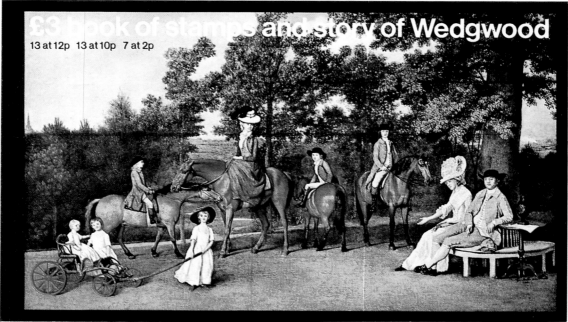

£3 book of stamps and story of Wedgwood

13 at 12p 13 at 10p 7 at 2p

Above and right, two colourful examples of stamp books

Stamps for Cooks

£1

TABLE OF STAMP-ISSUING AUTHORITIES

This table is arranged chronologically, according to the year when an authority first issued stamps. The other columns give the date of the first commemorative (Com), official stamp (Off), charity or semi-postal stamp (Char), airmail (Air) and postage due label (PD).

	Com	Off	Char	Air	PD
1840					
Gt Britain	1924	1882	1975	1928★	1914
1843					
Zürich, Geneva	—	—	—	—	—
Brazil	1900	1906	1931	1928	1889
1845					
USA					
(postmasters)					
Federal P.O.					
(1847)	1893	1873	—	1918	1879
1847					
Mauritius	1898	—	—	—	1933
1848					
Bermuda	1920	—	1918	—	—
1849					
Bavaria	1911	1916	1919	1912	1862
Belgium	1894	1929	1911	1930	1870
France	1923	—	1914	1927	1859
1850					
Austria	1908	—	1914	1922	1894
Austrian Italy	—	—	—	—	—
Br. Guiana	1898	1875	1918	—	1940
Hanover	—	—	—	—	—
New South Wales	1888	1879	1897	—	1891
Prussia	—	—	—	—	—
Saxony	—	—	—	—	—
Schleswig-Hol- stein	—	—	—	—	—
Spain	1905	1854	1938	1920	—
Switzerland	1900	1918	1913	1923	1878
Victoria	—	—	1897	—	1890
1851					
Baden	—	—	—	—	1862
Canada	1897	1949	1916	1928	1906
Denmark	1920	1871	1921	1925	1921
Hawaii	—	1896	—	—	—
New Brunswick	—	—	—	—	—
Nova Scotia	—	—	—	—	—
Sardinia	—	—	—	—	—

(★Private airline issue)

	Com	Off	Char	Air	PD
Trinidad	—	1894	1914	—	1885
Tuscany	—	—	—	—	—
Württemberg	1906	1881	—	—	—
1852					
Barbados	1897	—	1907	—	—
Brunswick	—	—	—	—	—
India (Scinde)	1931	1866	1971	1929	—
Luxembourg	1921	1875	1921	1931	1907
Modena	—	—	—	—	—
Netherlands	1907	1913	1906	1928	1870
Oldenburg	—	—	—	—	—
Parma	—	—	—	—	—
Reunion	1931	—	1915	1937	1889
Roman States	—	—	—	—	—
Thurn and Taxis	—	—	—	—	—
1853					
Cape of Good Hope	1900	—	—	—	—
Chile	1910	1928	1940	1927	1895
Portugal	1894	1938	1911	1937	1898
Tasmania	—	—	—	—	—
1854					
Philippines	1926	1926	1942	1926	1899
Western Australia	—	—	—	—	—
1855					
Bremen	—	—	—	—	—
Ceylon	1935	1895	—	—	—
Corrientes	—	—	—	—	—
Cuba & Puerto Rico	1914	—	1935	1927	1914
Danish West Indies	—	—	—	—	1902
New Zealand	1900	1907	1929	1931	1899
Norway	1914	1925	1930	1925	1889
South Australia	—	1868	—	—	—
Sweden	1903	1974	1916	1920	1874
1856					
Finland	1927	—	1922	1930	—
Macklenburg- Schwerin	—	—	—	—	—
Mexico	1910	1884	1919	1922	1908

	Com	Off	Char	Air	PD
St Helena	1934	—	1916	—	—
Uruguay	1896	1880	1930	1921	1902
1857					
Natal	—	1904	—	—	—
Newfoundland	1897	—	—	1919	1939
Peru	1897	1890	1964	1934	1874
Russia	1913	—	1905	1922	1924
1858					
Argentina	1892	1884	1944	1928	—
Buenos Aires	—	—	—	—	—
Cordoba	—	—	—	—	—
Naples	—	—	—	—	—
Romania (Moldavia)	1903	1929	1906	1928	1881
1859					
Bahamas	1920	—	1917	1935	—
Colombia	1910	1937	1935	1918	—
French Colonies	—	—	1943	1944	1884
Hamburg	—	—	—	—	—
Ionian Islands	—	—	—	—	—
Lübeck	—	—	—	—	—
New Caledonia	1903	1958	1915	1932	1903
Romagna	—	—	—	—	—
Sicily	—	—	—	—	—
Venezuela	1893	—	1937	1930	—
1860					
Jamaica	1935	1890	1923	—	—
Liberia	1923	1892	1918	1936	1892
Malta	1922	—	1918	1928	1925
Poland	1919	1920	1919	1925	1919
Queensland	1903	—	1900	—	—
St Lucia	1902	—	1916	—	1930
Sierra Leone	1933	—	—	1963	—
1861					
Bergedorf	—	—	—	—	—
British Columbia and Vancouver I	—	—	—	—	—
Confederate States of America	—	—	—	—	—
Greece	1896	—	1914	1926	1875
Grenada	1898	—	1916	1972	1892
Neapolitan Provinces	—	—	—	—	—
Nevis	1980	1980	—	—	—
Prince Edward Island	—	—	—	—	—
St Vincent	1935	—	1916	1979	—
1862					
Antigua	1932	—	1916	—	—
Costa Rica	1921	1883	1958	1926	1903
Hong Kong	1891	—	—	—	1923
Italy	1910	1875	1911	1917	1863
Nicaragua	1892	1890	1928	1929	1896
1863					
Bolivar	—	—	—	—	—
Russian P.O.s in Turkey	1913	—	—	—	—
Turkey	1908	1947	1935	1938	1863
Wenden	—	—	—	—	—
1864					
Dutch East Indies	1922	1911	1915	1928	1874
Holstein	—	—	—	—	—
Mecklenburg-Strelitz	—	—	—	—	—
Schleswig	—	—	—	—	—
Soruth	—	1929	—	—	—
1865					
Dominican Republic	1899	1902	1931	1928	1901
Ecuador	1896	1886	1921	1929	1896
Shanghai	1893	—	—	—	1892
1866					
Bolivia	1909	—	1939	1924	1931
British Honduras	1921	—	1916	—	1923
Egypt	1922	1893	1940	1926	1884
Honduras	1892	1890	1941	1925	—
Jammu and Kashmir	—	1878	—	—	—
Serbia	1904	1943	—	—	1895
Br. Virgin Islands	1935	—	1917	—	—
1867					
Austrian P.O.s in Turkey	1908	—	—	—	1902
El Salvador	1892	1896	—	1930	1895
Heligoland					
Straits Settlements	1922	—	1917	—	1924
Turks (and Caicos) Islands	1935	—	1917	—	—
1868					
Antioquia	—	—	—	—	—
Azores	1894	—	1911	—	1904
Fernando Poo	1929	—	1960	—	—
Madeira	1898	—	1925	—	1925
North German Confederation	—	1870	—	—	—
Orange Free State	—	—	—	—	—
1869					
Gambia	1935	—	—	—	—
Hyderabad	1937	1873	—	—	—
St Thomas and Prince Is	1938	—	1925	—	1904
Sarawak	1946	—	—	—	—
Transvaal	1895	—	—	—	—

	Com	Off	Char	Air	PD
1870					
Afghanistan	1920	1909	1938	1939	—
Alsace & Lorraine	—	—	—	—	—
Angola	1938	—	1925	1938	1904
Cundinamarca	—	—	—	—	—
Fiji	1935	—	1916	—	1917
Paraguay	1892	1886	1930	1929	1904
Persia (Iran)	1915	1902	1948	1927	—
St Christopher	—	—	—	—	—
Tolima	—	—	—	—	—
1871					
Guatemala	1897	1902	1927	1929	—
Hungary	1916	1921	1913	1918	1903
Japan	1894	—	1942	1919	—
Portuguese India	1898	—	1919	—	1904
1872					
German Empire	1919	1903	1919	1919	—
1873					
Curacao	1923	—	1941	1929	1889
Iceland	1911	1873	1933	1928	—
Porto Rico	1893	—	1898	—	1899
Surinam	1923	—	1927	1930	1885
1874					
Dominica	1935	—	1916		
Griqualand	—	—	—	—	—
Italian P.O.s in the Levant	—	—	—	—	1922
Jhind	—	1885	—	—	—
Lagos	—	—	—	—	—
Montenegro	1893	—	1944	1941	1894
1875					
Gold Coast	1935	—	1918	—	1923
1876					
Bhopal	—	1908	—	—	—
Montserrat	1932	1976	1917	—	—
Poonch	—	—	—	—	—
Johore	1896	—	—	—	1938
1877					
Alwar	—	—	—	—	—
Cape Verde Is	1921	—	1925	—	1904
Mozambique	1913	—	1916	1946	1904
Nowanugger	—	—	—	—	—
Samoa	1920	—	1966	1965	—
San Marino	1894	—	1917	1931	1897
1878					
China	1894	—	1932	1932	1912
Falkland Is	1933	—	1918	—	—
Panama	1913	—	1941	1929	1915
Perak	1948	1889	—	—	—
Selangor	1948	—	—	—	—
Sungei Ujong	—	—	—	—	—
1879					
Bhor	—	—	—	—	—
Bosnia and Herzegovina	1910	—	1916	—	1904
Bulgaria	1896	1942	1916	1927	1884
Faridkot	—	1886			
Labuan	1896	—	—	—	1901
Sirmoor	—	1890	—	—	—
Tobago	—	—	—	—	—
1880					
Cyprus	1928	—	1974	—	—
Rajpipla	—	—	—	—	—
1881					
Eastern Roumelia	—	—	—	—	—
Haiti	1929	—	1944	1929	1898
Nepal	1956	1960	—	1958	—
Portuguese Guinea	1946	—	1919	—	1904
1882					
Bangkok	—	—	—	—	—
Tahiti	—	—	—	—	1893
1883					
North Borneo	1922	—	1918	—	1895
Thailand	1908	1963	1920	1925	—
1884					
Guadeloupe	1931	—	1938	1945	1876
German P.O.s in Turkey	—	—	—	—	—
Macao	1948	—	1919	—	1904
Madagascar (British P.O.)	—	—	—	—	—
Patiala	—	1884	—	—	—
Santander	—	—	—	—	—
Stellaland	—	—	—	—	—
1885					
British Levant	—	—	—	—	—
French Levant	—	—	—	—	—
Korea	1902	—	—	—	—
Guanacaste	—	—	—	—	—
Gwalior	—	1895	—	—	—
Monaco	1921	—	1914	1933	1906
Nabha	—	1885	—	—	—
St Pierre and Miquelon	1931	—	1915	1942	1892
South Bulgaria	—	—	—	—	—
Timor	1898	—	1919	—	1904
1886					
British Bechuanaland	—	—	—	—	—
Chamba	—	1886	—	—	—
Cochin China	—	—	—	—	—

	Com	Off	Char	Air	PD
Congo (Belgian)	1928	—	1918	1930	1923
French Guiana	1931	—	1915	1933	1925
Gabon	1931	1968	1915	1960	1928
Gibraltar	1935	—	1918	—	1956
Holkar (Indore)	—	—	—	—	1904
Martinique	1931	—	1916	1945	1927
New Republic	—	—	—	—	—
Tonga	1899	1893	1982	1963	—
1887					
Jhalawar	—	—	—	—	—
Senegal	1931	1961	1915	1935	1903
1888					
Annam and Tonkin	—	—	—	—	—
Bechuanaland Protectorate	1935	—	—	—	1926
Formosa	—	—	—	—	—
Travancore	1931	1911	—	—	—
Tunisia	1938	—	1916	1919	1901
Wadhwan	—	—	—	—	—
Zululand	—	—	—	—	—
1889					
Bamra	—	—	—	—	—
Bogota	—	—	—	—	—
French Madagascar	1931	—	1915	1935	1896
Indo-China	1931	1933	1914	1933	1904
Nossi-Bé	—	—	—	—	1891
Swaziland	1935	—	—	—	1933
1890					
British East Africa	—	—	—	—	—
British South Africa Co.	1905	—	—	—	—
Diego Suarez	—	—	—	—	1891
Leeward Is	1897	—	—	—	—
Pahang	1948	—	—	—	—
Seychelles	1935	—	—	—	1951
1891					
British Central Africa	—	—	—	—	—
French Congo	—	—	—	—	—
French Morocco	1946	—	1914	1922	1915
Negri Sembilan	1948	—	—	—	—
1892					
Angra	—	—	—	—	—
Anjouan	—	—	—	—	—
Benin	—	—	—	—	1894
Cochin	—	1913	—	—	—
Cook Is	1935	1975	1968	1966	—
French Guinea	1931	—	1938	1940	1905
French Indian Settlements	1931	—	1916	1942	1923

	Com	Off	Char	Air	PD
Funchal	—	—	—	—	—
Horta	—	—	—	—	—
Ivory Coast	1931	1973	1915	1940	1906
Mayotte	—	—	—	—	—
Mozambique Company	1935	—	1917	1935	1906
Niger Coast (Oil Rivers)	—	—	—	—	—
Obock	—	—	—	—	1892
Oceania	1931	—	1915	1934	1926
Ponta Delgada	—	—	—	—	—
1893					
Cavalla	—	—	—	—	—
Datia (Duttia)	—	—	—	—	—
Dedeagatz (Dedeagh)	—	—	—	—	—
Eritrea	1922	—	1916	1934	1903
German East Africa	—	—	—	—	—
Portuguese Congo	—	—	—	—	—
Rajnandgaon	—	—	—	—	—
Vathy	—	—	—	—	—
1894					
Bundi	—	1918	—	—	—
Charkari	—	—	—	—	—
Djibouti (till 1902)	—	—	—	—	—
Ethiopia	1908	—	1936	1929	1896
French P.O.s in China	—	—	—	—	1901
French Sudan	1931	—	1938	1940	1921
Lourenzo Marques	1895	—	1918	—	—
Ste Marie de Madagascar	—	—	—	—	—
Zambezia	—	—	—	—	—
Zanzibar (French P.O.)	—	—	—	—	1897
1895					
Inhambane	1895	—	—	—	—
Majunga	—	—	—	—	—
Uganda	1962	—	—	—	1967
Zanzibar (Br. P.O.)	1936	—	—	—	1930
1896					
Bussahir	—	—	—	—	—
Cameroun	1931	—	1938	1941	1925
Romanian P.O.s in Turkey	—	—	—	—	—
1897					
Dhar	—	—	—	—	—
New Guinea	1935	1914	—	1931	—

	Com	Off	Char	Air	PD
Grand Comoro	—	—	—	—	—
Las Bela	—	—	—	—	—
Marshall Is	—	—	—	—	—
Nyassa Company	—	—	1925	—	1924
German S.W. Africa	—	—	—	—	—
Sudan	1935	1902	—	1931	1897
Togo	1931	—	1938	1940	1921

1898

	Com	Off	Char	Air	PD
British P.O.s in Crete	—				
German P.O.s in China	—				
Morocco Agencies	1935	—	—	—	—
Portuguese Africa	1898	—	1919	—	1945
Thessaly	—	—	—	—	—

1899

	Com	Off	Char	Air	PD
Alexandria (Fr. P.O.)	—	—	1915	—	1922
Boyaca	—	—	—	—	—
Caroline Is	—	—	—	—	—
Dahomey	1931	—	1915	1940	1906
German P.O.s in Morocco	—	—	—	—	—
Guam	—	—	—	—	—
Kishengarh	—	1918	—	—	—
Marianne Is	—	—	—	—	—
Rethymno	—	—	—	—	—
Russian P.O.s in China	—	—	—	—	—

1900

	Com	Off	Char	Air	PD
Cayman Is	1932	—	1917	—	—
China E.F.	—	—	—	—	—
Crete	1907	1908	—	—	1901
Federated Malay States	—	—	—	—	—
Italian P.O.s in Crete	—	—	—	—	1924
Japanese P.O.s in China	—	—	—	—	—
Kiatschau	—	—	—	—	—
Mafeking	—	—	—	—	—
Northern Nigeria	—	—	—	—	—
Turks & Caicos Is	1900	—	1917	—	—

1901

	Com	Off	Char	Air	PD
Canton	—	—	—	—	—
Hoi-Hao	—	—	—	—	—
Magdalena	—	—	—	—	—
Papua	1934	1931	—	1929	—
Southern Nigeria	—	—	—	—	—

1902

	Com	Off	Char	Air	PD
Australia	1927	1931	—	1929	1902

	Com	Off	Char	Air	PD
Cauca	—	—	—	—	—
French P.O.s in Crete	—	—	—	—	—
French Somali Coast	1931	—	1915	1941	1915
Niue	1935	1985	1980	—	—
Penrhyn I	1974	1978	—	—	—
Spanish Guinea	1929	—	1951	1941	—

1903

	Com	Off	Char	Air	PD
Aitutaki	1972	1978	1974	—	—
Austrian P.O.s in Crete	1908	—	—	—	—
British Somaliland	1935	1903	—	—	—
East Africa and Uganda	—	—	—	—	—
Elobey, Annobon and Corisco	—	—	—	—	—
French P.O.s in China	—	—	—	—	—
Italian Somaliland	1922	—	1915	1934	1906
Spanish Morocco	1929	—	1937	1936	—
St Kitts-Nevis	1923	1980	1916	—	—
Senegambia and Niger	—	—	—	—	—
Yunnan-Fu	—	—	—	—	—

1904

	Com	Off	Char	Air	PD
Canal Zone	1926	1941	—	1929	1914
Jaipur	1931	1929	—	—	—

1905

	Com	Off	Char	Air	PD
Rio de Oro	—	—	—	—	—

1906

	Com	Off	Char	Air	PD
Brunei	1922	—	—	—	—
Kouang Tcheou	1939	—	1939	—	—
Maldive Is	1960	—	—	—	—
Mauretania	1931	1961	1915	1940	1906
Mohéli	—	—	—	—	—
Upper Senegal and Niger	—	—	1915	—	1906

1907

	Com	Off	Char	Air	PD
British Solomon Is	1935	—	—	—	1925
Middle Congo	1931	—	1916	—	1928

1908

	Com	Off	Char	Air	PD
King Edward VII Land	—	—	—	—	—
New Hebrides	1949	—	—	—	1925
Nyasaland	1935	—	—	—	1950

1909

	Com	Off	Char	Air	PD
Rhodesia	1965	—	—	—	1965

	Com	Off	Char	Air	PD
1910					
South Africa	1910	1926	1933	1925	1914
Trengganu	1922	—	1917	—	1937
Tripoli	—	—	—	—	—
1911					
Gilbert and Ellice Is	1935	—	1918	—	1940
Kelantan	1922	—	—	—	—
Tibet	—	—	—	—	—
Victoria Land	—	—	—	—	—
1912					
Aegean Is	1932	—	1932	1932	1934
Kedah	1922	—	—	—	—
Libya	1922	1952	1915	1928	1915
Liechtenstein	1918	1932	1925	1930	1920
1913					
Albania	1913	—	1924	1925	1914
Orchha	—	—	—	—	—
Quelimane	—	—	—	—	—
Tete	—	—	—	—	—
Trinidad and Tobago	1935	1913	1915	1975	1947
1914					
Epirus	—	—	—	—	—
French Morocco	1946	—	1914	1922	1915
German Occ. Belgium	—	—	—	—	—
Indian Expeditionary Force	—	—	—	—	—
Nigeria	1935	—	1966	—	1959
1915					
Austrian Military Post	—	—	1918	—	1918
Bushire	1915	—	—	—	—
German Occ. Poland	—	—	—	—	—
Mafia Island	—	—	—	—	—
N.W. Pacific Is	—	—	—	—	—
Ubangi-Shari-Chad	—	—	1916	—	—
1916					
Bulgarian Occ. Romania	—	—	—	—	—
Cape Juby	1929	—	—	—	—
German E. and W. Commands	—	—	—	—	—
Hejaz	1924	—	—	—	1917
Kionga	—	—	—	—	—
Long Island	—	—	—	—	—
Nauru	1935	—	—	—	—

	Com	Off	Char	Air	PD
Rouad I	—	—	—	—	—
Ruanda-Urundi	1934	—	1918	—	1924
Salonika (Levant)	—	—	—	—	—
1917					
Baghdad	—	—	—	—	—
Br. P.O.s in China	—	—	—	—	—
German Occ. Romania	—	—	—	—	1918
Italian P.O.s in China	—	—	—	—	1917
Koritza	—	—	—	—	—
1918					
Czechoslovakia	1919	1945	1919	1920	1919
Estonia	1928	—	1920	1920	—
Fiume	1920	—	1919	—	1918
French P.O. Tangier	—	—	—	1928	1918
Iraq	1949	1920	1949	1949	—
Latvia	1919	—	1920	1921	—
Lithuania	1920	—	1924	1921	—
Palestine	—	—	—	—	1920
Poland	1920	1920	1919	1925	1919
South Russia	—	—	—	—	—
Trentino	—	—	—	—	—
Venezia Giulia	—	—	—	—	1918
Ukraine	—	—	1923	—	—
Yugoslavia	1918	1946	1918	1934	1918
1919					
Armenia	—	—	—	—	—
Azerbaijan	—	—	1921	—	—
Batum	—	—	—	—	—
Belgian Occ. Germany	—	—	—	—	1920
Central Albania	—	—	—	—	—
Cilicia	1919	—	1919	—	1919
French Occ. Hungary	—	—	—	—	1919
Georgia	—	—	1922	—	—
Italian Occ. Austria	—	—	—	—	1919
Mosul	—	—	—	—	—
N.W. Russia	—	—	—	—	—
Polish P.O.s in Turkey	—	—	—	—	—
Rarotonga	—	—	—	—	—
Romanian Occ. Hungary	—	—	1919	—	1919
Serbian Occ. Hungary	—	—	1919	—	1919
Siberia	1922	—	—	—	—
Don Cossacks	—	—	—	—	—
Crimea	—	—	—	—	—

	Com	Off	Char	Air	PD
Denikin Govt. S. Russia	—	—	—	—	—
Syria	1920	—	1926	1920	1920
USPO Shanghai	—	—	—	—	—
Western Ukraine	—	—	—	—	—
1920					
Allenstein	—	—	—	—	—
Arbe and Veglia	—	—	—	—	—
Carinthia	—	—	—	—	—
Castelrosso	1930	—	1930	—	—
Central Lithuania	1921	—	1921	—	1921
Danzig	1930	1921	1921	1920	1921
Eastern Silesia	—	—	—	—	1920
Far Eastern Republic	1922	—	—	1923	—
Jordan	1922	1924	1947	1950	1923
La Aguera	—	—	—	—	—
Marienwerder	—	—	—	—	—
Memel	1923	—	—	1921	—
North Ingermanland	—	—	—	—	—
Saar	1933	1922	1926	1928	—
Schleswig	—	—	—	—	—
Thrace	—	—	—	—	1919
Upper Silesia	1921	1920	—	—	—
Upper Volta	1931	1963	1962	1961	1920
Wallis and Futuna Is	1931	—	1939	1946	1920
Wrangel Govt., Russia	—	—	—	—	—
1921					
Barwani	—	—	—	—	—
Niger	1931	1962	1939	1940	1921
Spanish Tangier	1929	—	—	1938	—
1922					
Ascension	1935	—	—	—	1986
Barbuda	1968	—	—	—	—
Chad	1931	1966	1963	1960	1928
Ireland	1929	—	—	1948	1925
Kenya and Uganda	—	—	—	—	1928
League of Nations	1932	—	—	—	—
Tanganyika	1961	1961	—	—	—
Ubangi-Shari	1931	—	—	—	1928
1923					
Corfu	—	—	—	—	—
Cyrenaica	1923	—	1925	1932	1950
International Labour Office	1932	—	—	—	—
Kuwait	1948	1923	—	1933	1963
Saseno	—	—	—	—	—
South West Africa	1935	1927	1935	1931	1923

	Com	Off	Char	Air	PD
Transcaucasian Federation	—	—	—	—	—
Tripolitania	1923	—	1925	1930	1948
1924					
Algeria	1930	—	1927	1946	1926
Lebanon	1924	—	1926	1924	1924
Mongolia	1945	—	—	1961	—
Southern Rhodesia	1935	—	—	—	1951
Spanish Sahara	1929	—	1950	1943	—
1925					
Alaouites	—	—	—	1925	1925
Jubaland	1925	—	1926	—	1925
Territory of New Guinea	1931	1925	—	1931	—
Northern Rhodesia	1935	—	—	—	1929
Polish P.O. in Danzig	1938	—	—	—	—
1926					
Hejaz-Nejd	1926	—	—	—	1926
Tuva	1936	—	—	1934	—
Yemen	1939	—	1967	1947	1964
1927					
Kirin & Heilungchang	—	—	—	—	—
1928					
Andorra (Spanish P.O.)	1972	—	—	1951	—
1929					
Chinese Communist Posts	—	—	—	—	—
Vatican	1935	—	1933	1938	1931
1931					
Andorra (French P.O.)	1962	—	1964	1950	1931
Latakia	—	—	—	1931	1931
Morvi	—	—	—	—	—
1932					
Inini	1939	—	1939	—	1932
Italian Colonies (general issue)	1932	—	1932	1932	—
Manchukuo	1933	—	—	1936	—
Saudi Arabia	1932	1939	1934	1949	1937
1933					
Bahrain	1948	—	—	—	—
Basutoland	1935	—	—	—	1933
Dungarpur	—	—	—	—	—

	Com	Off	Char	Air	PD
1934					
International Court of Justice	—	—	—	—	—
1935					
Bijawar	—	—	—	—	—
East African P. & T. (Kenya, Uganda and Tanganyika)	1935	1959	—	1935	1935
1936					
French Equatorial Africa	1937	—	1938	1937	1937
Malayan Postal Union	—	—	—	—	1936
1937					
Aden	1937	—	—	—	—
Burma	1940	1937	—	—	—
1938					
Alexandretta	1938	—	—	1938	1938
Greenland	1945	—	1958	—	—
Italian East Africa	1938	—	1940	1938	1941
Sudetenland	—	—	—	—	—
1939					
Bohemia and Moravia	1941	1941	1941	—	1939
German Occ. Poland	1940	1940	1940	—	1940
Hatay	1939	—	—	—	1939
Idar	—	—	—	—	—
Slovakia	1939	—	1939	1939	1939
1940					
Alsace	—	—	—	—	—
Faeroe Is (Br. Occ.)	—	—	—	—	—
German Occ. Luxembourg	—	—	1941	—	—
Greek Occ. Albania	1940	—	—	1940	1940
Lorraine	—	—	—	—	—
Pitcairn Is	1946	—	—	—	—
1941					
Cephalonia and Ithaca	—	—	1941	1941	—
Corfu	—	—	—	—	—
Croatia	1941	1942	1941	—	1941
Eastern Karelia	—	—	1943	—	—
Fiume and Kupa Zone	1941	—	1941	—	—
German Occ. Estonia	—	—	1941	—	—
German Occ. Latvia	—	—	—	—	—
German Occ. Lithuania	—	—	—	—	—
German Occ. Ukraine	—	—	1944	—	—
German Occ. Vilna	—	—	—	—	—
German Occ. Ostland	—	—	—	—	—
German Occ. Guernsey	—	—	—	—	—
German Occ. Jersey	—	—	—	—	—
Ifni	1949	—	1950	1943	—
Italian Occ. Ionian Is	—	—	—	—	—
Serbia	1941	1943	1941	1941	1941
Slovenia (Italian Occ.)	—	—	1941	—	—
1942					
Free French Forces, Levant	—	—	1943	1942	—
Mengkiang	1943	—	—	—	—
Kwangtung	—	—	—	—	1945
Jap. Occ. N. China	1943	—	—	—	—
Jap. Occ. Malaya	1942	—	—	—	1942
Jap. Occ. Netherlands Indies	1943	—	—	1943	1942
Jap. Occ. North Borneo	—	—	—	—	—
Jap. Occ. Philippines	1942	—	1942	—	1942
Jap. Occ. Sarawak	—	—	—	—	—
Jasdan	—	—	—	—	—
Middle East Forces	—	—	—	—	1942
Seiyun	1946	—	—	—	—
Shihr and Mukalla	1946	—	—	—	—
1943					
Fezzan	—	—	1950	1943	1943
German Occ. of Zante	—	—	—	—	—
Thai Occ. Malaya	—	—	—	—	—
1944					
French West Africa	1945	—	1944	1945	1947
Graham Land	—	—	—	—	—
International Education Office	—	—	—	—	—
Italian Social Republic	1944	—	—	—	1944
Laibach	—	—	1944	1944	1944
Macedonia	—	—	—	—	—

	Com	Off	Char	Air	PD
Muscat	1944	—	—	—	1944
South Georgia	1972	—	—	—	—
South Orkneys	—	—	—	—	—
South Shetlands	—	—	—	—	—
1945					
Anglo-American Occ. Germany	1948	—	1948	—	—
French Zone of Germany (general)	—	—	—	—	—
Russian Occ. Germany	1949	—	1948	—	—
Indonesia	1945	—	1945	1947	1950
Malaya (Br. Mil. Admin.)	—	—	—	—	—
Taiwan (Formosa)	1946	—	—	—	1948
Venezia Giulia and Istria	—	—	—	—	1948
Vietnam	1945	—	1945	1952	1952
1946					
B.C.O.F. Japan	—	—	—	—	—
Falkland Islands Dependencies	1946	—	1982	—	—
North Korea	1946	—	—	1958	—
North Vietnam	1953	1952	—	1959	1952
South Korea	1946	—	1957	1947	—
1947					
French Occ. Baden	1949	—	1949	—	—
French Occ. Rhineland Palatinate	1949	—	1948	—	—
French Occ. Württemberg	1949	—	1949	—	—
Greek Occ. Dodecanese	—	—	—	—	—
Norfolk I	1956	—	—	—	—
Pakistan	1948	1947	—	1962	—
Saar	1948	1949	1948	1948	—
Trieste	1948	—	—	1947	1947
1948					
Bahawalpur	1948	1945	—	—	—
Br. P.O.s Eastern Arabia	1948	—	—	—	—
Channel Is	1948	—	—	—	—
Gaza	1957	—	—	1948	1948
Israel	1948	1951	1957	1950	1948
Jordanian Occ. Palestine	1949	—	1950	—	1948
Malacca	1948	—	—	—	—
Penang	1948	—	—	—	—
Perlis	1948	—	—	—	—
Ryukyu Is	1951	—	—	1950	—

	Com	Off	Char	Air	PD
Singapore	1948	—	—	1955	1968
Tokelau Is	1953	—	—	—	—
West Berlin	1949	—	1949	—	—
Yugoslav Occ. Trieste	1948	—	1948	1948	1948
World Health Organisation	1962	—	—	—	—
1949					
China Peoples Republic	1949	—	—	1951	1950
Republic of China (Taiwan)	1951	—	1954	1959	1950
German Democratic Republic	1949	1954	1949	—	—
German Federal Republic	1949	—	1949	—	—
Ghadames	—	—	—	1949	—
Netherlands Antilles	1949	—	1951	—	1952
Rajasthan	—	—	—	—	—
Spanish West Africa	1949	—	—	1951	—
Travancore-Cochin	—	1949	—	—	—
1950					
Comoro Is.	1952	1979	1962	1954	1950
Council of Europe	1978	—	—	—	—
Netherlands New Guinea	1959	—	1953	—	1957
International Refugees Org.	—	—	—	—	—
N. Korean Occ. S. Korea	—	—	—	—	—
United Nations (Geneva)	1955	—	—	—	—
1951					
Cambodia	1955	—	1952	1953	1957
Laos	1952	—	1953	1953	1952
United Nations (New York)	1952	—	—	1951	—
1952					
Papua New Guinea	1961	—	—	—	1960
St Christopher-Nevis-Anguilla	1953	1980	—	—	—
Tristan da Cunha	1953	—	—	—	1957
1953					
Indian Custodian Forces, Korea	—	—	—	—	—

	Com	Off	Char	Air	PD
1954					
Indian Forces in Indo–China	1965	—	—	—	—
Rhodesia and Nyasaland	1955	—	—	—	1961
Riau–Lingga Is	—	—	—	—	—
1955					
French S. & Antarctic Terr.	1957	—	—	1962	—
Hadhramaut	1966	—	—	—	—
South Vietnam	1955	—	1960	1955	1955
1956					
Morocco	1956	—	1960	1956	1965
World Meteorological Office	1973	—	—	—	—
1957					
Australian Antarctic	1961	—	—	—	—
Galapagos Is	—	—	—	1959	—
Ghana	1957	—	—	1958	1958
Malayan Federation	1957	—	—	—	—
Qatar	1957	—	—	1970	1968
Ross Dependency	—	—	—	—	—
Universal Postal Union	—	—	—	—	—
1958					
Christmas I	1965	—	—	—	—
French Polynesia	1958	1977	—	1960	1958
Guernsey	1969	—	—	—	1969
Isle of Man	1973	—	—	—	1973
Jersey	1969	—	—	—	1969
International Telecommunications Union	1973	—	—	—	—
Malagasy Republic	1958	—	1960	1960	1962
Northern Ireland	—	—	—	—	—
Scotland	—	—	—	—	—
United Arab Republic	1958	1958	1958	1959	—
Wales	—	—	—	—	—
1959					
Central African Republic	1959	1965	1962	1960	1962
Congo (Brazzaville)	1959	1968	1962	1960	1961
Guinea	1959	—	1960	1959	1959
Mali	1959	1961	1962	1959	1961

	Com	Off	Char	Air	PD
1960					
Congo (Kinshasa)	1960	—	1963	1967	—
Islamic Rep. Mauritania	1960	1961	1962	1960	1961
Katanga	1960	—	—	—	1960
Rio Muni	1961	—	1960	—	—
South Cameroons	—	—	—	—	—
1961					
South Kasai	—	—	—	—	—
Trucial States	—	—	—	—	—
Uganda	1962	—	—	—	1967
UNESCO	—	—	—	—	—
1962					
Bhutan	1962	—	1964	1967	—
Burundi	1962	—	1963	1964	—
Indian Forces in Congo	—	—	—	—	—
Rwanda	1962	—	—	1971	—
Western New Guinea	—	—	—	—	—
1963					
Br. Antarctic Territory	1966	—	—	—	—
Cocos (Keeling) Is	1965	—	—	—	—
Dubai	1963	—	—	1963	1963
Kenya	1963	1964	—	1967	—
Malaysia	1963	—	—	—	1966
Nat. Front for the Liberation of South Vietnam	1963	—	—	—	—
Sharjah	1963	1966	—	1963	—
South Arabian Federation	1963	—	—	—	—
South Georgia	1972	—	—	—	—
West Irian	1963	—	—	—	1963
1964					
Abu Dhabi	1968	—	—	—	—
Ajman	1964	1965	—	1965	—
East Africa	1964	—	—	—	—
Fujeira	1964	1965	—	1965	—
Malawi	1964	—	—	1972	1967
Ras al Khaima	1965	—	—	—	—
Sabah	—	—	—	—	—
Umm al Qiwain	1964	1965	—	1965	—
Zambia	1964	—	—	—	1964
1965					
Indian Forces in Gaza	—	—	—	—	—
Khor Fakkan	1965	—	—	—	—
Tanzania	1966	1965	—	—	1967

	Com	Off	Char	Air	PD
1966					
Botswana	1966	—	—	—	1967
Guyana	1966	—	—	—	1967
Lesotho	1966	—	—	—	1966
Manama	1966	—	—	—	—
Muscat and Oman	1969	—	—	—	—
1967					
Anguilla	1968	—	—	—	—
Fr. Terr. of Afars and Issas	1968	—	—	1969	1969
Mahra (Qishn and Socotra)					
Upper Yafa	1967	—	—	—	—
1968					
Biafra	1968	—	1968	—	—
Br. Indian Ocean Terr.	1971	—	—	—	—
Equatorial Guinea	1968	—	—	—	—
Southern Yemen	1968	—	—	—	—
1970					
Bangladesh	1971	1973	—	—	—
Khmer Republic	1971	—	1972	1973	1974
Oman	1971	—	—	—	—
Yemen P.D. Republic	1971	—	—	—	—
Zaire	1971	1975	—	—	—
1972					
Sri Lanka	1972	—	—	—	—
1973					
Belize	1973	—	1982	—	1976
Grenadines of Grenada	1973	1982	—	—	—
Grenadines of St. Vincent	1973	1982	1980	—	—
United Arab Emirates	1973	—	—	—	—
1974					
Guinea-Bissau	1976	—	—	—	—
Turkish Cypriot Post	1974	—	—	—	—
1975					
Faeroe Is	1976	—	—	—	—
Solomon Islands	1975	—	1982	—	—
1976					
Benin Peoples Republic	1976	—	—	1976	1978
Gilbert Is	1976	—	—	—	—
Tuvula	1976	1981	1982	—	1981
Soc. Rep. Vietnam	1976	—	—	—	—
1977					
Bophuthatswana	1977	—	—	—	—
Central African Empire	1977	1977	—	1977	—
Djibouti Republic	1977	—	—	1977	—
Transkei	1977	—	—	—	—
1979					
Kiribati	1979	1981	—	—	1981
Kuala Lumpur	—	—	—	—	—
Redonda	1979	—	—	—	—
U.N. (Vienna)	1980	—	—	—	—
Venda	1979	—	—	—	—
1980					
Madeira	1980	—	—	—	—
Azores	1980	—	—	—	—
Kampuchea	1982	—	—	1984	—
Nevis	1980	1980	—	—	—
St Kitts	1980	1980	—	—	—
Vanuatu	1980	—	—	—	—
Zil Eloigne Sesel	1980	—	—	—	—
Zimbabwe	1980	—	—	—	1980
1981					
Ciskei	1981	—	—	—	—
Caicos Islands	1981	—	—	—	—
1983					
Alderney	1985	—	—	—	—
Niuafo'ou	1983	—	—	—	—
Palau	1983	—	—	1985	—
1984					
Åland Islands	1986	—	—	—	—
Bequia	1984	—	—	—	—
Burkina Faso	1985	—	—	1984	—
Cayes of Belize	1984	—	—	—	—
Funafuti	1984	—	—	—	—
Marshall Islands	1984	—	—	1986	—
Micronesia	1984	—	—	1984	—
Nanumaga	1984	—	—	—	—
Nanumea	1984	—	—	—	—
Niu	1984	—	—	—	—
Niutao	1984	—	—	—	—
Nukufetau	1984	—	—	—	—
Nukulaelae	1984	—	—	—	—
Union Island	1984	—	—	—	—
Vaitupu	1984	—	—	—	—
1986					
Aruba	1986	—	1986	—	—
South Georgia & South Sandwich Is	1986	—	—	—	—

Egypt, 'Sphinx and Pyramids', 1867

Definitive stamps were anticipated by other issues in Australia, which issued postage due stamps in 1902, eleven years before the first definitive set, and in Bahawalpur which issued stamps for use on official correspondence in 1945, three years before stamps for general public use were released.

RARITIES

The world's rarest stamps have been issued in British Guiana and Russia. Contrary to popular belief, the British Guiana 1 cent black on magenta of 1856 is *not* the world's rarest stamp, being no rarer than any other stamp of which only one example is recorded.

There are, in fact, two examples of rarities of which only *half* a stamp exist. In 1866 British Guiana cut 4 cent stamps in half for use as the local 2 cent rate. Normally these bisects were issued perforated, but one imperforate sheet was produced by accident. The combination of bisection and no perforations was theoretically possible but no example was recorded until 1965, when an example on a cover dated 16 April 1868 was found. This stamp is now listed by the Gibbons catalogue (S.G. 90b).

The zemstvo stamps (see page 175) issued by the Russian district of Kotelnich comprised two parts, one affixed to the letter and the other retained by the post office as a counterfoil. Only one example of the 3 kopek black on yellow paper of 1869 has ever been found, and of this only the counterfoil portion exists. Curiously enough, an intact specimen *must* have existed in philatelic hands at one time, since an illustration of one appeared in *Timbres Poste* published by the Belgian dealer J B Moens in the late nineteenth century.

Unique stamps of the world include:
British Guiana: 1 cent black on magenta, 1856
Cameroons: 3 shilling surcharged on 1 mark, surcharge double 1915
Canada: 3d postmaster's provisional, New Carlisle, Gaspé, 1851
Confederate States local issues from Mount Lebanon (Louisiana), New Smyrna (Florida) 10 on 5c, and Uniontown (Alabama) 2c blue on blued paper.
France: 15c and 1fr 1849, the Hulot *tête-bêche* pairs (only one of each known); 5fr Napoleon III, value omitted, mint (only two known in used condition).
Gold Coast: 1d surcharged on 4d magenta, 1883
Great Britain: 1d Venetian red, watermark inverted, 1880 2d Tyrian plum, May 1910 – only one used (on cover addressed to King George V).
Indochina PO in Mengtsze 75c of 1903-6 and 1906-8 issues with INDO-CHINE inverted – one of each.
Kenya, Uganda and Tanganyika: 5c black and brown, 1954 with centre inverted.
Lagos: ½d on 2d (instead of 4d) – one mint and one used.
Russia: zemstvo issue of Byezhetsk 3 kopek, 1872 black on rose.
Spain: 10c 1873 *tête-bêche* pair, mint.
Sweden: 3 skilling-banco yellow instead of green, 1855.
Togo: 1 mark carmine overprinted for the French occupation, 1915.
USA: postmasters' provisional issues of Alexandria (Maryland) 5c black on blue paper, 1846; Boscawen (New Hampshire) 5c blue, 1846; and Lockport (New York) 5c red and black on buff paper, 1846.

The Pembina Twins was the nickname given to a pair of 7½d Canadian stamps of 1857, uniquely used at Pembina, North Dakota in November 1858. Unfortunately the stamps were soaked off the envelope and separated, and sold into separate collections. It was not until almost a century later

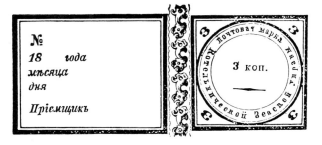

Kotelnich bi-partite stamp (from the illustration in the Moens catalogue, 1880)

that the two stamps were re-united by consent of the owners (two prominent Canadian philatelists) to constitute a unique philatelic treasure.

SIZE

The smallest stamps in the world were issued by the Colombian department of Bolivar in 1863-6. The stamps, in denominations of 10 centavos and 1 peso, measured only 8×9.5 mm. Colombia has also been responsible for some of the smallest stamps of modern times, the obligatory tax stamps issued since 1940 including such minuscule examples as the 5 centavos of September 1952, which measures 15×10 mm. The majority of these stamps measured 25×15 mm.

Britain's first halfpenny stamp, introduced in 1870, was designed to be approximately half the size of the corresponding penny stamp, and had a horizontal design measuring only 17.5×14 mm. This idea was adopted by Victoria (1874) and South Australia (1883) for vertical-format halfpenny stamps. As a wartime economy measure South Africa reduced the size of its entire low-value (½d–1s) definitive series. The so-called 'Bantams' were in use from 1942. As late as 1948 a 1½d stamp (gold mine design) was issued in the Bantam format.

The size of American definitives, usually approximate to the British format, was reduced drastically in January 1978 when a 13c stamp (reproducing the Indian head cent) measured only 17×20 mm, perforation to perforation. This was followed by the equally tiny Dolley Madison 15c of 1980. Other small stamps include Spain ¼ centimo, 1872-6 (15.5×15.5 mm) and the stamps issued by Mecklenburg-Schwerin (1856-64) and Brunswick (1857). Each stamp measured 24×24 mm, but could be divided into quarters, each of which was a ¼

schilling or ¼ gutegroschen (3 pfennig) stamp in its own right. These tiny stamps measured 12×12 mm.

The largest stamps in the world were issued by China for use on express letters. The first issues (1905-12) measured 210×65 mm and were issued imperforate but divided by rouletting into four parts. The first part served as a counterfoil and the fourth was given to the sender as a receipt. The second part (dragon's head) was signed by the addressee and returned to the post office by the postman, who was paid for his services against delivery of the third part (dragon's body). A second issue appeared in 1913-14 and measured 248×70 mm. It was divided into five parts by rouletting, with a flying goose motif on the second and fourth parts. These ungainly stamps were demonetised in February 1916 and thereafter served mainly as receipts without franking validity. Four of the five sections were overprinted with the letters A, B, C and D to denote their use as receipts.

The Arab sheikdom of Fujeira issued 10 rial stamps in 1972 in honour of the Apollo Moon-landing. These measured 78×143 mm (design) or 81×147 mm (perforation to perforation) and would undoubtedly rank as the largest stamps ever issued, but for the fact that their authenticity has been cast in doubt. They do not even rate a mention in the appendix of the Stanley Gibbons catalogues, wherein are listed other stamps of questionable validity.

The largest stamps to be issued in an orthodox sheet format, and recognised by all catalogues, were the 5, 10 and 25c newspaper stamps issued by the United States in 1865. These stamps measured 51×95 mm.

The largest stamps regularly issued for ordinary postal purposes have all been produced by the Soviet Union:

Barguzin Nature Reserve 4, 6 kopek, 1966

80×26 mm

Tiny stamps from South Australia (1883), Colombia (1952), GB ½d (1870), Spain ¼c (1872-6), Brunswick (1857), South Africa ½d (1942), USA 'Indian Head' (1978) and Dolley Madison (1980)

Cedar Fall Nature Reserve 10k, 1967   80×26 mm

10th anniversary Sputnik I 30k, 1967   75×27 mm

A 1 rouble stamp of 1962 honouring Soviet cosmonauts measured 151×70 mm and is considered as a large stamp rather than a miniature sheet (see page 156) because it was perforated all round.

Poland has issued several stamps notable for their length. The longest stamps were:

5.60 zloty B70 Tanker, 1961   108×21 mm

7.10 zl. Horses series, 1965   104×22 mm

In 1964 Sharjah issued a triptych for the New York World's Fair, the centre stamp (1 rial) measuring 85.5×44.5 mm (design) or 89×48 mm (perforation to perforation).

The largest British stamp was the 50p for the

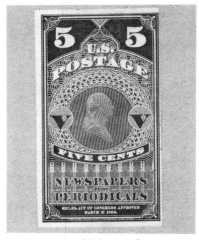

USA 5c newspaper stamp, 1865 (reduced)

London International Philatelic Exhibition, 1980 – 39×55 mm.

The largest Commonwealth stamps were issued by Western Samoa:

Captain Cook 30 sene, 1970   83×25 mm

Interpex Stamp Exhibition, 70s, 1971   84×26 mm

Jacob Roggeveen 30s, 1972   85×25 mm

UPU centenary 50s, 1974   87×29 mm

The only postal administration ever to issue each stamp in a different size was the German city of Bergedorf whose postal service was jointly operated by Hamburg and Lübeck. Between 1861 and 1867 Bergedorf issued a series of five stamps whose size increased in ascending order of value.

The size of British definitive stamps was changed twice in two years. The George V low values, printed by Harrison and Sons in photogravure, 1934-6, were first produced in the size 22.25×18.3 mm (1d and 1½d), but it was found necessary to have a wider space between them to facilitate perforation. Accordingly these denominations, as well as the ½d and 2d, were printed in the reduced dimensions of 21.8×18.1 mm. Even this proved to be not enough, so finally the size was reduced to 21.5×17.5 mm. This format was also used for the remaining denominations of the series.

The Irish 3d and 5d definitives were issued in 1966-7 printed in photogravure instead of letterpress, and reduced from the usual 22.5×18 mm to only 21×17 mm.

The only country to vary the size of its stamps on numerous occasions was Afghanistan. Stamps commemorating the end of the civil war were issued in the dimensions 39×47 mm (1920-), 23×29 mm or

Poland Horses, 1965, 7.10zl; Samoa UPU centenary, 1974

Sharjah New York World's Fair triptych, 1964

GB London 1980 Stamp Exhibition 50p

22.5×28.25 mm (1921-7). The Independence Day commemoratives of 1924, originally 24×32 mm, were subsequently enlarged to 29×37 mm (1925) and reduced again to 26×33 mm (1926). Newspaper stamps were issued in 1928 (38×22.75 mm) but enlarged the following year (42.5×25 mm). Official stamps were issued in 1939 sized 22.5×28 mm, increased to 24.5×31 mm (1954-73) and reduced again to 24×30.5 mm (1964-5).

SHAPE

The shape of the first adhesive postage stamps was determined by the gummed labels which secured tax stamps to parchment legal documents. This was an upright rectangle approximately 18 mm across and 24 mm deep. This format has been used for the vast majority of British definitive stamps since 1840, the exceptions being the embossed stamps of 1847-54, the halfpenny of 1870 and all stamps above the face value of two shillings, which were produced in a larger upright format (1867-1913), or various large horizontal formats – confined to the pound values (1884 onwards). The Queen Victoria £5 stamp was produced in twice the size of the high values of 1867-83. A double-size format (i.e., twice the size of the low-value definitives) was used for the George V high values and many subsequent issues, while a treble-size format was used for the Victorian and Edwardian pound stamps (1884-1913). Various sizes larger than the ordinary definitive format have been used for commemoratives since 1924.

Many of the early stamp-issuing countries followed the British format. The United States, France, Switzerland, Belgium, Austria and many of the British colonies followed Britain's lead, and the British upright rectangular format is the shape most widely used for definitive stamps to this day. Over the past 140 years, however, many shapes other than the rectangular have been used for stamps.

The first polygonal stamps were embossed shilling stamps of Great Britain, printed at Somerset House in 1847. These stamps had an upright octagonal format, which was subsequently used for the tenpence stamp of 1848-54. The sixpenny stamp, introduced in 1854, also had a polygonal shape, but with the top and side panels raised from the main frame which was slightly curved. These stamps were usually cut square. Regrettably many early collectors later trimmed their specimens to shape, in order to fit the printed octagons in their stamp albums. The four annas indigo and red of India, 1854, was produced in the same format and also tended to be cut to shape, but this was done mainly by Indians intent on reducing the weight of their letters as far as possible!

The first triangular stamps were issued by the Cape of Good Hope in September 1853. The instructions from the Cape Legislative Council to Charles Bell, the colony's Surveyor-General, were to prepare designs of a 'device and stamp so different from those of English postage stamps as to catch the eye at a glance'. Bell prepared both triangular and polygonal designs but only the former was used by the printers, Perkins Bacon. It is popularly believed that this shape was chosen in order to help semi-literate sorting clerks in Cape colony to recognise their own stamps and thus sort the mail more efficiently. The stamps were engraved in London by William Humphrys and intaglio-printed by Perkins Bacon in denominations of 1d, 4d, 6d and 1s. They were in use until 1864. During a shortage of stamps a provisional issue was made locally. Known to collectors as the 'Woodblocks' they were, in fact, engraved on steel by C J Roberts and printed from stereotyped plates by Saul Solomon of Cape Town. The 1d was printed in vermilion and the 4d in blue. Both values are known in the wrong colour, due to clichés (see p.189) being inadvertently inserted in the wrong plate. Curiously enough, the South African government revived the design of the Cape Triangulars for a 4d grey-blue stamp, issued in 1926. This was intaglio-printed by Bradbury Wilkinson and, like its famous predecessors, was issued imperforate – an anachronism in the 1920s, but numerous private perforations are known.

The triangular format did not find much favour in Commonwealth countries, Newfoundland being the only other colony to issue a stamp of this type in the nineteenth century (3d, 1857). New Zealand revived the fashion in 1943 with triangular stamps portraying Princesses Elizabeth and Margaret, and in more recent years the occasional triangular stamp has been

GB 6d, 1854

issued for commemorative purposes by Jamaica (1964), Malaysia (1962, 1966) and East Africa (1976). Triangular stamps have also been produced from time to time by Hungary, Monaco, San Marino, Israel, Mongolia and the countries of Latin America.

The smallest triangular stamp was the 2½ centavos black on lilac, issued by Colombia in 1865 and measured only 18 mm on each side. It was an equilateral triangle (each side of equal length) whereas most triangulars have a longer side (usually the base).

The only scalene triangular stamp was also issued by Colombia. In this form each side of the triangle is of a different length. This was the 2½ centavos of 1869-70.

Triangular stamps with the apex at the foot were first issued by Latvia which produced airmail stamps in 1921 and 1928 and air charity stamps in 1932 and 1933 in this unusual format. Other countries to follow suit were Iceland (10 aurar airmail of 1930) and Tuva (1t and 5t airmails of 1935).

The first circular stamps were the Scinde 'Dawks' of 1852-4 (see page 78). Only the first printing was a

Triangular stamps from Nicaragua (1947), Iceland (1930) and New Zealand (1943)

circular stamp in the true sense, since the later versions were issued in sheets and usually cut square. Circular designs were also used by the Indian native states of Indore (1889) and Kashmir (1866–78), the registration stamps of Colombia (1865) and the first issues of Afghanistan (1871–90) but were invariably cut square. The first true circular stamps since 1852 were the 'beermats' (as they have been derisively nicknamed by collectors) issued by Tonga in June 1963 to commemorate the introduction of the first gold coinage of Polynesia. The stamps were embossed on gold foil backed with paper bearing an overall inscription TONGA THE FRIENDLY ISLANDS in microscopic print. The stamps were in three sizes, according to face value, and the largest (depicting the 1 koula coin) measured 80 mm in diameter. This was followed by a second series (again reproducing coins) in July 1967, but similar circular metal-foil embossed stamps were also issued by Sierra Leone, Bhutan, Qatar, Sharjah, Umm al Qiwain and Jordan in the 1960s. In 1973 Bhutan produced the ultimate in philatelic gimmickry, when a set of stamps was issued in the form of circular gramophone records (see also page 200). Circular stamps perforated all round were issued by Malaysia in May 1971, and by Singapore in 1978 and 1980, the latter being perforated both round the design and square round the stamps.

Circular stamp from Kashmir (1866)

Circular gold-foil series of Tonga, 1963

The first diamond-shaped stamps were issued by Nova Scotia on 1 September 1851 and consisted of 3d, 6d, and 1s stamps featuring the heraldic flowers of the United Kingdom and the mayflower of Nova Scotia, with the imperial crown in the centre. Similar stamps were issued in the sister colony of New Brunswick four days later. Both sets were intaglio printed by Perkins Bacon. Two years later Nova Scotia added a penny denomination but turned the design round so that it appears as a square, with the Chalon portrait of Queen Victoria in the centre.

Diamond shapes were popular with the Russian zemstvos and the stamps of the German local posts in the late nineteenth century. Until recently, the best-known exponent of diamond-shaped stamps was Tuva which issued many large pictorial stamps in this format between 1927 and 1940. Since the 1960s, however, there has been a revival of this fashion, many stamps emanating from Commonwealth countries and even the United States (Mineral Heritage series, 1974).

The first oval stamp was the half-anna red issued by the Indian state of Bhor in 1879, in a horizontal format. The 1881 registration stamp of Colombia was in an upright oval format. Both stamps were issued imperforate but usually cut square. The best-known example of stamps with an oval design was the numeral definitive series issued by Mexico in

Singapore circular perforated issue, 1980

1886. This series, however, was perforated in the orthodox upright rectangular shape.

The first trapezoidal stamps were issued by Malaysia on 2 December 1967 to celebrate the centenary of the first stamps of the Straits Settlements. The stamps were printed *tête-bêche* (head to tail), with the top and bottom sides parallel, and the sides sloping upwards and inwards. The only other trapezoid stamps to date have also been issued by Malaysia. A set of three publicising the Earth Satellite Station was issued in April 1970 and had the

Nova Scotia 3d, 1851

parallels at the sides and the sloping sides at top and bottom.

The only irregular polygons were issued by Malta in October 1968 for Christmas. The design, by E V Cremona, shows the Star of Bethlehem and the Angel waking the Shepherds. The shape is an irregular pentagon, rectangular on three sides, with a raised apex towards the left. The shorter side at the top and the long side at the bottom were both perforated 14½ while the other three sides gauge 14. The stamps were issued in sheets of 60, arranged in ten strips of six, alternately upright and inverted.

The first free-form postage stamps were issued by Sierra Leone on 10 February 1964 to commemorate the World's Fair in New York. The set of fourteen stamps was printed in combined intaglio and lithography by the Walsall Lithographic Company and stamped out in the manner of Victorian

Tuva, 1934-5, triangular and diamond-shaped stamps

French Somali Coast 50fr, 1884

scraps. The stamps were shaped like the map of the country which, in fact, formed the background to each design. The stamps were also the world's first self-adhesive (see page 201) and were issued in sheets of 30 on backing paper which had the butterfly logotype of the paper-makers, Samuel Jones, on the reverse. Later free-form stamps in the same genre from Sierra Leone used the backing paper for advertising. Tonga followed with a set of stamps on 19 October 1964. These stamps were embossed on metal foil but were in free-form shapes – either heart-shaped or in the outline of Tongatapu (irreverently dubbed by collectors 'the Hearts and Boots' issue). Later free-form issues from Tonga followed the same self-adhesive pattern as Sierra Leone. Sierra Leone abandoned this gimmick in 1972 and Tonga in 1980. Several sets from Norfolk Island between 1974 and 1978 were in the free-form, self-adhesive style, all produced by the Walsall company.

Two attempts have been made to produce free-form stamps in a more orthodox manner. De La Rue intaglio-printed a set of four stamps for the Bahamas in 1968, kidney shaped and depicting obverse and reverse of a set of gold coins. The stamps were perforated round each stamp, but were usually cut square with scissors. Harrison and Sons produced a

Malta Christmas, 1968, irregular polygon

set of four stamps for Gibraltar in July 1969 perforated in the shape of the rock of Gibraltar. Additionally, however, each stamp was perforated in the normal rectangular shape. Neither experiment has so far been followed up.

VALUE

The lowest face value expressed on stamps and actually postally valid was $\frac{1}{10}$ of a cent, on stamps of French Indochina, 1922-39, equivalent at that time to 0.01 penny sterling. Other very low value stamps were:

Puerto Rico ½ milesima, 1881-98	0.025d
Cuba ½ milesima, 1888-94	0.025d
France ½ centime, 1919-22	0.05d
Travancore 2 cash, 1943	0.08d
Dhar ½ pice, 1897	0.125d
Cochin 2 pies, 1909-46	0.16d

Malaysia, trapezoidal stamps of 1967 and 1970

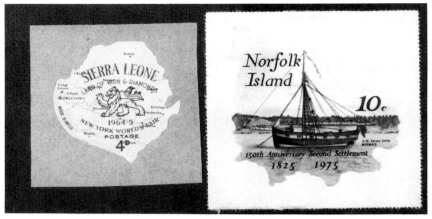

Gibraltar, 1969 stamps perforated in the shape of the Rock

The lowest postal rate in the United Kingdom was a halfpenny, on newspapers, printed matter and postcards, introduced 1870. This was in reply to the circular delivery companies who infringed the Postmaster General's monopoly in 1865-7 by offering services at rates as low as a farthing (¼d). Apart from some of the Indian native states listed above, British India had a 3 pies (¼d) rate for inland postcards from 1879 till 1921 and farthing rates, prepaid by distinctive stamps, were also current in Malta and the Cayman Islands before the Second World War.

The most worthless stamp ever issued was the 3000 pengö definitive of Hungary issued on 5 February 1946. Originally intended as the top value of a postwar series, the stamp was delayed several months after the rest of the series. By the time of its issue, however, the pengö had plummeted in value in the worst case of hyper-inflation this century. By February 1946 the value of the pengö had dropped to the equivalent of 150 000 000 000 000 to 1p in modern British decimal currency.

The highest values, in real terms can be found on certain British Commonwealth stamps which were intended mainly for revenue purposes, but are regarded as postage stamps because of their inscription 'Postage and Revenue'. Pride of place goes to East Africa (Kenya, Uganda and Tanganyika) which, in 1925, issued stamps with face values of £75 and £100, the highest denominations ever issued with a postal inscription.

In the same year Ceylon issued a stamp valued at 1000 rupees. At the then rate of exchange (1 rupee=1s 6d sterling) this stamp was worth £75. The Straits Settlements $500 stamps of 1910, 1912 and 1923 were worth £58.33 sterling.

The highest face value of any British stamp is £5 (issued in 1887 and demonetised in 1915). No further £5 stamps were issued for postage until 1977.

The highest face value of any US stamp was $100, the highest denomination of the newspaper stamp series of 1895. The highest face value of any American stamp issued for ordinary postage is $10.75 (1985).

Lowest face value: French Indochina (1922-39), Cuba (1898), France ½c (1919-22), Travancore 2 cash (1943)

Hungary, 3000p (1946)

Germany 50 billion marks (1923), Hungary
500 000 000 000 000 pengös (1946)

The highest values expressed on stamps appeared during times of severe inflation and had consequently little real value in relation to other currencies at the time. During the German inflation of 1923 the most astronomical value ever to appear on a stamp (the top denomination of the October–November issue) was 50 000 000 000 marks.

In 1946, however, Hungary easily topped this. In 13 July of that year a stamp with a face value of 500 000 000 000 000 pengös was issued, but superseded by stamps valued in 'tax pengös' only three days later.

Undenominated stamps were issued in the 1850s by several British colonies as a means of cutting costs since only one die or plate was required. The different values were indicated by altering the colour. Three colonies used identical designs, showing Britannia seated on sugar bags, distinguished only by having the name of the colony at the foot. These stamps were issued without any value expressed by Trinidad (1851–79), Barbados (1852–73) and Mauritius (1858–62). Mauritius had actually commissioned these stamps as far back as 1848 but for some inexplicable reason preferred to issue local makeshifts instead. When the Britannia stamps were first released in Mauritius (April 1854) they were overprinted locally FOUR-PENCE. The undenominated stamps were not released till four years later. The stamps of the Ionian Islands (1859-64) were issued undenominated, in different colours for each value.

St Helena's first stamp was a sixpenny, prepaying the postage on letters to Britain. When other values

were required (1863) these sixpenny stamps were printed in various colours and surcharged appropriately with the new values. This curious system continued until 1884.

Undenominated stamps during severe inflation have been issued on two occasions. They were first used in Hungary in 1946 when it was pointless to produce stamps with an actual monetary value. Instead, obsolete stamps were overprinted to denote their purpose and sold at the rate prevailing on the day. Stamps were overprinted ANY or NYOMTATV (sample post), HLP or HELYI LEV. LAP. (local postcard), HL. or HELYI LEVÉL (local letter), TLP or TÁVOLSÁGI LEV. LAP. (inland postcard), TL or TÁVOLSÁGI LEVÉL (inland letter), AJL or AJANLAS (registered letter), CS or CSOMAG (parcel). Numeral suffixes indicated the issue.

In March and April 1949 the gold yuan currency of China was ravaged by inflation which spiralled so sharply that it was impossible to keep pace with it and stamps were worthless before they came off the press. In May-July 1949, therefore, a set of four undenominated stamps was released. Each stamp had a pictorial motif which symbolised the service for which it was intended (ordinary mail, airmail, express and registered letters). Like their Hungarian predecessors, these 'unit' stamps were sold at the rate for the day. Subsequently other stamps and even revenue stamps were overprinted in the various Chinese provinces and used in the same manner.

Other examples of undenominated stamps have resulted from milder cases of inflation. The United

Mauritius undenominated stamp (1848), St Helena 1d (1863), Hungary inflation provisional (1946)

USA Christmas undenominated stamp, 1975

Canada, undenominated rate 'A' stamp, 1982

States issued two Christmas stamps in October 1975 without any value expressed, as an increase from 10 to 13c in the inland rate was imminent, and it was not known at the time of production whether Congress would agree the increase asked by the Post Office. In the end the increase was delayed and the stamps were sold for 10c. History repeated itself in November 1981 when the two Christmas stamps were issued undenominated but sold for 20c. They were restricted to inland postage.

Uncertainty over the implementation of proposed increases in postal rates led the US Post Office to introduce undenominated stamps in May 1978. These stamps, depicting the American eagle, were lettered A and were issued as 15c stamps following an increase in the inland letter rate, to cover an anticipated shortage of that denomination pending production of supplies. Similar stamps lettered B and C were issued in 1981 when the letter rate was raised, first to 19c and then (28 October) to 20c. Undenominated stamps lettered A were issued by Canada in 1982 for the same reason.

Sweden has issued undenominated stamps since 1979 inscribed INRIKES POST (inland post). They were issued in booklets of twenty sold at 20 kronor or supplied in exchange for tokens distributed to all Swedish households. They are known as rebate stamps since the prevailing letter rate at the time has been either 1.30 kr or 1.70 kr.

Stamps have been sold at a discount on several occasions. The first such issue was the bipartite stamp issued by the Swiss canton of Geneva in

September 1843 (see page 135). A discount of 50 per cent was allowed on bulk postings of twenty letters or more. It is not known to what extent this concession was used; as the stamps are exceedingly rare it is conjectured that the scheme was not a success.

The *Lady McLeod* steamship stamp of Trinidad, 1847 (see page 49) was sold at 5c, but a hundred cost only $4 – a discount of 20 per cent. Despite this powerful inducement these stamps appear to have been little used.

Between 1885 and 1891 the stamps of Costa Rica were sold at a discount to encourage vendors to stock large quantities. The stamps issued in the province of Guanacaste were sold at twice the national discount to encourage the vendors in an area which was relatively remote from the capital. For this reason the stamps sold in Guanacaste had to be overprinted with the name of the province to distinguish them from those released at the higher rate. Between 1905 and 1913 certain Turkish stamps were overprinted in Arabic *Behié* to signify sale at a discount.

Following changes in postal rates introduced on 20 May 1946 Belgian stamps were overprinted '–10%' to indicate that they were to be sold at a discount off face value. They were nicknamed 'Van Ackers' after the then Minister of Posts.

Stamps with values expressed in two currencies have been issued by:
Canada 1855-9 local currency and sterling. Heligoland 1859-90 German and British currency. Holstein 1864-5 Holstein and Danish or Lavenburg currency. Rhodesia 1967-8 Sterling pence and cents during the transistion to decimal currency.

Stamps with a postal value in one currency and a charity premium in another were issued by St Helena on 12 October 1961. The stamps were four of the definitive stamps of Tristan da Cunha, with values expressed in South African cents. They were overprinted ST HELENA/TRISTAN RELIEF and surcharged in sterling (the currency used in St Helena) and sold on St Helena to raise money for the refugees from the volcano which erupted on Tristan da Cunha. This unorthodox action was promptly repudiated by the Foreign and Commonwealth Office in London, and the stamps were withdrawn from sale on 19 October. Only 434 sets were sold, raising some £205 for the refugees. Today a set is catalogued by Stanley Gibbons at £4000 mint and £1500 used.

Stamps with values in the wrong currency were issued by Fiji in November 1871. Although notices regarding the postal rates were given in US currency (which was then in circulation in Fiji) the stamps, printed in Sydney, Australia, bore values in pence.

These stamps were only in use for 41 days before they were surcharged in cents. Conversely, Fiji adopted sterling currency in 1874, but all stamps up to 1876 continued to be surcharged in cents.

Stamps with values in three currencies were prepared in 1916, for use by military forces of the joint Anglo-Russian expedition to occupy Mount Athos. The stamps were unique in several respects, having been printed photographically aboard a ship (HMS *Ark Royal*) in time of war, and inscribed in three alphabets, three languages (English, Greek and Russian) and three currencies – pence, lepta and kopeks. The expedition was cancelled owing to a dispute between the British and Russian high commands. A few examples of mint stamps are known, and three covers bearing various denominations, used at the British Field Post Office in Salonika.

A stamp denominated in centigrammes of gold dust was issued by Julius Popper in 1891 for the use of gold miners in Terra del Fuego, to prepay mail to the mainland of Chile.

PORTRAITS

The first person portrayed on a stamp was Queen Victoria whose profile by Henry Corbould, based on a medallic effigy by William Wyon in 1837, when she was eighteen years old, was used for the Penny Black and Twopence Blue of 1840. Incredibly, the profile remained in use throughout the next 62 years – even after the Queen's death at the age of 82. The Wyon profile, however, survived on the stamps of New South Wales, Queensland, South Australia and Victoria as late as 1913.

The first person other than a head of state (living or dead) portrayed on a stamp was Benjamin

Belgium, 'Van Ackers' 10% discount stamp (1946)

Rhodesia 25c/2s 6d (1967)

Mount Athos, 1916, inscribed in Greek, British and Russian currencies

Franklin whose portrait (from a drawing by James B Longacre) appeared on the 10c stamp issued by the United States in July 1847. Franklin (first Postmaster General of the United States) shares with George Washington the distinction of having appeared in every American definitive series until the present issue appeared in 1975.

The first person, other than the reigning monarch, to appear on a stamp from the British Commonwealth was Prince Albert, the Prince Consort, on the 6d stamp issued by Canada in 1851.

The first living person, other than royalty, to appear on a Commonwealth stamp was Lord Carrington, Governor of New South Wales (20s of 1888). Charles Connell Postmaster General of New Brunswick put his own portrait on the 5c stamp (1860) but it was never issued and he was forced to resign.

By an Act of Congress in 1866 the portrayal of living persons was forbidden on American stamps, banknotes and security documents. The nearest to a portrayal of a living person, however, was the 5c stamp of 1967, showing an astronaut walking in space from Gemini IV, Lieutenant Colonel Edward White and the 10c stamp of 1969 showing an astronaut, Neil Armstrong, setting foot on the Moon. As this honour went to Neil Armstrong it can be argued that he is the person in the picture. Previously, the 10c airmail stamp of 1927-8, inscribed LINDBERGH, showed the *Spirit of St Louis* over a map of the North Atlantic, and also the 3c stamp of 1933 honoured the Byrd Antarctic Expedition, depicting a map thus inscribed.

The first person other than royalty to appear on a British stamp was William Shakespeare, in 1964.

No living person, other than members of the Royal Family, has been portrayed on a British stamp. The nearest to this, however, was the 1s 9d stamp of 1967 honouring the world voyage of Sir Francis Chichester and depicting his yacht *Gypsy Moth IV* under full sail with, presumably, Sir Francis himself at the helm.

The most portrayed person of all time is Her Majesty Queen Elizabeth II. Of the 40 000 stamps

USA, 1847, 5c portraying Benjamin Franklin

New Brunswick 5c, 1860, portraying Postmaster General Charles Connell

issued in the British Commonwealth since her accession on 6 February 1952, some 8739 had borne her portrait by the end of 1987. Britain (including regionals) has contributed 1017 – every postage stamp bearing a portrait or effigy of the Queen. Next in descending order of loyalty are Guernsey (354), Jersey (315), Antigua (279), Isle of Man (279), Tristan da Cunha (266), Bermuda (254), British Virgin Islands (253), Solomon Islands (250) and Fiji (232).

Prior to her accession, Queen Elizabeth was portrayed on 28 stamps from eleven Commonwealth countries. Newfoundland was the first to portray her, as a 6-year-old princess (6c, 1932). New Zealand portrayed her as princess on four occasions between 1943 and 1950, a total of six stamps (including the only triangular bearing her portrait). Canada (4c, 1951) was the only country to portray her as Duchess of Edinburgh. Australia, Canada and Newfoundland alone issued stamps for her 21st birthday and/or wedding, and Malta honoured her stay on the island when Prince Philip was stationed there with the Mediterranean Fleet in 1950. The Queen has also

been portrayed on stamps of several non-Commonwealth countries including two from Iran (1961), three from Ethiopia (1965), two from Togo (1977) and one each from Brazil (1968), Comoro (1977) and Bhutan (1978) – plus an incalculable number from the sheikdoms of the Arabian Gulf during the short but highly prolific period 1967–72.

The person (other than British monarchs) most portrayed on stamps has varied from time to time. At the end of the nineteenth century the record was held by Christopher Columbus. Chile, which portrayed no one else between 1855 and 1910, contributed no fewer than 130 Columbus stamps, and from 1892 till 1900 he was honoured by many American and Caribbean countries who celebrated the quatercentenary of his voyages of discovery with a further 101 stamps. If one includes all the stamps honouring Columbus, directly or indirectly, however, the number amounts to 701. This includes numerous overprints, stamps showing his ships, his mausoleum, memorial lighthouse and places named after him, but not actually bearing his portrait. The fewest stamps honouring Columbus, issued by any of the 37 countries, are one each from the Turks and Caicos Islands, Hungary and Italy – the last being the country of his birth.

In the twentieth century, however, he was overtaken by Sir Winston Churchill, the subject of worldwide issues after his death in 1965, and again in his centenary year (1974). Churchill even appeared (in cartoon form) on Nazi field postcards of the Second World War, and on a West German commemorative of 1968. To date a total of 474 stamps have honoured Churchill.

The most portrayed person on the stamps of any one country is Queen Elizabeth, who has been portrayed on 1017 British stamps (including regional issues) since December 1952.

Dr Sun Yat-sen has appeared on at least 913 Chinese stamps since 1912. All of the definitives issued by China from 1931 till 1949 bore his portrait.

Ghost stamps are those in which a portrait has

Iran 1r, 1961, portraying the Shah and Queen Elizabeth

unintentionally manifested itself in some detail of the design.

The first example of a ghost portrait occurred in 1881 when Haiti's first definitive issue, depicting the allegorical effigy of Liberty, was deemed to show (in the folds of Liberty's headdress) the profile of Madame Salomon, wife of the country's president.

The most celebrated example occurred in 1904. The previous year a coup was staged in Serbia and King Alexander Obrenovich and his consort, Draga Mashin, were brutally murdered in bed. The coronation of the new ruler, Peter Karageorgevich, was commemorated by a set of stamps whose low values showed the conjoined profiles of King Peter and his ancestor Karageorge. The stamps were designed by the Serb artist D Jovanovich, but the dies were engraved by Eugène Mouchon and the stamps printed in Paris. When the stamps reached Belgrade it was found that, by turning them upside down, a third portrait could be seen where the profiles overlapped. There, for all to see, was a grotesque face, and the rumour spread like wildfire that this was the death-mask of the murdered king. In vain did Mouchon protest that he had only followed instructions and that the 'death-mask' was quite fortuitous. The stamps became so popular with collectors that they were soon extensively forged.

Ghost portraits of Adolf Hitler can be seen in the roses featured on the Austrian Christmas stamps of 1937 – later regarded as an ill omen, since the stamps were the last issued by Austria before the Nazi invasion on 11/12 March 1938. Hitler can also supposedly be seen in the trees featured at the left side of the vignette on the West German 50 pfennig definitive of 1964.

PICTORIAL STAMPS

The first pictorial stamps were issued in 1843. D O Blood & Co of Philadelphia issued stamps showing a postman leaping over the city. Featured prominently in the foreground was the façade of the Exchange building. Two other American local services, the Broadway Post Office and Wyman's Post (both 1844) featured early steam locomotives on their stamps.

The first pictorial stamp issued by a government was the 3d of Canada, 1851, designed by Sir Sandford Fleming. The stamp shows a beaver in its natural habitat rather than a stylised, heraldic interpretation. A strong counter claim has been made on behalf of New South Wales since its stamps issued in 1850 (depicting the great seal of the colony) showed settlers landing at Botany Bay. These stamps are popularly known to collectors as the Sydney Views.

The first pictorial series with a different motif on each value was issued by the United States in 1869. Apart from the mandatory portraits of Franklin and Washington this series also portrayed Abraham Lincoln, and featured heraldry (the American eagle, shield and flags) on two stamps, while the

Haiti, 1881 definitive series: ghost portrait of the president's wife in the fold's of Liberty's head-dress

Dr Sun Yat-sen, on nine of the Chinese definitive issues (1931-49)

Ghost portraits of Adolf Hitler on Austria Christmas stamp (1937) and West Germany definitive 50pf (1964)

remaining designs featured a post rider, a locomotive, a steamship (SS *Adriatic*) and reproductions of two paintings – the landing of Columbus by Vanderlyn and the declaration of independence by Trumbull.

The first pictorial stamps in Europe were issued by the Turkish Admiralty in 1859 and featured a steamship. The first from the British Commonwealth was David Bryce's steamship stamp of 1847 featuring the *Lady McLeod*. Steamship companies, such as the St Thomas and La Guaira and the Custendje & Czernavoda service, were among the first to use pictorial stamps. The Swiss hotel posts (1872-80), the Norwegian town posts (from 1881), the German local posts and the Russian zemstvo issues also emulated the American carrier companies in using pictorial designs, but government issues were slow to follow suit. Britain's first pictorials were issued by the Express Parcels Delivery Company (1864-6) but the Post Office did not produce a

USA Broadway local post (1844) showing a locomotive

Canada 3d, 1851, depicting a beaver

pictorial design in the true sense till 1951, when the 2s 6d and 5s definitives featured HMS *Victory* and the cliffs of Dover respectively. Previously, the 1924-5 British Empire Exhibition stamps (showing the Wembley lion), the Victory issue of 1946 (symbols of reconstruction) and the 3d value of the UPU series of 1949 (the UPU monument in Berne) were more heraldic than pictorial in approach. Two stamps of 1948 showed islanders gathering seaweed, but were confined to the Channel Islands.

The first stamps to depict a historic subject were issued by Egypt in 1867 and featured the Sphinx and Pyramids. This motif appeared on all Egyptian stamps until 1914.

The first stamps, other than portraits, to be derived from paintings were two of the US 1869 series. The 15c reproduced the landing of Columbus by Vanderlyn in the Capitol, Washington, while the 24c showed the declaration of independence by Trumbull, in Yale Art Gallery, New Haven, Con.

The first stamps to be derived from photographs were issued by the Confederate States of America in 1861 and portrayed President Jefferson Davis. The first stamp based on a photograph, issued on the Union side, was the 15c of 1866 portraying Abraham Lincoln. The same photograph was used for the 90c stamp of the 1869 series. The United States was an early and enthusiastic exponent of photographically inspired stamps. Other pioneer issues in this medium include the Zachary Taylor and James Garfield 5c stamps of 1875 and 1882 (based on daguerrotypes), the Lincoln 4c, Grant 5c, Garfield 6c, Sherman 8c, Webster 10c and Clay 15c stamps of 1890 and the 2c and $2 stamps of the Trans-

USA 15c (1869): Landing of Columbus, after Vanderlyn

Mississippi Exposition series of 1898 showing farming in the west and the Mississippi Bridge at St Louis respectively.

The earliest photographically inspired stamp from the British Commonwealth was the North Borneo wildlife series of 1894, printed by Waterlow and Sons. The dollar values of the issues from the Malay States (1895) showed a group of elephants, from a photograph. Other early Commonwealth examples include the Tasmanian scenery set (1899), the Llandovery Falls 1d of Jamaica (1900) and the Valletta Harbour ¼d of Malta (1901).

Economy in stamp production resulted in a strange coincidence. In 1897 Newfoundland issued a 10c stamp which purported to show John Cabot's ship *Matthew* (1497). The self-same ship, however, had appeared on the American 3c stamp four years earlier, in the guise of the *Santa Maria* of Christopher Columbus. It had a remarkable resurrection in 1936 when it turned up on stamps of Costa Rica commemorating Cocos Island. It was actually a stock engraving of the American Bank Note Co.

STAMPS AS AN ADVERTISING MEDIUM

Advertising through the post was first used in 1840 when many of the Mulready wrappers and envelopes (see Chapter 6) bore advertisements and were sold at a discount on packs of twelve. Advertising agencies, insurance companies and even the Inland Revenue tax offices used this medium, but the Mulready design was unpopular and was soon discontinued. In 1857 the Post Office offered companies an advertising ring round the embossed stamp on postal stationery. Only nine companies used this facility before it was discontinued in 1893. Some other companies had these advertising rings applied privately.

The first attempt to put commercial advertising on stamps occurred in 1862, when an American local postal service issued 10c stamps inscribed: 'Wedding cards, Notices and Letters delivered by the California City Letter Express Co Office at Hoogs & Madison's, Real Estate, House Brokers & Rent Collectors, 418 Montgomery St.'

The first attempt to transmit advertising on stamps issued by a government postal administration took place in 1887 when Pears Soap had their name printed in double-lined capitals on top of the gum on the back of British ½d and 1d stamps. This was only an experiment and never secured official sanction.

The first country to permit commercial advertising on the back of its stamps was New Zealand whose definitive series of 1893 has been nicknamed 'Adsons' by collectors. A different advertisement appeared on the back of each stamp in a sheet and it is therefore possible to reconstruct the entire sheet. Beecham's Pills, Sunlight Soap, Fry's Cocoa, Cadbury's Chocolate, Bonnington's Irish Moss ('for coughs and colds') and a Christchurch dentist, S Mayers, who extolled the use of nitrous oxide for painless extractions, were among the advertisers. The overprint was applied to stamps prior to gumming, but the public objected to the stamps on the grounds that they would be liable to lick off the ink. The advertising campaign was discontinued within two years.

Advertising on the backs of stamps was revived by Sierra Leone in 1964 when the Butterfly brand logotype of Samuel Jones Ltd appeared on the backing paper of the self-adhesive stamps. This privilege was extended to other firms in 1965 but discontinued in 1972 when Sierra Leone reverted to stamps of more orthodox appearance. Usually a separate advertisement appeared on the back of each stamp, but a 7c stamp featuring a diamond necklace was issued in November 1965 in sheets of 25, with a single large advertisement on the back, covering the entire sheet, and publicising the New York diamond merchant, Harry Winston.

A loophole in Swiss postal regulations enabled A Kocher et Fils of La Chaux de Fonds and Vevey to have private postal stationery franked with impressions of contemporary postage stamps in 1909. By

Confederate States of America 5c (1861); North Borneo scenery and wildlife (1894)

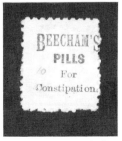

New Zealand, 1893, with advertisement for Beecham's Pills on reverse

exploiting the letter, if not the spirit, of the regulation, this company had gummed advertising labels prepared with the stamps printed within a frame. When the Swiss postal authorities tumbled to this ruse they promptly withdrew the privilege of stamping private stationery – but not before some 16 000 of these unique 'stamps on stickers' were issued.

The commonest form of advertising consists of coupons or labels attached to stamps issued in booklets. This practice began in the German Empire and Bavaria in 1911, advertisements for Pelikan ink, Delaunay cars, honey, apple wine and various stamp dealers appearing alongside Germania and Prince Regent Luitpold definitives. Advertising of a less commercial, more blatantly propagandistic kind was to be found in the coil stamps issued by the Third Reich. British stamp booklets contained advertising on the interleaving from 1908, but this was extended to the stamps themselves in February 1924 when a pane of four 1½d stamps had a pair of labels bearing advertising, to make up the pane of six subjects. This form of advertising has continued down to the present time.

Commercial advertising was also permitted on the selvedge of sheets issued in Germany and on the selvedge of booklet panes in France, New Zealand and South Africa from the 1920s onward. Belgium issued stamps with publicity labels in normal sheet format from 1927 till 1938, advertising Persil, the national lottery, the Dover-Ostend ferry and cod liver oil. Italy issued stamps in 1923 with advertising panels as an integral part of the stamp, though the advertisements were usually printed in different colours from the stamp. These advertisements publicised Campari, Singer sewing machines and other consumer goods.

Advertising on postal stationery was widely used by the German local posts, in the same manner as the Mulready wrappers, but New Zealand was the only country to do so nationally, particularly advertising the postal and telecommunications services in the interwar period.

A bill before Congress in 1981, promoted by Barry Goldwater Jr, would have permitted the issue of American definitive stamps advertising commercial products, as a way of eliminating the deficit in the postal budget. This was strongly opposed by philatelists on the grounds that it would lead to an unnecessary proliferation of issues – estimates running as high as several thousand each year!

Advertisements on German coil stamps, booklet panes from GB, Belgium, USA and South Africa, and Italian stamp of 1923 with an advertisement panel

In 1923 Costa Rica overprinted the 5c definitive with a slogan advertising Costa Rican coffee.

INSCRIPTIONS

The earliest stamps bore no country name – an unnecessary feature since they could only be used on internal mail in their respective countries. Many of the early stamps of the world were issued without a country name inscribed, but one of the first regulations promulgated by the UPU in 1874 was the compulsory use of some form of identification. In deference to Britain's position as premier user of adhesive stamps, this rule was waived for British stamps alone, and since then the effigy of the reigning monarch has been regarded as sufficient identification. Occasionally, however, the rule is flouted. A notable example in recent years was the US 5c definitive of 1963 showing the Stars and Stripes over the White House – both subjects which might have been regarded as sufficiently well known worldwide as to require no caption. Subsequent stamps with similar motifs (1968-71) have been properly inscribed UNITED STATES. The set of three stamps honouring the Tercentenary of the Pilgrim Fathers (1920) was the only commemorative issue from the United States to be unnamed.

The first stamps to bear a country name were issued in 1842-5 by the City Despatch Post of New York. Although they were inscribed UNITED STATES, they were limited in validity to New York City. The first government issues to bear a name defining the limits of validity were the cantonal stamps issued by Zürich and Geneva (1843). The first stamps with country-wide validity to bear a country name were issued by Mauritius (September 1847), France (January 1849) and Bavaria (November 1849). The stamps produced by William Perot, postmaster of Hamilton, Bermuda, in 1848 consisted of his office datestamp, minus the date slugs, and since the name of the island appeared at the foot they may be regarded as 'national' stamps, although their validity may have been local.

The first stamps to be inscribed in two languages were the cantonal stamps of Geneva, 1843, which bore the Latin motto POST TENEBRAS LUX (After the darkness comes light), in addition to inscriptions in French. In the same manner the first stamps of New South Wales (1850) had *two* Latin inscriptions, but the only English words were POSTAGE/ONE PENNY. The first stamps to be inscribed in two languages, denoting the usage or value, were issued by Zürich in March 1850. They were inscribed ORTS POST (German) and POSTE LOCALE (French) for use pending the introduction of the federal issue in May that year.

'Anonymous' stamps from USA: Pilgrim Fathers tercentenary (1920) and 5c Stars and Stripes over White House (1963)

Stamps issued simultaneously in two language versions were first produced by Switzerland in 1850. Stamps of 2½ rappen value were issued in French-speaking areas inscribed POSTE LOCALE and in the German-speaking areas inscribed ORTS POST. No attempt was made to accommodate the Italian-speaking areas at the time. These stamps were printed in separate sheets and not in bilingual pairs (see below). Subsequently Switzerland got around the language problem by inscribing stamps FRANCO (franked) which was understandable in French, German and Italian, and rendered the country name in Latin – HELVETIA OR CONFOEDERATIO HELVETICA.

In 1982 the USA planned stamps in English and Spanish versions, the latter being confined to those states with substantial Hispanic population. The issue, however, never took place.

Stamps issued simultaneously in three language versions were produced by Switzerland between 1939 and 1942. The first such issues publicised the Swiss National Exhibition in Zürich and were inscribed in French, German and Italian. In 1940 stamps for the National Exhibition and Red Cross fund were inscribed in one or other of the three languages, according to the face value of the stamps, but there was no attempt on that occasion to issue each denomination in all three languages. In March 1942 stamps publicising the national salvage campaign were inscribed TO SURVIVE, COLLECT SALVAGE in either French, German or Italian. Subsequent Swiss stamps have tended to be inscribed in all three languages or merely in Latin, as before.

Bilingual inscriptions, in countries with two major languages, were first used in Belgium (French and Flemish) in 1893, and in Canada (French and English) in 1927. In the latter case, the first concession to the Francophone population was the inscription TERCENTENAIRE DE QUEBEC on the series of 1908, English on that occasion being confined to the value and word POSTAGE. In 1927 a set celebrating the diamond jubilee of the Confederation had the words POST and POSTES in the side panels. Since cents, dollars and the country name are the same in both languages Canada has neatly solved the

Switzerland, National Exhibition, Zürich (1939), in Italian, French and German

problem of bilingualism by confining other inscriptions to a minimum, and then showing considerable ingenuity in the use of words common to both languages or arranging the inscriptions in such a way as to minimise the repetition of words common to both languages.

Bilingualism is a common feature of stamps from many Slavonic and Oriental countries where, in accordance with UPU regulations, inscriptions are rendered in French or English as well as the local script.

The first stamps with inscriptions in two different alphabets were issued by the Grand Duchy of Finland in 1856. The value (in kopeks) was rendered in the Roman and Cyrillic alphabets. The first stamps issued by Moldavia (now part of Romania) were likewise inscribed in Roman and Cyrillic (1858–62).

The first stamps in Roman and Oriental scripts were issued by Hong Kong in 1862 (English and Chinese), followed by Shanghai in 1865 (English and Chinese), Egypt in 1866 (Roman and Arabic). Jammu and Kashmir was the first country to issue stamps in two different Oriental scripts – Arabic and Hindi (1866).

The first British stamps in two languages were the Menai Bridge stamp (1968), the Welsh stucco cottage stamp (1970), the University College of Wales stamp (1971) and the Eisteddfod pair (1976): all in English and Welsh. The first (and so far the only) stamp inscribed in Scottish Gaelic as well as English was the Highland Games 11p stamp of 1976.

Stamps in bilingual pairs, inscribed alternately in different languages, were first issued by South West Africa in 1923. South African stamps – themselves inscribed bilingually in English and Dutch – were alternately overprinted SOUTH WEST AFRICA or ZUID-WEST AFRIKA. The latter language was changed to Afrikaans (Suidwes Afrika) in 1926 – the year in which South Africa introduced stamps printed alternately in the two main languages. This practice continued in South Africa and South West Africa till 1951, but since then the majority of stamps have been inscribed bilingually. A solitary issue was made

by East Africa (Kenya, Uganda and Tanganyika) in 1941-2, using South African stamps with suitable overprints and surcharges in East African currency. Similarly, the Victory stamps issued by Basutoland, Bechuanaland and Swaziland in 1945, being overprints on South African stamps, were printed in bilingual pairs.

Outside Southern Africa this practice has been confined so far to a single issue from Ceylon (now Sri Lanka). A pair of 60c stamps was issued in 1964 to commemorate the centenary of the railways and these were inscribed alternately in Tamil and English as well as Sinhala.

Trilingual inscriptions on stamps were first issued by Switzerland in 1854, the denominations being expressed in centimes (French), centesimi (Italian) and rappen (German). They were superseded in 1862 by stamps showing the numeral of value alone. Some of the National Fête stamps, from 1938 to 1944, were inscribed trilingually, but in general Switzerland avoided the complications of using three languages simultaneously until 1960. Since then many of the Publicity stamps and commemoratives for international events have been thus inscribed.

Other examples of trilingualism on stamps are:
Finland: 1867, 1889-94 Finnish, Swedish, Russian
Soruth: 1877-1913 English, Urdu, Hindi
Djibouti: 1894-1902 French, Amharic, Arabic
North Borneo: 1897 English, Chinese, Arabic (Malay)
Yugoslavia: 1933 Serb, Croat, Slovene
Yugoslavia: 1938 Serb, Croat, Latin
Bhopal: 1935-9 English, Arabic, Hindi
Italy: 1954 Italian, Chinese, Latin
India: 1948 English, Urdu, Hindi
Pakistan: 1956-62 English, Urdu, Bengali
Ceylon: 1950- English, Tamil, Sinhala
Cyprus: 1960- English, Greek, Turkish
South West Africa: 1980 English, Afrikaans, Latin

Multilingual stamps, with inscriptions in four or more languages, were first issued by Hyderabad in 1871. From then until 1948 the majority of stamps

Bilingual pairs from South West Africa
(1923), South Africa (1926) and Ceylon
(1964)

were inscribed in English, Mah-
ratti, Telugu and Urdu – four different scripts.

The set of seven stamps issued
by the USSR in 1927 to mark the
tenth anniversary of the Revolution were variously inscribed in
Russian, Ukrainian, Georgian,
Armenian and Arabic. Most
stamps had three languages but
the 28k was inscribed in four (all
but Arabic).

The majority of the definitive
issues of the United Nations since
1951 have been inscribed simul-
taneously in English, French, Spanish, Russian and
Chinese – the five most widely spoken languages in
the world.

The stamps issued by Eastern Roumelia (South
Bulgaria) from 1881 till 1885 were inscribed in
Turkish, Greek, Bulgar and French – four languages
and four scripts (Arabic, Greek, Cyrillic and Roman), a record for different alphabets until 1966 (see
below). The 1945 Red Cross set of Yugoslavia was
inscribed in Serb, Croat, Slovene and South Slav
(Macedonian).

Trilingual Triplets have only been issued by South
West Africa. In 1968 3c and 15c stamps honouring
President Swart were printed alternately in English,
Afrikaans and German (the language of the original
settlers). In 1978 a set of six stamps publicising
universal suffrage was overprinted in the three
languages in *se-tenant* (side-by-side) strips of three.

The greatest number of languages on any stamp
was recorded in November 1987 when South Africa

issued a 16c stamp as part of a set marking the 150th
anniversary of the Bible Society. In Africa the Bible
is available in 111 languages. The stamp shows the
title in 75 languages, beginning with *Die Bybel* (Afrikaans) and ending with *The Bible* (English). Inscriptions are given in three scripts – Arabic, Amharic and
the Roman alphabet. The word BIBLIA appears twice,
to represent its use in nine indigenous African
languages. Among the titles is that of the only Bible
in the world with the title *Word of God* – ELOBMIS in
Nama.

The runner-up is a pair of stamps from Denmark
on behalf of the Red Cross, 1966, inscribed in
Latin PER HUMANITATEM AD PACEM (through human-
ity towards peace) and the name of the organisation
in 32 languages.

**The only stamps issued in two languages and
currencies for use in two countries simultaneously** were released jointly by Romania and

Switzerland trilingual 10c (1854), Hyderabad and Eastern Roumelia – 4 languages and scripts; United Nations – 5 languages, 4 alphabets
(1951)

South West Africa trilingual triplet 3c, 1968

Romania and Yugoslavia Derdap Hydro-electric Project (1965)

South Africa, Bible Society 16c, 1987

Yugoslavia on 20 May 1965 to celebrate the inauguration of the Derdap Hydro-electric Project. They bore the names of both countries and were valued at 30 bani (25 dinar) and 55 bani (50 dinar). A miniature sheet accompanied this issue and contained two Romanian and two Yugoslav stamps – the only bi-national sheet issued so far.

Unusual languages or alphabets on stamps have occurred on several occasions.

Cyrillic (the alphabet of Russia, Bulgaria and Yugoslavia) was used for a solitary stamp, issued by Czechoslovakia on 15 March 1939 to mark the inauguration of the Carpatho-Ukrainian or Ruthenian parliament in Jasina. It was withdrawn after only one day as a result of the German invasion of Prague.

Two German issues are known with Cyrillic inscriptions. Hitler Head definitives were overprinted in the town of Herrnhut in 1945 with the name rendered in Cyrillic, following occupation by the Red Army. The first stamp issued in Dresden under Soviet occupation was inscribed POCHTA in Cyrillic, but withdrawn on the very day of issue (23 June 1945) because the appearance of Cyrillic in the inscription violated a Four-Power agreement. A total of 14 500 stamps were sold out of the 1 030 000 printed.

Chinese has appeared on two Italian stamps of 1954 commemorating the seventh centenary of the birth of Marco Polo, and on an American 5c stamp of 1942 publicising the Chinese nationalist war effort.

Hebrew, normally confined to stamps of Palestine (1920–48) and Israel, appeared on a stamp issued by the Hansa local post in Breslau (now Wroclaw, Poland) in 1897 to celebrate the Jewish New Year. Hebrew also appears on two of the stamps issued by Czechoslovakia in 1967 featuring historic aspects of Jewish culture and a set from Surinam in 1968.

Inscriptions in Chinese, Japanese, Hebrew, Sanskrit and Arabic appeared on a Mexican 1p60 airmail

Czechoslovakia, Carpatho-Ukrainian parliament (1939); Jewish culture (1967); Italy, Marco Polo (1954)

stamp of 1976 honouring the 30th International Asian-North American Congress.

The only stamps with meaningless inscriptions were issued by Macao in 1936 for airmail purposes. Two lines of Greek characters were included:

ξοωηθεζωνδϑ/εαιοωρωνlu

This blundered inscription, together with a curious mixture of accents, breathings and diaeresis marks, was included merely in a laudable attempt to make forgery more difficult!

MISCELLANY

The only stamps prepared as an unofficial local issue but issued instead by a government postal administration were the first stamps of Peru. Perkins Bacon of London recess-printed a quantity of stamps for the Pacific Steam Navigation Company, a British firm trading along the west coast of South America. The stamps were never actually used by the company, owing to objections raised by the Peruvian authorities. In 1857, however, the Peruvian Post Office considered the introduction of adhesive postage stamps and the company thereupon offered its unused stamps to the government for circulation pending the supply of a regular issue. The stamps, bearing the initials of the company (PSNC) in the corners, were in use from 1 December 1857 till March 1858, when they were superseded by a series specifically inscribed with the country name.

Local stamps, usually ignored by government postal administrations, have been reproduced on government issues on several occasions. In 1912 a local set of stamps portraying Apollo was prepared for issue in the Dodecanese Islands, but the stamps were suppressed by the Italian military authorities. The design was reproduced on two of the stamps issued by Greece in 1947 to celebrate the transfer of the Dodecanese Islands to Greece.

In 1964 one of the Stamp Day stamps issued by Cuba reproduced the 10 centavo stamp issued by the guerillas in the war against Spain in 1898. A set of stamps issued by Tristan da Cunha for the centenary of the death of Sir Rowland Hill (1979) featured the famous 'Potato' local stamp on the 50p denomination.

In October 1967 the Irish Republic issued two stamps commemorating the centenary of the Fenian insurrection and reproduced two stamps which purported to be Fenian stamp essays of 1867. It has since been discovered that the 'essays' were a hoax perpetrated by the notorious philatelic swindler, Samuel Allen Taylor of Boston, Massachusetts. Ireland thus has the dubious distinction of being the only country to reproduce bogus stamps on its issues.

A newspaper founded a country's postal service. In 1870 the *Fiji Times* organised a postal service and heralded it with a jingle:

'Remember, remember the First of November
The day you'll have reason to bless.

For then we commence a thing quite immense
To be called the *Fiji Times* Express.'

The newspaper's proprietor, G L Griffiths, not only provided enlarged premises for a post office at Levuka, the islands' capital, until 1882, but also mailbags, an inter-island mailboat and an issue of stamps (1d, 3d, 6d, 9d and 1s). The stamps were composed of printers' type and perforated by lines of printers' dashes, producing a rouletted effect. The service in fact operated between 8 October 1870 and May 1872 when it was taken over by the Fiji government.

Stamps have been used as money during shortages of coinage on several occasions. The first time was during the American Civil War (1861-5), the stamps being encapsulated in small metal cases with a mica window and firms' advertisements on the back. This was the invention of John Gault, a sewing-machine salesman from Boston. Similar instances of encased postage stamp currency occurred in France, Monaco, Belgium, Austria, Germany, Argentina, Greece, Italy and Norway during and immediately after the First World War. Stamps affixed to cards and circulated in lieu of coins were issued in Rhodesia (1898-1900), Madagascar (First World War) and Spain (during the Civil War of 1936-9). Stamps were printed on card and circulated in lieu of coins in Russia (1915-17) and the Ukraine. Only two examples are known from the Second World War. The Indian state of Bundi printed 3 pies and 1 anna tokens, consisting of cards reproducing the current stamps overprinted CASH COUPON BUNDI STATE. Filipino guerillas operating in Japanese-held territory in 1942 produced 5 peso notes to which revenue stamps of the appropriate value were affixed.

Stamps were the principal weapon in a cold war between Britain, Argentina and Chile which lasted more than thirty years. It was sparked off in 1933 when the Falkland Islands celebrated their centenary

Irish Republic, Fenian centenary reproducing bogus 'stamps', 1967

as a British colony with a lengthy set of stamps which included one (3d) showing a map of the islands. Argentina, which has laid claim to the islands as the heir to the Spanish empire, retaliated by issuing a 1 peso stamp in 1936 showing a map of South America, with Argentinian territory (including the Falklands) shaded. At first this stamp also showed the boundaries of the other South American countries, but it was superseded by one omitting the boundaries, on account of the sensitivity of certain countries (notably Bolivia and Paraguay) to the delineation of their frontiers. The battle switched to the Antarctic in 1944 when Britain arranged for separate issues of stamps to be made in Graham Land, South Georgia, South Orkneys and South Shetland, followed by a joint issue for the Falkland Islands Dependencies in 1946 showing a map of the polar regions with British territory delineated. Again Argentina retaliated by issuing various stamps depicting maps of Argentina and *her* Antarctic possessions. The first of these appeared in 1947 and commemorated the 43rd anniversary of the first Argentinian Antarctic mail. Even the prewar 1 peso stamp was redesigned to show the Antarctic territory, and in 1954 a stamp honoured the 'Orcadas del Sur' as the Argentinians called the South Orkneys. Although territorial claims in the Antarctic were suspended under the terms of the Antarctic Treaty of

Russia and Bundi: stamps printed on card and circulated in place of coinage

1961 both sides continued to snipe at each other philatelically. Many of the stamps of South Georgia, British Antarctic Territory, the Falkland Islands and its dependencies down to the present day have featured maps stating unequivocally British sovereignty. Equally, Argentina has continued to depict its Antarctic territory on stamps and in 1964 went so far as to issue a set of three featuring maps of the Antarctic and 'Islas Malvinas' (the Falklands) with Argentinian flags superimposed. Chile's claim to a slice of Antarctica, overlapping with those of

Falkland Islands Dependencies ½d (1944), and 1d (1980); Chile 2.50p (1947); Argentina 20c (1947) and 4p (1964)

Britain and Argentina, was registered by stamps issued between 1947 and 1958.

Stamps provoked a disastrous war between Bolivia and Paraguay. Both countries laid claim to a wilderness called the Gran Chaco, but Bolivia had the temerity to issue stamps in 1930 featuring a map with the disputed area captioned 'Chaco Boliviano'. Incensed by this, Paraguay issued large stamps showing a more detailed map of the area, now entitled 'Chaco Paraguayo' and bearing the slogan 'Has been, is, and will be'. This was shortly followed by the outbreak of fighting between Bolivian and Paraguayan forces in the Chaco. The Chaco War dragged on, decimating the population on both sides and precipitating the economic ruin of Bolivia. Further Chaco map stamps were issued by Bolivia in 1935 and by Paraguay in 1934-6. After a conference of American states in Buenos Aires in 1938-9 awarded the territory to Paraguay the latter issued two further sets (1939-40) featuring maps and scenery in the Gran Chaco.

Boundary disputes between Haiti and the Dominican Republic, Nicaragua and Honduras, Ecuador and Brazil, Venezuela and Guyana, Guatemala and Belize and Chile and Peru have also made use of postage stamps to make claims and counter claims. The 1900-map series of the Dominican Republic distorted the boundaries with Haiti, provoking a wave of anti-Dominican feeling which almost resulted in war between the two countries. The matter was only resolved at the highest diplomatic level and the Dominican Republic speedily replaced the offending stamps with an innocuous heraldic series.

Stamps sparked off an insurrection and changed the history of a country. In 1884 the Japanese (whose influence had been increasing) were instrumental in introducing adhesive postage stamps in Korea. This upset the Koreans who staged an uprising, burned down the post office in Seoul and scattered the sheets of new-fangled stamps through the streets. On the pretext of restoring law and order Japanese troops moved in and occupied the country – an occupation which lasted till 1945.

Stamps have changed the economic and political history of countries. At the end of the nineteenth century, when French and American financiers were trying to decide the location of the canal to link the Pacific and Atlantic Oceans, one group voted for cutting it through the isthmus of Panama, while another wanted it cut through Nicaragua. The Nicaraguan Post Office made the mistake of issuing a new definitive series in 1900 showing Mount Momotombo. This volcano had been extinct for years but, with proud artistic licence, it was depicted with fire and smoke belching

Bolivia 2c, 1930, showing the Bolivian Chaco

from its crater. That was all the Panamanian lobby needed. The stamps were circulated to every US senator. The Senate was alarmed at the prospect of a canal being cut through unstable terrain and vetoed the Nicaraguan proposal. But for the stamps, the canal might have run 500 miles north of Panama.

The series of stamps issued by Spain in June 1930 to commemorate the centenary of the death of the painter Goya depicted his famous *La Maja Desnuda*, a nude portrait of the Duchess of Alba, on the three top values. Subsequently these stamps were allegedly used by republican agitators. 'Your king is consorting with loose women' they told the uneducated peasants, and Alfonso's reputation was destroyed. This widely held story does not accord with the facts, however, that in the municipal elections in April 1931 the monarchists got 22 150 seats while the republicans only gained 5875 – mainly in the cities, indicating that the 'uneducated peasantry' were not so moved by the canard of the nude stamps as is popularly supposed. Faced with an ultimatum from the republicans, Alfonso XIII left the country to avert civil war.

The strangest theft of stamps occurred on 7 September 1914 when the German cruiser *Nürnberg*

Paraguay 1.50p, 1932, showing the Paraguayan Chaco

Dominican Republic 5c, 1900, distorting the boundary with Haiti

Guatemala 5c of 1936 and 1948, the latter showing Belize incorporated in Guatemalan territory

raided the New Zealand dependency of Fanning Island, cutting the telegraph cable and removing £33 6s 8d worth of New Zealand stamps from the island's cable station. When the cable was reconnected the first request was for a supply of stamps, from ½d to 2s, to cover the urgent requirements of the island on letters and parcels to New Zealand.

The only postal service operated by criminals was the so-called Bandit Post between Tsaochwang and the Paotzeku Mountains in China in May-June 1923. On 6 May bandits forced 120 passengers off the Blue Express on the Tientsin-Pukow line and held them hostage in the mountains. Carl Crow, of the American Red Cross, organised a messenger

service for letters and parcels to the hostages. Two stamps were prepared locally – 5c (erroneously inscribed 50c) and 10c with the inscription PAO TZU KU BANDIT POST (*sic*) and a crude outline of the mountains. A Chinese inscription also appeared on the lower denomination. About 500 stamps were printed and used by both inward and outward services. The service ceased by 13 June when the last of the hostages had been released.

Stamps, the mere possession of which was a criminal offence, have been issued on two occasions. British stamps overprinted for use on the mail of government departments (1882-1904) were very strictly controlled and even postally used examples were supposed to be returned to head offices for destruction. Following the conviction of a prominent philatelist in 1904 for dealing in mint official stamps they were abruptly withdrawn from use and replaced by 'Official Paid' stationery.

Stamps issued by the German Democratic Republic since 1947 for the *Zentraler Kurierdienst* (Central Courier Service), handling the confidential correspondence of government departments, are subject to very rigorous control and the possession of mint or used examples renders citizens of the GDR liable to a maximum of 5 years imprisonment. Nevertheless both mint and used examples have leaked out and have been noted frequently in the stocks of dealers in the West.

People have allegedly been murdered for their stamps on two occasions. Of the fifteen examples of the 2c Hawaiian 'Missionary' of 1851 only one has ever been found in unused condition. In 1892 this stamp reposed in the collection of the Parisian philatelist Gaston Leroux. One day he was found murdered in his apartment, the crime being apparently motiveless as no money or valuables had been taken. At first detectives were baffled by the crime but one, who had some knowledge of philately, discovered Leroux's collection of Hawaiian stamps and, checking it against a catalogue, discovered that the 2c stamp was absent. A round of the dealers failed to yield up the missing stamp. Eventually, however, suspicion fell on Hector Giroux, an ardent philatelist and a close friend of the murdered man. The detective posed as a collector, made Giroux's acquaintance, and eventually tricked him into boasting of owning a 2c 'Missionary'. Giroux was arrested the following day and questioned over the manner in which he had come by the stamp. Eventually he broke down and confessed to the murder of Leroux who had refused all offers to part with the stamp. Giroux is said to have been convicted in due course and to have paid the supreme penalty for his crime. This story, repeated by several writers (notably L N and M

Korea 5mon (1884),
Nicaragua Momotombo 10c
surcharged 15c (1904),
Spain 'La Maja Desnuda'
(1930)

Williams) as recently as 1970, has been repudiated as untrue but the story persists. The stamp, incidentally, passed into the Ferrary and Burrus collections, making $41 000 at the Burrus sale in New York, 1963.

In 1896, however, Paris was the venue for the murder of Julien Emile Delahaeff, a young stamp dealer, by a collector named Aubert and his accomplice Margaret Dubois. The motive for the crime is unclear, but Aubert killed Delahaeff with a blow to the head and subsequently disposed of the corpse in a trunk. The police eventually connected Aubert with Delahaeff's disappearance and he was arrested, tried and convicted. He evaded the guillotine on the grounds of diminished responsibility but was sentenced to penal servitude for life, while his accomplice received three years' imprisonment.

The monopoly of the New Zealand Post Office was circumvented ingeniously in 1930-1 by Dominion Airlines Ltd, which operated an air service between Hastings and Gisborne in the North Island. Letters were carried for sixpence each, and the company produced special stamps for the purpose. The Post Office objected to this and ordered the company to terminate the service. The company managed to continue the service, within the letter of the law, by re-issuing the labels without any denomination expressed. Technically the letters were carried free of charge, but they had to be signed by the pilot, G B Bolt, who charged sixpence for his autograph.

Kinds of stamps

The world's first stamps were labels signifying the prepayment of postage, and until the 1960s many postal administrations (Britain included) were inclined to regard them merely as receipts denoting payment by the sender. The workhorses of the postal system are these stamps, known variously as permanent or definitive stamps, which remain in use for relatively long periods – as opposed to commemorative and thematic sets which are generally on sale for a limited time. The growing sophistication of postal services over the past 140 years has created a need for special stamps of many kinds. Furthermore, the circumstances in which stamps are issued often create issues with some special quality. All of these kinds of stamps are discussed in this chapter.

Acknowledgement of Receipt is a system whereby the sender of a registered item may receive acknowledgement that it has been delivered to and received by the addressee. Special forms prominently inscribed AR have been used in Britain for this purpose since 1895.

Special stamps were first issued by Colombia in 1865 in pairs inscribed A (*Anotacion*) and R (*Rejistro*) denoting registration and acknowledgement respectively (the opposite to what one might expect, judging by the initials). Stamps inscribed AR (*Aviso de Recepcion*) were issued by Colombia from 1894 till 1917. Stamps for this service were also issued by Chile (1894), El Salvador (1897) and Montenegro (1895-1913).

Airmail stamps, produced in connection with the transmission of letters by air, have a surprising antiquity. The first airmail stamp was a 5c adhesive label issued in 1877 by 'Professor' Samuel King for use on mail carried by the balloon *Buffalo* from Nashville, Tennessee. Printed in blue, it showed a picture of the balloon in flight.

In November 1898 blue shilling stamps were issued by the Original Great Barrier Pigeongram Service (see page 39). The stamp showed a bird carrying a letter in its beak. Among subsequent issues was a stamp overprinted for use on the pigeon post to Marotiri Island, and a pair of triangulars (1899-1901).

In the years immediately following the Wright Brothers' first flights by heavier-than-air machines, aviation meetings were all the rage in Europe and many of them produced souvenir labels, some of which enjoyed semi-official status as airmail stamps. The first of these labels was issued in June 1909 for the meeting at Bar-sur-Aube and depicted a female allegorical figure of aviation. The following month the Douai air meeting had the first souvenir postcard and the first label depicting an aircraft – albeit semi-symbolic (a female figure with biplane wings fixed to her back). In August 1909 the meeting at St

Acknowledgement of Receipt stamps of Antioquia (1902), Panama (1904) and Montenegro (1895)

Malo les Bains had the first label to depict an identifiable aircraft – a hydroplane.

The first label to have actual franking validity was issued in August 1910 in connection with the Nantes aviation meeting. The 10c red and blue stamp was closely modelled on the Basle Dove stamp of 1845, with a monoplane substituted for the dove. Used examples on souvenir cards were cancelled with a two-ring postmark inscribed NANTES AVIATION. It is doubtful whether these souvenir cards were actually flown.

The first semi-official air stamps were produced in Germany in connection with the flights between Bork and Brück by the aviator Grade. Three different labels (none bearing any indication of value) were issued, and are known on cards and covers with a variety of airmail cachets. Other semi-official German air stamps followed rapidly, including the Margareten-Volksfest 50 pfennig of May 1912, the Rhine airmail (for the airship *Schwaben* and the monoplane *Gelber Hund*) in June 1912, the Gotha airmail (July) and the Bavarian Aero Club and Regensburg mail flights (both October).

The first airmail stamp issued by a government postal service was the Italian 25 centesimi Express Delivery stamp, overprinted in May–June 1917 for the Rome-Turin air service. The world's first airmail definitive stamps were issued by the United States in May 1918 and featured a Curtiss Jenny. The 24c with inverted centre was the first airmail error.

The United States was also the first country to issue a stamp featuring an aircraft, though not indicating airmail usage. This was the 20c stamp in the parcel post series of December 1912. Other early examples of non-airmail stamps which depicted aircraft were: Cuba 10c express delivery (1914), Austria 35h + 3h war charity (1915), Dominican Republic special delivery 10c (1920), Brazil 100, 150 and 200 reis definitives (1921) and Russian famine relief 20 rouble + 5 rouble (1922).

Automatic stamps, sometimes known as Frama labels (after the FRAMA Co. which produced some machines), were pioneered by Switzerland in 1976 and are now widely used. By inserting coins in a slot and tapping out the value on a keyboard, the customer gets stamps of the required denomination.

Bipartite stamps are those which comprise two portions which can be separated and used individually. The earliest example was the 'Double Geneva' of 1843. Each portion could be used as a 5c stamp for local mail, while the whole served as a 10c stamp for cantonal mail. A horizontal band across the top of the two parts signified the 10c value. Other early examples of bipartite stamps include the Kotelnich zemstvo stamps of Russia (1869–70) and the Drammen local stamps of Norway (1868). Since 1914 Italy

Above Automatic stamp of West Berlin depicting Charlottenburg Castle *Below* Bipartite parcelstamps of Italy (1946)

has issued bipartite stamps for parcel post, the left-hand portion being affixed to the packet card and the right-hand portion to the receipt given to the sender. Similar stamps have been issued by San Marino since 1928. Bipartite stamps have been produced by Romania since 1947, the left-hand portion being retained by the postman and the right-hand portion affixed to the unpaid or underpaid item.

Bisects are stamps divided in half and used postally at half their face value. Among the earliest examples recorded are the British 6d of 1854 cut in half and used to pay the 3d late fee on a letter from London to Ashby de la Zouch (R M Phillips Collection, National Postal Museum). The 3d and 6d stamps of New Brunswick, 1851, were bisected and used with other denominations to make up the 1s 3d and 7½d rates. Probably the best known case of bisection occurred in the Channel Islands in 1940 when British 2d stamps were cut in half and used as penny stamps, during a shortage following the German occupation.

Canadian 3c stamps were divided into ⅓ and ⅔ for use as 1c and 2c stamps at Port Hood in January 1895. Each 'split' was handstamped with the appropriate numeral to denote its new value.

New Brunswick also furnishes the earliest instance of quartering stamps – the 1s of 1851 being thus divided for use as a 3d stamp, while the Papal States cut 6 bajocchi stamps into sixths (1852).

The greatest use of fractional stamps was made by Mexico. The 8 reales stamps of 1856 were split four ways to provide lesser denominations: ¾ = 6r, ½ = 4r, ¼ = 2r, and ⅛ = 1r. The 1861 series provided an even greater range: half of the 1r (½r), half of the 2r (1r), half of the 4r (2r) and quarter of the 4r (1r) in addition to the ⅛, ¼, ½ and ¾ of the 8r as before. In the 1864–6 series ¼ and ¾ 4r stamps were used as 1r and 3r stamps.

Booklets of stamps were first considered as long ago as November 1878 when the British Board of Inland Revenue commissioned De La Rue to produce an experimental booklet containing four panes of six 1d revenue stamps. These were secured, in an ingenious manner, by means of white cotton threaded through the perforations between the upper and lower rows of stamps. The booklet's cover was printed in lilac and bore the royal coat of arms together with the price – 2s ½d – the additional halfpenny defraying the cost of production. Although actual examples were submitted to the Board the idea was never implemented. It was not until 1904 that Britain introduced booklets of postage stamps, although permission was given in 1891 to a private syndicate to do so, the cost of production in this case being defrayed by commercial advertising on the covers.

The first country to issue postage stamps in booklets was Luxembourg, in 1895. Other countries quickly adopted the idea. The first British booklets were priced at 2s ½d – the additional halfpenny again covering production costs. This was a source of irritation to the public and made accounting more difficult, so in 1906 the price was lowered to 2s, but one less halfpenny stamp was included and its place in the booklet pane was taken up by a label bearing a green saltire of St Andrew's cross. In August 1911, when booklets containing King George V stamps were issued, the halfpenny charge was dropped. Purely commercial advertising was introduced in 1909 and since 1968 British booklets have had

pictorial covers, the designs being issued in thematic sets changed every few months. Another British innovation has been the sponsored booklet, in which all the advertising matter has pertained to one sponsor. This was tried experimentally in February 1959, a 2s booklet being sponsored by the Bacon Information Council and including bacon recipes. This was revived in December 1969 for a £1 booklet entitled *Stamps for Cooks*, and containing twelve recipes printed on gummed labels attached to the panes of stamps. On 24 May 1972 a £1 booklet was issued telling the story of the famous pottery Josiah Wedgwood & Sons Ltd. The interleaves were printed in full colour and showed examples of Wedgwood ware. A second booklet, containing £3 worth of stamps, was issued in January 1980 to mark the 250th anniversary of the company. Since November 1978 Britain has also issued Christmas Greetings booklets, containing *se-tenant* strips of the first and second class letter rate stamps, intended as Christmas gifts.

In May 1982 Stanley Gibbons sponsored a £4 booklet which contained panes of nine stamps attached to gummed sheets outlining the history of the world's oldest philatelic business, as a belated commemoration of the company's 125th anniversary celebrated in 1981.

Below and right, various covers of stamp booklets. The colourful covers of the British Post Office's *Stamps for Cooks* and the Wedgwood booklets mentioned above may be seen on page 96

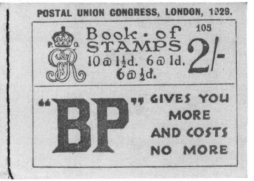

Bus parcel stamps are issued by the Finnish Post Office for use on parcels carried on motor coach services (including private companies). They were introduced on 1 January 1949, the first issue comprising five values inscribed in Finnish (*Auto-pakketti*) and Swedish (*Bilpaket*), with a posthorn motif, value and serial number. A pictorial design, showing a motor coach, was substituted in 1952 and the Swedish inscription changed to *Busspaket*. Other sets were issued in 1963 and 1981.

Carriers' stamps are those issued by local carrier services, most of which operated in various parts of the United States and covered the fees payable for delivering letters to or from the post offices. The US Post Office at first undertook to convey mail only from office to office and people either had to collect their mail from the nearest office or make use of a local carrier service. The first of these was the City Despatch Post, established in New York in February 1842 (see page 75). Over the ensuing decade numerous carrier services sprang up all over the United States, the majority issuing distinctive stamps. In September 1851 the US Post Office began local delivery of mail in New York, Philadelphia and New Orleans, and issued its own 1c carrier stamp for this purpose to pay the local delivery fee. This stamp portrayed Benjamin Franklin and was undenominated. It was superseded on 17 November 1851 by a

Bus parcel stamp of Finland, 1963

denominated 1c stamp showing the American eagle. Whereas the Franklin stamp was inscribed CARRIERS STAMP, the Eagle stamp was inscribed U.S.P.O. DESPATCH PRE-PAID ONE CENT. Most of the carrier services and their stamps disappeared in 1863 when the US Post Office introduced free delivery in the towns and cities, but a few lingered on for several months. Among the last to discontinue its letter carrier service was Wells Fargo whose pony express had the distinction of issuing $4 stamps – at that time a world record for high face value.

Charity stamps are stamps which combine an indication of postal prepayment and a premium in aid of some good cause.

The first issue of this nature comprised a stamped pictorial envelope issued by Britain in 1890 to celebrate the Golden Jubilee of Penny Postage. It was sold for a shilling, but only paid 1d postage, the remaining 11d being credited to the Rowland Hill Benevolent Fund for Post Office Widows and Orphans. A penny postcard, sold for sixpence, was

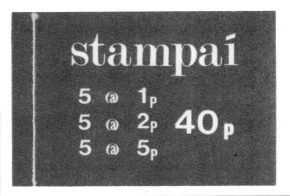

US Carriers' stamps of September and November 1851, and Brown & McGill's local stamp based on the latter

also issued. Two labels were issued in 1897 in Britain to raise money for the Prince of Wales' Jubilee Appeal Fund, but though they had official approval they had no postal validity.

In the same year, however, New South Wales produced two stamps (June 1897) in aid of a consumptives home (TB sanatorium). These were sold for 1s and 2s 6d but prepaid postage of 1d and 2½d only, the balance being given to the charity. The idea was speedily adopted by the neighbouring state of Victoria which issued two Hospital charity stamps in October 1897, also priced at 1d (1s) and 2½d (2s 6d). Three years later 1d (1s) and 2d (2s) stamps were issued on behalf of the Boer War Patriotic Fund by both Victoria and Queensland. Neither the Australian states nor the federal postal administration ever issued charity stamps again.

The first charity stamps were issued in Europe in 1905 when Russia issued a set of four with premiums in aid of war charity at the time of the Russo-Japanese War. In 1906 the Netherlands issued three stamps for the Amsterdam Anti-TB Federation, while Romania released no fewer than four sets of four stamps the same year. Such excesses were roundly condemned by collectors who boycotted them. They virtually died out, being superseded by non-postal labels such as the Christmas seals pioneered by Einar Holboell of Denmark in 1904, but got a new lease of life during the First World War when many countries issued stamps with premiums in aid of the Red Cross, war relief, widows and orphans. Since 1920 they have been widely used for all kinds of charities. Many commemorative stamps of Belgium, Italy and Romania in particular have been issued with charity premiums, while other countries, such as Switzerland, the Netherlands, Luxembourg and New Zealand produce annual charity issues of a particular nature. The United States has never issued any at all, while Britain's sole charity stamp (4½p + 1½p) was issued in January 1975. It was not successful and the experiment has never been repeated.

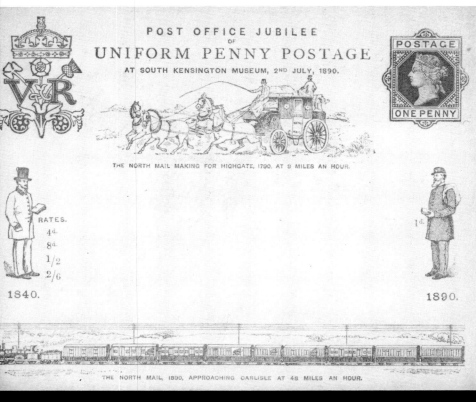

Souvenir envelope of the Jubilee of Uniform Penny Postage, 1890

Russo-Japanese war charity stamp (1905), Romania social welfare issue (1906), Denmark – first Christmas seal (1904) and portrait of its inventor, Einar Holboell on a Belgian stamp of 1955

The longest running charity issues are:

Pro Juventute (Latin 'for youth') issued annually by Switzerland since 1913.

Wohlfartsmarken (welfare stamps) by Germany since 1922.

Kinderzegels (children's stamps) by the Netherlands since 1924.

Health stamps by New Zealand since 1929.

Zomerzegels (summer stamps), by the Netherlands since 1935.

National Relief Fund stamps, by France since 1935.

Some of the unusual charities for which specific stamps have been issued:

Flood relief – Austria (1921), Belgium (1926), Liechtenstein (1928), Bulgaria (1939), Hungary (1940), Netherlands (1953), Indonesia (1961), Morocco (1970).

Fréjus Dam burst – France (1959).

Avalanche victims – Austria (1954).

Earthquake victims – Greece (1953).

Volcano victims – St Helena (1962), Indonesia (1963), Philippines (1967-8).

Hurricane victims – British Honduras (1962), Samoa (1966), Cook Islands (1968, 1972), St Vincent (1980).

Juvenile delinquents – Costa Rica (1958).

Milk for children – Grenada (1968).

Clothing for army reservists – Sweden (1916).

Dole money for unemployed intellectuals – France (1935-40)

Charity stamps: for unemployed intellectuals (France), children (Switzerland), pro-Austrian vote in plebiscite (Carinthia), prisoners of war (Austria), children (Netherlands), Kingston earthquake victims (Barbados), hurricane relief (Cook Islands), flood damage (Neth. Antilles) and restoration of church windows (Netherlands)

Unemployed artists – Hungary (1940)
Restoration of Gouda Cathedral stained glass windows – the Netherlands (1931).
Help for people in another country – Barbados (1907) for victims of the earthquake in Kingston, Jamaica; Denmark, for victims of flooding in Holland (1953) and Hungarian refugees (1956); German Democratic Republic, for victims of Anglo-French aggression in Egypt and 'socialist Hungarians' (both 1956).
Caisse d'Amortissement (sinking fund) – France (1927-31), to raise funds to reduce the national debt.
Victims of adulterated cooking oil – Morocco (1960).
Victims of an air raid on Piraeus – Greece (1944).
Victims of poison gas attacks – Yemen (1967).
Widows and orphans of the crew and passengers of the *Hans Hedtoft*, lost at sea on 30 January 1959 – Denmark (1959).
Prisoners of war – Hungary (1920), France (1940), Belgium (1942-5), Austria (1947).
Memorial to General Patton – Belgium (1957).
Displaced persons – Belgium (1959).
Austrian stamps overprinted for use in Carinthia during the plebiscite of 1920 bore a premium for a fund to promote a vote in favour of remaining Austrian. The result was, in fact, a vote for Austria instead of Yugoslavia.

The largest premiums on any charity issues. A set of four stamps issued by China in 1932 had a face value of 20c but sold for $5 to raise funds for Sven Hedin's North-west Scientific Expedition. The stamps did not bear any indication of the 2400 per cent premium – the largest ever recorded. Runner-up is the Heligoland Cession stamp of 1940, issued by Nazi Germany. Postally valid for 6 pfennige, it had a premium of 94 pfennige or 1566 per cent. The premiums on the British postal stationery (1890) and 1100 per cent. In recent years charity premiums have been much more moderate, largely as a result of the action of the Fédération Internationale de Philatélie which has declared a boycott of stamps with a premium of more than 50 per cent of the postal value. Nevertheless, the Falklands and Dependencies each issued a £1 stamp with a £1 premium in 1982.

The worst offender in the issue of charity stamps was Nazi Germany. Of the 110 stamps issued for ordinary postage between 9 September 1941 and the collapse of the Third Reich in April 1945, all but five definitives (March 1942) and a solitary 6pf for the SA Military Training Month (August 1942) bore charity premiums, the majority being considerably in excess of the postal value.

Compulsory charity stamps have been issued by several countries for use on mail posted on certain days of the year in addition to the normal postage. They were pioneered by Portugal which issued them from 1911 till 1928 to raise money for the poor, the Lisbon festival, the Portuguese troops in Flanders, a memorial to the Marquis de Pombal and the Portuguese athletes attending the Amsterdam Olympic Games. Greece adopted this principle in 1914 to raise money for the Red Cross and patriotic funds during the Balkan Wars, and continued the practice till 1956, aiding such charities as the Patriotic Charity League, social welfare, postal staff TB fund, the Ionian Islands earthquake victims and the Macedonian cultural fund. Similar stamps have also been used by Romania (1915-36), Yugoslavia (since 1933), Colombia (1935-70) and Ecuador (1920-61). Postage due stamps have been issued by Portugal, Romania and Yugoslavia for the surcharging of mail not bearing these compulsory charity stamps. Compulsory charity stamps have also been issued by several countries for a specific occasion, all mail being thus surcharged over a considerable period. Many British colonies issued War Tax stamps (q.v.) to raise money during the First World War. In more recent years compulsory tax stamps have been issued by West Germany (for the Berlin airlift, 1948), Iraq (Palestinian relief, 1949), Bahrain (Palestinian relief, 1974), Cyprus (refugee relief, 1974, 1977) and India (Bangladesh refugee relief, 1971). Mexico issued a 1c stamp in 1923 to raise money for a campaign to stamp out plagues of locusts.

Cheque stamps were embossed on cheques drawn in Britain and its colonies until 1971. The only instance of a cheque stamp officially utilised for postage occurred in British Central Africa (now Malawi) in 1898. During an acute shortage of penny stamps the embossed oval cheque stamps were struck within a rectangular frame and overprinted INTERNAL POSTAGE. They were not sold direct to the public but were affixed to letters by counter clerks on payment of cash and are thus scarce in mint condition.

Christmas stamps were first issued – apparently unintentionally – by Canada in 1898. The Canadian Post Office reduced their imperial rate from 3 to 2c

Postage due stamps for failure to use compulsory charity stamp (Azores, 1925)

in December 1898. William Mulock, the Postmaster General, himself devised a stamp to commemorate the occasion. This showed a map of the world with the British Empire in red, and included the caption XMAS 1898. Originally it was intended to issue it on 9 November, the birthday of the Prince of Wales. It is said that when a court official told Queen Victoria that the stamp was to be issued on the Prince's birthday, she suspiciously asked, 'Which Prince?' The courtier saved the situation by replying, 'Why, ma'am, the Prince of Peace.' And so the issue was delayed till 7 December.

The first stamps issued specifically for the postage on Christmas greetings cards appeared in Austria in December 1937. Ominously, the stamps – the last to be issued by an independent Austrian postal administration prior to the *Anschluss* – depicted a nosegay and a curious ghost portrait appeared in the design, one of the roses in the vase bearing an uncanny resemblance to Adolf Hitler. Austria resumed the issue of Christmas stamps in 1948, appropriately celebrating the 130th anniversary of *Silent Night*. Hungary issued Christmas stamps in 1943 and Cuba from 1951 onwards. The first Commonwealth country to do so was Australia (1957), which has also issued a Christmas air letter since 1961. Britain adopted Christmas air letters in 1965 and Christmas stamps in 1966.

The oddest Christmas issue was made by Cuba in 1960 and took the form of a sheet of 25 stamps with different designs, showing various flowers. Sixteen of the stamps were arranged in groups of four, surrounded by an oval border on which was inscribed the words and music of a Christmas hymn.

Australia's 7c stamp of 1971 was issued in seven different colour combinations. Each half pane of 25 was laid out in such a way that five stamps were repeated four times, and the others only twice or three times.

Since 1958 Costa Rica has issued obligatory tax stamps in aid of children's charities; these stamps, inscribed *Sello de Navidad* (Christmas stamp) are for compulsory use on greetings cards.

Circular delivery stamps were local issued made in Britain in the 1860s. In 1865 Robert Brydone, an Edinburgh printer and stationer, formed the Edinburgh and Leith Circular Delivery Company and undertook the delivery of circulars and other forms of printed matter in the Edinburgh area for a farthing (¼d). Stamps of this denomination were produced in 1865 and halfpenny stamps added the following year. Similar companies were established in Aberdeen, Glasgow, Liverpool and the London area in 1866-7 and their considerable success was due to the fact that the British Post Office's minimum rate at the time was a penny. In August 1867 the Postmaster General brought an action against Edward Smith, a messenger of the London and Metropolitan companies, on the grounds that his activities infringed the Postmaster General's monopoly on the delivery of letters. Smith was duly convicted and it seemed that the circular delivery companies would be forced out of business. Manuel Eyre, who had purchased Brydone's chain of companies, tried to circumvent the court ruling by issuing sets of stamps with the word 'Circular' omitted. In May 1868 the companies were prosecuted again. Conviction was upheld, despite an appeal, and in June 1869 the companies went into liquidation. Nevertheless, their action forced the Post Office to review the situation and in October 1870 the minimum rate on postcards, newspapers and printed matter was reduced to ½d.

College stamps were issued by the Oxford and Cambridge colleges and also by several business schools in the United States in the nineteenth century. Between 1871 and 1886 Keble, Merton, Lincoln, Hertford, Exeter, All Souls, St John's and Balliol (Oxford) and Queens', St John's and Selwyn (Cambridge) produced stamps which franked letters carried by the college porters within the university precincts. The first to do so was Keble, which issued stamps in 1871. These adhesive stamps were suppressed by the Postmaster General in 1885, but Keble flouted this by issuing envelopes with the college crest on the flap, and regarding this as a 'frank' which permitted transmission by porter as before. In 1970 Keble even produced an adhesive label to celebrate

Canada, Christmas 1898

Edinburgh and Leith Circular Delivery Company stamp, 1867

Queens' College, Cambridge, local stamp

Keble College, commemorative label, 1971

the centenary of the college, and examples of this have been seen on envelopes transmitted by college post. All of the Oxford and Cambridge stamps featured the coat of arms of the respective colleges.

Several aspects of these stamps are noteworthy. The Hertford stamps, lithographed by Spiers & Son, had a marginal imprint in minuscule lettering giving the name and address of the printer – a feature of many American stamps of the period but not adopted by the British Post Office until 1966. While most stamps were printed in sheets, both Merton and Balliol produced stamps in strips. The Merton stamps came in strips of 13, while those of Balliol were printed in strips of 17 containing one *tête-bêche*, the two end stamps being inverted.

British Penny Red stamps were issued between 1859 and 1880 overprinted or underprinted OUS as a security device. These stamps were intended for the use of members of the Oxford Union Society.

Stamps issued by the Friends' Boarding School, Barnsville, Ohio and Westtown School, Pennsylvania, were sold to the students to pay fees on mail taken to the nearest US post office or taken by coach to the railway station. The majority of American college stamps, however, were merely imitation stamps used by the students of business schools in connection with practical exercises in office administration. Several bogus issues of college stamps were made in the 1870s by Samuel Allen Taylor of Boston, purporting to emanate from colleges in the United States and Canada.

COMMEMORATIVE STAMPS

Both adhesive stamps and special postal stationery have been issued to commemorate an event or personality or to celebrate a historic anniversary. Nowadays such stamps are usually on sale for a limited period, concurrent with the definitive (permanent) series, but in the nineteenth century stamps wholly or partly commemorative in character or inspiration might be used for an indefinite period. The distinction between 'commemorative' and 'definitive' therefore tends to become blurred.

Among the contenders for the title of the first commemorative stamps are the following: The first stamps of *Baden* (1851-8) and *Württemberg* (1851-7) bear a tiny inscription in the side panels in German signifying 'German-Austrian Postal Union, 1850', but as this has been held to be authority by which the stamps were issued they are not regarded as commemoratives in the strict sense.

New Brunswick issued a set of pictorial stamps in 1860 and two of these may be regarded as quasi-commemorative. The 1c stamp featured locomotive No 9 and celebrated the completion of the European and North American Railway, 1860, while the 17c, portraying the Prince of Wales in Highland dress, commemorated his visit to the colony in August 1860. Neither stamp, however, drew attention to the commemorative aspect in the inscription. These stamps remained in use till 1868.

France re-issued its definitive stamps in 1863 with a laurel crown added to the brows of the Emperor Napoleon III in commemoration of his victories in the Italian campaign of 1859-60. These stamps remained in use till the downfall of the Second Empire in 1870.

Peru issued a 5c stamp in April 1871 which the Stanley Gibbons catalogue claims as the world's first commemorative. It is inscribed CHORILLOS LIMA and CALLAO on three sides and features a locomotive above the national coat of arms. Since a railway line between Lima and Callao was opened in 1851 it has been deduced that this stamp commemorated the

Peru 5c, 1871, for Lima, Chorillos and Callao local service

twentieth anniversary of the railway. In fact the stamp was inspired solely by the fact that the revolution of 1869 and the overthrow of the dictatorship led to the suppression of the stamps produced by the American Bank Note Company. This, in turn, necessitated new stamps produced locally and these included a 5c specifically intended for the low rate on mail in the Lima, Callao and Chorillos area. This stamp was authorised on 15 September 1869 in a decree stating 'The postage of letters between Lima, Callao and Chorillos is hereby reduced by half; consequently the director-general is authorised to print postage stamps of five centavos, destined for the prepayment of such postage.' The director-general stated on 12 September 1870 that a matrix had been prepared and then went on to describe the design in detail. Significantly no mention was made of any commemoration. The stamp was illustrated and fully described in the contemporary philatelic press but no mention was made of the railway or its anniversary. It would appear, therefore, that the issue of the stamp around the time of the twentieth anniversary was purely coincidental and was not planned for that reason. The stamp remained in use till 1877.

The first issue consciously commemorative in nature consisted of two 3c stamped envelopes, in green or red, issued by the United States in May 1876 to celebrate the Centennial Exposition in Philadelphia. The design showed a horse postman and a train, representing mail transportation old and new, with the dates 1776 and 1876. Quite clearly these embossed stamps celebrated both the Exposition, a current event, and the hundredth anniversary of American Independence, a historic event.

The first adhesive commemorative stamp was a 2pf value produced by the Privat Brief Verkehr of Frankfurt-am-Main in July 1887 in honour of the Ninth German Federal and Jubilee Shooting Competition.

The first adhesive commemorative stamps produced by a government postal administration were those inscribed ONE HUNDRED YEARS, issued by New South Wales in 1888 to mark the centenary of the British settlement at Sydney Cove. The series

comprised ten values, from 1d to 20s, and though clearly commemorative in inscription and subject matter, the stamps were retained in use for 12 years, undergoing numerous changes in colour, watermark and perforation. Thereafter adhesive commemoratives were issued in:

Asia Hong Kong Golden Jubilee (1891) – an overprint on the current 2c stamp.

America El Salvador and Nicaragua both issued sets on 1 January 1892 to celebrate the quatercentenary of Columbus' discovery of America, while Honduras (31 July), Argentina and Paraguay (both 12 October) also commemorated this event.

Europe Montenegro, quatercentenary of printing (1893).

Africa South African Republic (Transvaal), introduction of Penny Postage (1895).

Anxiety at the proliferation of unnecessary stamps of a high face value led to the Society for the Suppression of Speculative Stamps (the four-S League) in 1895, followed by a resolution at the UPU Congress in Washington (1897) that 'stamps issued for a special object peculiar to the country of issue, such as stamps called commemorative stamps and available for a limited time only, should no longer be valid for international postage.' This was never implemented although some countries volun-

USA 3c stamped envelope celebrating the centenary of independence, 1876

New South Wales 4d, 1888, portraying Captain James Cook

tarily restricted the validity of such stamps (e.g., the Central American Exhibition series of Guatemala, 1897, and the Auckland Exhibition set of 1913, restricted to letters and cards in New Zealand and to Australia).

No commemoratives were issued by Germany till 1919, by France till 1923, or by Great Britain till 1924.

The first historic event to be commemorated simultaneously by several countries was the Columbus quatercentenary in 1892 (see above). Stamps were issued by many countries in Latin America, as well as the United States (1893) and two British colonies – Grenada and Trinidad (both 1898) – celebrated this event. In 1897-8 seven countries of the British Empire issued a total of 44 stamps in celebration of Queen Victoria's Diamond Jubilee.

The first omnibus issue, comprising uniform designs issued simultaneously by several countries, appeared in 1898 and celebrated the quatercentenary of Vasco da Gama's discovery of the sea route to India. Stamps were issued by Portugal and her overseas colonies, intaglio-printed by Waterlow and Sons of London. This idea was slow to catch on; France first issued an omnibus series in 1931 for the Colonial Exposition in Paris, while the first British colonial omnibus series appeared in 1935 to celebrate the Silver Jubilee of King George V.

The fastest release of a commemorative stamp after the event was achieved by Czechoslovakia on 13 April 1961 when it succeeded in releasing two stamps to celebrate the first manned space flight which took place on the previous day. The basic stamps, showing an astronaut in space, were designed by F Hudeček and engraved by Ladislav Jirka and recess-printed in anticipation of the event, but an

The first British adhesive commemorative stamp: British Empire Exhibition, 1924

inscription, including the date of the actual launch, was added at the last moment.

The longest commemorative set was issued by Chile on 6 December 1948 and consisted of 25 stamps each of 60 centavos, 2.60 pesos and 3p celebrating the centenary of Claude Gay's book on Chilean fauna and flora. All 75 stamps had different botanical or zoological motifs. Runner-up was a set of 50 stamps issued by the United States in 1976 as part of the Bicentennial programme. The stamps, all of 13c value, featured the flags of all 50 states and were printed side by side in the same sheet. In 1982 the United States issued a sheet of 50 different 20c stamps, each showing the heraldic bird and flower associated with each state.

Philatelic commemoration of Afghan independence became something of a movable feast. The actual declaration took place on 28 February 1919. Stamps were issued annually to celebrate the day rather than the anniversary. At first the same

The earliest commemorative stamps in Asia (Hong Kong, 1891), America (Argentina and El Salvador, 1892), Europe (Montenegro, 1893) and Africa (Transvaal, 1895)

First omnibus issue (Vasco da Gama, 1898) and first British
Commonwealth omnibus (Silver Jubilee, 1935)

design was used each year, but the size of the stamps
varied. To confuse matters, in February 1926 the
seventh *anniversary* was commemorated, the inscriptions being suitably amended and the size reduced
again. Thereafter new designs were used each year.
In 1927-8 the eighth and ninth anniversaries were
commemorated, but no stamps appeared in 1929-30
and when commemoration was resumed in 1931 the
day was celebrated, though there was some confusion in later years when some stamps were wrongly
inscribed ANNIVERSARY. Moreover, in 1931 the
celebration was changed to 24 August (the date of the
armistice), mainly because the weather was more
suitable for the celebration. Exceptionally, however,
the celebration in 1937-9 took place in May because
August was too hot. As the stamp issues coincided
with the beginning of the celebrations the issue dates
tended to move around somewhat disconcertingly.

The longest-delayed commemorative set was
the series of four stamps intended for issue by
Sarawak in 1941 to celebrate the centenary of the
White Rajahs. The stamps were recess-printed by
Bradbury Wilkinson in 1941 but their issue was
postponed on account of the Japanese invasion in
December that year. They were not, in fact, released
until 18 May 1946, a year after the country was
liberated from Japanese rule and 4½ years after the
intended date.

A set of eleven stamps was printed by Harrison
and Sons for Haiti and delivered to that country at
the beginning of 1966 to commemorate Sir Winston
Churchill. The issue was scheduled for 1 February
but was postponed as the entrepreneur master-
minding the deal had failed to complete his part of
the bargain with the postal authorities. The stamps
were eventually released on 23 December 1968 –
almost three years late. Examples of the stamps were
actually circulated to philatelic journalists at the
beginning of 1966.

**Odd anniversaries commemorated by stamps
include:**
19th anniversary of the Faculty of Medicine (Afgha-

nistan, 1950).
27th, 29th and 34th birthdays of the Maharaja
(Travancore, 1939-46).
43rd anniversary of Antarctic postal service (Argentina, 1947).
67th birthday of Chief Justice Fred Castro (Philippines, 1981).
76th anniversary of the UPU (Afghanistan, 1951).
81st anniversary of the execution of medical students
(Cuba, 1952).
82nd anniversary of Henry Lawson (Australia,
1949).
85th anniversary of postal services (Afghanistan,
1955).
104th anniversary of adhesive stamps and 110th
anniversary of the postal service (Sierra Leone, 1963)
112th anniversary of first stamps (Azores and
Madeira, 1980)
207th anniversary of the birth of Robert Burns
(Great Britain, 1966)
Sets commemorating the 441st anniversary of the
departure of Columbus from Palos were issued in
1933 by Brazil, Nicaragua, Paraguay and Uruguay.
550th anniversary of the birth of Mowlana Jami
(Afghanistan, 1964).

**The only instance of definitive and com-
memoratives printed side by side** occurred in
Denmark in January 1937, when a set of three charity
stamps was issued to raise money for the memorial
to H P Hansen, the North Slesvig patriot. The
stamps were issued in booklets which included
ordinary definitive stamps of the same face value (5,
10 or 15 øre). The 5 øre in green (instead of the
normal yellow-green) only exists from these Hansen
booklets. The 10 øre was re-issued, with wider
margins, in a special printing of September 1940, in
booklets side by side with a 10 + 5 øre Red Cross
charity stamp.

**Commemoratives retained as part of the defini-
tive series** have been issued in only one instance in
modern times. Ireland issued ½d and 1s stamps on 30
June 1944 to commemorate the tercentenary of the
death of Michael O'Clery, author of *The Annals of
the Four Masters*. The stamps show a monastic scribe
and were captioned in Gaelic 'To the Glory of God

Ireland Constitution 2d (1937) and Annals of the Four Masters ½d
(1944)

USA block of four 2c stamps depicting the Cape Hatteras National Seashore Park, 1972

and the Honour of Ireland'. Though clearly temporary in nature, they were retained in place of the corresponding definitives (Sword of Light design) and, in fact, remained in use for 24 years.

Ireland also provides an unique example of commemoratives re-issued more than twenty years later in an identical design. Two stamps depicting an allegorical figure of Ireland holding the new constitution, were issued in December 1937 to celebrate the constitution which altered the status from a free state to an independent country. In December 1958 the 21st anniversary of the republican constitution was celebrated by re-issuing the design of 1937 in new values and colours (to take into account increased postal rates) and printed on the 'e' watermarked paper which had been introduced in 1940.

Composite stamps, in which the design is spread over two or more stamps, were first issued by Poland in April 1957. Two 60 groszy stamps were printed side by side showing duelling fencers. In June 1960 Poland went a stage farther with a set of Olympic stamps issued in blocks of four different subjects which together made up a complete circuit of the racing track. Cuba followed this example, in December 1960, with Christmas stamps arranged in blocks of four to make up the words and music of a Christmas hymn (see page 141).

Britain had issued multiple strips and blocks of stamps (each with separate designs) from 1965, but the first true composite issue was the strip of five 12p stamps marking the 150th anniversary of the Liverpool and Manchester Railway (1980). The first US issue of this kind was a block of four stamps in 1972 depicting the Cape Hatteras National Seashore Park.

St Lucia's Easter series of 1970 depicted the Hogarth Triptych and was not only spread over the three stamps, but simulated the staggered effect of the original by having the side stamps positioned lower in the sheet than the centre stamp.

Concentration camp stamps were issued on two occasions during the Second World War. An undenominated green stamp showing an innocuous country scene was issued in July 1943 by the Nazis to the inmates of the Theresienstadt (Teresin) camp in Czechoslovakia. These stamps could then be sent to friends and relatives in order to frank parcels to the camp.

The Jewish Council in the ghetto of Lodz were permitted to organise a local post and issued stamps in March 1944 inscribed in German JUDENPOST LITZMANNSTADT GETTO (Jewish post Lodz ghetto).

After the war Polish displaced persons interned in the former concentration camp at Dachau-Allach organised their own postal service and issued stamps in pfennig denominations, showing the Polish eagle and flag. These stamps were re-issued a month later (September 1945) as a miniature sheet with a premium in aid of the Red Cross. The Dachau stamps were withdrawn at the end of 1945.

Concessional letter and parcel stamps have been issued by Italy since July 1928. They are an admirable way out of the age-old problem of protecting the postal monopoly from enterprising organisations and individuals who are capable of offering a more efficient service at a purely local level. These stamps are issued by the Italian Post Office for the use of private companies and agencies which are permitted to deliver mail on payment of a small fee per item. These stamps are inscribed RECAPITO AUTORIZZATO (Authorised Delivery). Since 1953 bipartite (q.v.) stamps have been issued for concessional parcel post (*trasporto pacchi in concessione*).

Departmental stamps, for the use of government departments, were first issued by South Australia which overprinted definitive stamps between 1868 and 1874 with the initials of no fewer than 54 different departments, in red, blue or black ink.

Dachau-Allach Polish camp post 3m, 1945

Italy 35L concessional letter post, and 900L concessional parcel post stamps

Europa stamps of West Germany (1956) and Italy (1957)

They ranged alphabetically from A (Architect) to W (Waterworks) and included B.G. (Botanic Garden), G.T. (Goolwa Tramway), I.S. (Inspector of Sheep), L.A. (Lunatic Asylum), M.R.G. (Main Roads, Gambier), P.A. (Protector of Aborigines) and V.A. (Valuator and Auctioneer). These stamps were superseded by a general issue overprinted O.S. (Official Service).

Government departments in the United States were allowed to send mail post free, but this franking privilege was so abused that it was abolished by Act of Congress on 1 July 1873. Instead, each of the nine executive departments got their own stamps. Each series ranged from 1c to 90c (except the Agriculture Department whose set terminated at 30c) and the Department of State (which went up to $20). These stamps portrayed a different president or political figure for each denomination, the same person appearing on the corresponding value of each set. Each department, however, had stamps in a distinctive colour. The Post Office Department also had its own stamps, printed in black and bearing the numerals of value instead of portraits. These stamps were superseded by penalty envelopes on 1 May 1879, the envelopes showing the amount of the penalty for misuse. Special stamps were again issued (1910-11) for use by the US Postal Savings Bank.

USA Department of the Interior 3c, 1873

Britain issued stamps for certain government departments at various times from 1882 till 12 May 1904. They consisted of definitive stamps overprinted to denote Inland Revenue, Office of Works, Army, Admiralty, Board of Education and Royal Household. In addition, stamps were overprinted for use on government parcels.

Argentinian stamps were overprinted with the initials of eight government departments, between 1913 and 1938.

Europa stamps are issued annually by member countries of the CEPT (*Conference Européen des Postes et Telecommunications*). The concept of a joint issue arose in 1956 when the six members of the Coal and Steel Community – Belgium, Netherlands, Luxembourg, France, West Germany and Italy – issued a pair of stamps in a uniform design showing scaffolding around a tower inscribed EUROPA (Europe). Uniform designs were used in 1957-9 by the same six countries, but since 1960 the Europa theme has been taken over by CEPT. In that year Britain was among the nineteen member countries to use Pente Rahikainen's wheel with nineteen spokes emblem for two stamps. In 1961 a motif showing nineteen doves was devised by Theo Kupershoek of Holland and again Britain took part in the issue, but then dropped out until 1980. Uniform designs of a symbolic nature were used by the member countries until 1974 when it was decided that stamps should be issued in a common theme, but avoiding the monotony of the uniform designs. In that year sculpture was selected, and in subsequent years paintings, traditional crafts, scenery, architecture, communications history, cultural celebrities and folklore have been used. The stamps are generally issued in May-June each year.

Exile stamps have been issued by governments temporarily forced to flee their own country due to invasion by enemy powers. In August 1914 Belgium was invaded and rapidly occupied by German forces east of Ypres and the river Yser, and the Belgian government was forced to evacuate Brussels, and make its headquarters at Le Havre, France on 13 October 1914, where it remained until late in 1918. Belgian stamps portraying King Albert were printed by Waterlow and Sons in England and used by the government-in-exile at Le Havre. In 1916 the Serbian government and armed forces, having retreated through Albania, took up their abode on the Greek island of Corfu and used French stamps overprinted POSTES SERBES. Similarly French stamps were overprinted for the use of the Montenegrin government in exile at Bordeaux in 1916. Czech and Slovak soldiers in the Austro-Hungarian armies surrendered to the Russians and more than 70 000 of them were formed into the Czechoslovak legions which fought the Bolsheviks in Siberia in 1919-20. They issued stamps for their own postal service, based on Irkutsk, and also sold them to civilians for use along the route of the Trans-Siberian Railway which they controlled.

During the Second World War stamps were issued on behalf of governments-in-exile in several countries. Stamps inscribed for use in Czechoslovakia, the Netherlands, Norway and Yugoslavia were printed in England and used by military units, embassies and ships at sea.

The most diverse of these exile posts were operated by the Poles who used military franchise stamps of France (1939-40), special stamps printed by Bradbury Wilkinson or De La Rue for use on Polish ships and at certain military camps in Britain (1941-5), a 50 kopek stamps at Jangi-Jul near

Tashkent, USSR (1942) and a series in Italian currency for use at Bari (1944).

Express Delivery stamps were pioneered by private companies in the United States and Canada to denote the prepayment of fees on letters, business papers, packets, parcels and luggage transmitted by their services. The express system was founded in 1839 by William Frederick Harnden, a conductor on the Boston and Worcester Railway who began carrying small parcels as a sideline but soon left to form his own express company. Private express companies proliferated in the 1840s and seriously undermined the US Post Office and in 1872 an Act of Congress attempted to limit their activities. Nevertheless the express companies continued to thrive until 1912 when the US introduced a parcel post and thereafter their operations were more limited.

The first government stamps for express or special delivery services were issued by the United States on 1 October 1885, a 10c stamp being provided for a service which had been inaugurated as a result of a law enacted on 4 March 1885. The stamp showed a running messenger and was inscribed SECURES IMMEDIATE DELIVERY AT A SPECIAL DELIVERY OFFICE. At first special delivery could only be offered at special offices in towns with more than 4000 inhabitants but an amendment was enacted on 4 August 1886 making special delivery available for all classes of mail at all free delivery offices and within a mile of all other post offices. The stamp was consequently re-issued with the inscription altered to read AT ANY POST OFFICE.

Stamps inscribed SPECIAL DELIVERY or EXPRESS, or their equivalents in other languages, were subsequently issued by Canada (1898), New Zealand, Italy

Czech Legion in Siberia (1919-20), French stamps perforated for Polish military use (1939), stamps issued in wartime Britain for use by Norwegian, Dutch, Polish and Yugoslav forces

Express Delivery stamps of USA (1888), and Canada (1898); Air
Express stamp of Canada (1942)

and Mauritius (all 1903), China, Spain (1905), and
Mexico (1919). Airmail express and special delivery
stamps have also been issued by Italy, Canada,
Colombia and the United States, express parcel
stamps by the Vatican and express newspaper and
printed matter stamps by Czechoslovakia.

First Day Covers are covers bearing stamps
postmarked on the first day of issue. Although
covers are known from the Penny Black (1840)
onwards used on the first day of issue, the deliberate
practice of posting covers in this manner for
philatelic purposes is believed to have started in the
United States on 25 September 1909 when souvenir
envelopes were prepared by a private stationer in
connection with the Hudson-Fulton 2c stamp issued
on that date. This practice did not become widespread in America till the 1920s, but isolated
examples have been recorded from Europe, and
souvenir envelopes are known in connection with

the first George V stamps of Great Britain, issued in
May 1911.

**The first postmark inscribed FIRST DAY OF
ISSUE** was issued in the United States in 1937.
France, Germany, Italy and Sweden adopted First
Day cancellations in the early 1940s.

Britain adopted First Day of Issue cancellations in
May 1963, for the Paris Postal Conference stamp.
Special first day covers were adopted in April 1964,
in connection with the Shakespeare Festival series.

Foreign mail stamps have been issued in certain
countries for use on mail going abroad, to distinguish them from mail destined for internal delivery.
The first country to produce separate sets for inland
and internal mail was Turkey, which issued such
stamps, mainly for printed matter, between 1901 and
1911. The first issue in particular was often used
indiscriminately on both inland and external mail.

A first day cover commemorating the historic adoption of the
Northwest Ordinance under the Articles of Confederation

Haiti issued stamps between 1906 and 1919 for overseas mail, with denominations in 'strong' currency (piastres) instead of local currency or gourdes.

Both Guatemala (1931-45) and Chile (1934-52) issued separate sets of airmail stamps for foreign and inland mail.

Forgeries of stamps have been made on many occasions for various reasons, to defraud the postal administration, to cheat collectors, and for propaganda purposes. **The first instance of a forged stamp** occurred in 1840 when an attempt was made to counterfeit Penny Blacks using a wood engraving. Sir Rowland Hill referred to this in his diary as 'a miserable thing which could not possibly deceive any except the most stupid and ignorant'. The Penny Black was forged again, in March 1841, this time from an electrotype. In one case the perpetrator was never caught. In the other the counterfeiter, an Irish youth, was convicted after the forgery was detected on a letter to his girlfriend and was found to contain an unused specimen which he had enclosed for her use in reply.

The earliest forgeries were all postal, intended to defraud the revenue. The biggest problem was encountered by the Spanish Post Office which was reduced to changing the design of its stamps virtually every year from 1850 till 1879 to defeat the forgers. Other notable examples of postal forgeries are:

France 20c (1870), 15c (1886), Sower 25c (1923).
Germany 10pf (1902), 10pf (1909).
Great Britain 1s (1872), 4d World Cup Winners (1966).
Australia 2d Sydney Harbour Bridge (1932).
USA 13c Liberty Bell (1980).

By the 1860s the development of stamp-collecting had encouraged the fraudulent imitation of stamps by unscrupulous dealers for sale to philatelists. As early as 1862 the Belgian dealer J B Moens published his book *De la falsification des timbres-poste* shortly followed, in England, by *Forged Stamps: How to Detect Them* by E L Pemberton and *Album Weeds* by W B Earee. The earliest forgers in this market were the Spiro Brothers of Hamburg, followed by Foure (Paris), Panelli (Italy), Benjamin, Sarpy and Jeffryes (the 'London Gang'), François Fournier (Geneva), Georg Zechmeyer (Nuremberg), Erasmus Oneglia (Italy), Samuel Allen Taylor (Boston), Jean de Sperati (Aix-les-Bains) and Raoul de Thuin (Mexico).

Stamps have been forged by postal administrations for various reasons. As early as 1856 the British Post Office commissioned an engraver to forge 1d stamps to see whether the various safety features incorporated in the design were fraud-proof. In 1876 the US Post Office commissioned forgeries of the 1847 5c and 10c stamps from the Bureau of Engraving and Printing for inclusion in an exhibit of American stamps at the Centennial Exposition. As the plates and dies of the original issue had been destroyed it was necessary to forge them, whereas later issues could merely be reprinted from the existing plates.

Stamps have been forged for propaganda purposes since 1918 when the British government authorised the counterfeiting of the low-value definitives of Austria, Bavaria and Germany. These forgeries were used to frank leaflets, brochures and postcards purporting to emanate from these enemy countries. These forged documents were then meant to be air-dropped on neutral countries – Holland and Switzerland – in an attempt to influence them in favour of the Allies, but it seems that the project was abandoned. The only examples known to have been used postally were circulated in Germany after the Armistice and during the Allied occupation of 1919-20.

During the Second World War British Intelligence arranged for the forgery of contemporary German (Hitler Head) and Vichy French (Marshal Pétain) stamps. German stamps were also forged for espionage and propaganda purposes in Switzerland and the Soviet Union. The British even produced a counterfeit 6pf portraying Heinrich Himmler instead of Hitler, and circulated examples on postcards in the Third Reich with a view to sowing the seeds of dissension in the Nazi ranks. The Germans, for their part, countered with crude forgeries of British definitive and commemorative stamps (Silver Jubilee 1935 and Coronation 1937), but none of these came to light till after the war.

In more recent years West German forgeries of East German stamps, inscribed UNDEUTSCHE UNDEMOKRATISCHE REPUBLIK (Ungerman Undemocratic Republic), have been produced, while the Rhodesian stamp celebrating the Unilateral Declaration of Independence (1965) was forged in England, allegedly for propaganda reasons but mainly intended for sale to collectors.

Guerilla stamps were first issued by the 'Black Flag Republic' in Taiwan in September-October 1895, following the cession of the island to Japan after the third Sino-Japanese War. This was a Chinese underground movement which refused to acknowledge the terms of the surrender. The Republic and its stamps were speedily and brutally suppressed by the Japanese.

Later issues include the KKK stamps of the Aguinaldo partisans in the Philippines (1898), the Boer Commando issues in the South African War (1899-1902), the IRA stamps used in Co. Cork during the Irish Civil War (1922-3), the prolific issues of the Communist partisans in China from

Commando Brief stamp of the Orange Free State, 1899

1929 onwards, the stamps of the National Front for the Liberation of South Vietnam (1963-76) and the republican overprints in 'free Derry' (1972).

Health stamps, bearing premiums on behalf of children's health camps and TB sanatoria, have been issued by New Zealand since 1929, but had their origin in the New South Wales charity stamps of 1897 which bore a premium in aid of a consumptives' home (see page 138). The only other country to issue health stamps was Fiji (1951, 1954).

Interpostal seals were issued in Egypt between 1864 and 1890 for use on internal mail. They were circular and affixed to the backs of envelopes. The labels were inscribed in Egyptian across the centre, and in Italian, or latterly French, round the upper part of the circumference, with the name of the issuing post office round the foot. They were introduced by Giacomo Muzzi in 1864, when he was granted a 10-year monopoly of the Egyptian posts provided he carried all government mail free of charge. The interpostal seals were attached to these government letters. Muzzi's service was so successful that the Khedive Ismail bought the concession back from

Fiji Health stamp, 1951

New Zealand Health stamp, 1929

him, granted him a title of nobility and appointed him first Postmaster General.

Journal Tax stamps were issued by Austria between 1853 and 1890. They did not prepay postage as such but denoted a tax on newspapers collected by the Post Office and, like the handstruck stamps in Britain, permitted the transmission of newspapers by post without further charge. These stamps were inscribed ZEITUNGS-STÄMPEL (newspaper stamp). Confusingly, stamps prepaying the postage on newspapers and periodicals were also issued at the same time and apart from the initial issue of 1851-6, had no inscription at all, the portrait of Mercury being sufficient identification. An inscription denoting their purpose – ZEITUNGSMARKE (newspaper stamp) was not added to the design till 1916.

Similar stamps, combining postal and fiscal charges on newspapers, were issued by France in 1868 in denominations of 5 centimes (for use in the Department of the Seine and Oise) and 2 centimes (for use everywhere else). These stamps were affixed to the newspapers prior to printing, so that the typescript effectively cancelled them.

Keyplate designs were used by the various colonial powers in the nineteenth and early twentieth centuries in their overseas territories, as an economic way of printing stamps for many countries at the lowest possible cost. The idea originated in the period 1848-54 when Perkins Bacon produced stamps for Mauritius, Barbados and Trinidad using a standard design showing Britannia seated on sugar bags. Separate plates were engraved for each colony, using the same master die. This was taken to its logical conclusion in 1879 when De La Rue produced head and duty plates for a series of stamps issued by Nevis. The Queen's profile was contained in an octagon, with the name of the colony in a panel at the top and the value in a panel at the foot. This standard design, with only the names of the colonies and the values altered, was also used later the same year for stamps released by Antigua. The Virgin Islands (1880), Cyprus and Turks Islands (1881) and St Lucia (1882) also used this keyplate design and, in a modified form, it was also adopted by Natal and Grenada (1883).

A second keyplate design was evolved by 1889 and this remained in use, with changes of royal profile, as late as 1956 (Leeward Islands).

Colonial key types were adopted by the other European imperial powers. Spain (1855) and Portugal (1870) at first adopted the 'Britannia' principle, with identical designs in the various colonies and the mother country, derived from the same master die but keyplates, with separate head and duty plates, were not adopted by Portugal till 1897. France followed Britain's lead with the 'Tablet' design

Keyplate stamps used by the French, German, Portuguese and British colonies

(1892) and the Palms-Faidherbe-Ballay designs confined to the colonies in West Africa (1906-8). In 1900-1 Germany adopted the 'Hohenzollern' key types in her overseas territories. Spain, Belgium, Denmark and the Netherlands preferred uniform designs rather than standard keyplates.

Labels have been attached to stamps for various reasons. Advertising labels, printed alongside stamps, first appeared in stamp booklets in Germany in November 1910, followed by Bavaria in 1911. Other countries adopted this practice: Great Britain (1924), Belgium (1927), Ireland (1931) and the United States (1962). In 1924-5 Italy issued definitive stamps with advertising labels alongside, as an

Bohemia and Moravia Red Cross 60+40h, 1940

Belgium prisoner of war charity 5+45fr, 1942

integral part of the stamp (i.e., without perforations separating the stamp and the label). This was revived in 1942 for a series with war propaganda labels alongside.

Commemorative stamps with labels alongside were first issued by Czechoslovakia on 1 March 1935. These stamps, celebrating the 85th birthday of President Masaryk, were issued in sheets of 100 stamps with twelve blank labels. Other issues also had blank labels, but from the mourning issue for Masaryk (September 1937) onwards, the labels bore a commemorative inscription. Though only used intermittently by Czechoslovakia since 1949 it has since been used by other countries, notably Israel whose definitive and commemorative stamps since 1948 have invariably had descriptive 'tabs' attached to the bottom row of stamps.

Charity stamps with labels denoting the surcharge or the purpose of the issue were first issued by Hungary in 1913-16, descriptive labels being printed below the contemporary definitive stamps. A similar principle was used by Germany in 1922 for a pair of stamps with a premium in aid of the elderly and the very young. In this case, however, an entirely new design was used, with the charity inscription on a white label at the foot. In 1926 Belgium modified the St Martin charity stamps of 1910 and incorporated a label with a premium for flood relief at the foot.

Both definitive and commemorative stamps with dominical labels were issued by Belgium from 1893 till 1914. These labels, inscribed in French and Flemish 'Do not deliver on Sunday' are known as bandalettes or dominical labels. They provided a method whereby the sender could indicate (by leaving the label intact) that the letter or card was not to be delivered to the addressee on Sundays, since many people's Sabbatarian principles were offended by such secular matters. Where no objection was raised to Sunday delivery, the sender merely detached the label.

Postage stamps with labels converting them to fiscal usage were issued by the Mexican state of Sonora in 1913. The fiscal labels were supposed to be

Israel 'Operation Magic Carpet' 30a (1970) and tab with
biblical text; Hungary charity 10f (1913); Belgium, 10c with
dominical label (1894)

removed before the stamps were used on mail, but
postally used examples of the stamps, with labels
intact, have been recorded.

Labels for airmail incorporating postage were
issued by Mozambique in 1932, a space being
provided for the manuscript insertion of the airmail
fee. In 1937 the airmail fee was combined with the
ordinary postal charge and the label then reverted to
being merely an indication of the service.

Late Fee stamps, denoting the additional charge
levied on mail posted after the normal collection
hours, have been issued by several Latin American
countries: Colombia (1888-1914), Ecuador (1945),
Panama (1903-16) and Uruguay (1936). These
stamps are usually inscribed RETARDO.

Life Insurance stamps have been issued by New
Zealand since 1891. These are intended for the postal
use of the Government Life Insurance Department.
A unique feature of these stamps is that their motifs
have always depicted lighthouses. A stylised lighthouse appeared on the stamps from 1891 till 1947 but
since then pictorial designs, featuring actual lighthouses, have been employed. The 1947 series
included a stamp showing Eddystone Lighthouse off
the southwest coast of England, but all the others
have been around the coasts of New Zealand.

**The only stamp combining postal validity with
participation in a lottery** was issued by Norway
on 1 June 1964. It depicted the UN emblem and was
inscribed PORTO BETALT LYKKEBREVET (Postage
Paid – Chain [Good Luck] Letter). It had a franking
value of 50 øre but was sold for 2.50 kroner, the
balance being given to the Refugee Fund. In
addition, each stamp bore a serial number representing participation in a lottery which took place in
September. The stamp remained on sale till 15 July
and was postally valid till 10 August.

Mexico (Sonora) 2c, 1913

Belgian stamps of 1893-1914 with dominical labels
attached

New Zealand, First Day cover for the Government Life Insurance series of 1947

Marine Insurance stamps were issued by the Netherlands and the Netherlands Indies in 1921 in connection with a special service known as the DRIJVENDE BRANDKAST (floating safe). This was a special steel container attached to the boat deck of ships plying between Holland and the Far East. The safe was secured to the deck by four arms which were automatically released if the ship sank. The safe then floated free, to be salvaged later. A special tariff for floating safe letters was promulgated at the Madrid Congress of the UPU in 1920. This was proposed as a result of the loss of ships from mines and torpedoes in the closing years of the First World War. The idea was conceived by the Dutch firm of Van Blaaderen who constructed the safes. The service was little used and postally used examples of the stamps are very rare. The 1924 UPU Congress abolished the floating safe tariff. A similar service known as *Simmande Kassaskåp,* was provided by the Swedish Post Office on ships plying between Grisslehamn in Roslagen and Ekerö in the Åland Islands, but no stamps were provided for this purpose.

Military Post stamps, for the use of troops on active service, were first issued on 1 July 1879 in the Turkish districts of Bosnia and Herzegovina, following Austrian occupation the previous year. Due to

insurrection by the local Slav population as well as Turkish rebels, the postal service was at first restricted to the military field post, Austrian and Hungarian stamps being thus used. On 9 January 1879 the service was partially extended to civilian use and Austrian and Hungarian stamps were withdrawn when the distinctive stamps were introduced on 1 July. These stamps featured the Habsburg coat of arms and numerals of value, but were otherwise uninscribed. The name of the territory did not appear on the stamps till 1906 and from 1912 onwards the words K.U.K. MILITÄR POST (Royal and Imperial Military Post) were also inscribed. Some of the later issues omitted the names Bosnia and Herzegovina, but can be identified by the reference to the military post.

Rather confusingly, the Austrians also issued stamps during the First World War inscribed K.U.K. FELDPOST, but these were confined to areas occupied by Austro-Hungarian forces, and were overprinted (and sometimes surcharged in the local currency) for use in Italy, Montenegro, Romania and Serbia.

Other instances of stamps being issued for the use of troops in the field:

1900 Indian stamps overprinted C.E.F. (China Expeditionary Force), for use during the Boxer Rebellion.

1914 Indian stamps overprinted I.E.F. (Indian Expeditionary Forces); Anglo-French occupation of Togoland and Cameroons.

Military Post stamps for the China Expeditionary Force (1900), Bosnia (1914), Austrian-occupied territory (1915), Liberian Field Force (1918), Nyasaland Field Force (1918), Polish Corps in Russia (1918), East African Forces (1943), Yugoslav military occupation of Trieste (1947) and Indian UN Forces in the Congo (1962)

1916   British fieldpost Salonika, Long Island.
1918   German 9th Army (Romania); German 10th Army (Ukraine); Liberian Field Force; Nyasaland Field Force; Polish Army Corps (Russia).
1919   Czechoslovak Army in Siberia; Northern Army, Northwestern Army and Western Army (Russia).
1920   Petlyura fieldpost in Western Ukraine.
1923   Italian naval occupation of Corfu.
1940   German occupation of northern France.
1941   Flemish Legion, French Volunteers (Waffen SS).
1942   Walloon Legion (Waffen SS); Middle East Forces (UK); Polish fieldpost in Russia; Free French Forces (Levant).
1943   East African Forces (Somalia).
1944   Danish Legion (Waffen SS); Italian naval base (Bordeaux); Festung Lorient; German military forces in Macedonia.
1945   German fieldpost in Courland.
1953   Indian Custodian Forces (Korea).
1954   Indian forces with the International Commission in Indo-China (Laos, Cambodia and Vietnam).
1962   UN Force (India) in Congo.
1965   UN Force (India) in Gaza.

Military Franchise stamps, permitting troops on active service to send letters, cards and parcels free of postage, were first issued by Brazil during the war of 1865-70 against Paraguay. The stamps bore a typeset inscription EXERCITO EN OPERACOES CONTRA O PARAGUAY (Army on operations against Paraguay). During the Spanish expedition against Morocco (1893-4) free postage was granted to troops on active service. Labels inscribed FRANQUICIA POSTAL ESPANA CORREOS EJERCITO EXPEDICIONARIO MELILLA 1893 (Postal Franchise, Spanish Posts Expeditionary Army Melilla 1893) were produced privately and distributed free to the troops, apparently with the permission of the Spanish government. These labels, despite their inscription, were purely unofficial and not strictly necessary, but were very popular on account of their attractive patriotic motifs. Different sets were produced for each regiment as well as the battle fleet.

A set of three labels produced by the Paymaster of the US Volunteer Army, Major Brewster Cox Kenyon, in 1898 during the Spanish-American War, was also unofficial, despite its design – the American eagle and shield, and inscriptions – ARMY FRANK, OFFICIAL BUSINESS ONLY. Other semi-official stamps include the very prolific issues of the Swiss Army, and the labels produced by various British regiments in Northern Ireland in the 1970s.

Between 1932 and 1936 British forces in the Canal Zone of Egypt were permitted to send letters home at reduced rates, denoted by special seals sold in the NAAFI canteens. They were superseded in 1936 by special stamps, inscribed ARMY POST, provided by

France FM (*Franchise Militaire*) undenominated stamp (1946)

the Egyptian Post Office.

Stamps overprinted or inscribed F.M. (*Franchise Militaire*) have been issued by France since 1901. Danish stamps overprinted SF (*Soldater Frimaerke*) were issued in 1917. Other countries which have issued military franchise stamps include Finland, Germany, Vietnam and Japan. In 1929 Sweden introduced military reply franks which were attached to the flaps of military letters and needed only to be cut out by the recipient and affixed to ordinary letters sent in reply. Nazi Germany issued franks for use by the Afrika Korps (1942) and parcel franks permitting the transmission of parcels up to 2 kg from troops on active service to their families. Military airmail franks were issued in 1942-5 to airlift soldiers' mail from beleaguered garrisons, especially on the Eastern Front. In 1968 the US Post Office issued a $1 stamp inscribed AIRLIFT FOR OUR SERVICEMEN, permitting a reduced parcels rate to military and naval personnel stationed in Alaska, Hawaii and Puerto Rico.

Miniature sheets are small sheets containing a single stamp, pair, block of four, strip or set, with wide margins, often with a special inscription or ornamental device, issued as a commemorative souvenir, and often sold at a premium over face value.

Forerunners of miniature sheets are the definitive series issued by Ethiopia in 1894, often claimed as the world's first miniature sheets since the stamps were issued in blocks of four. As these stamps were never put on sale, however, they can only be classed as essays (trial designs, which are not issued). The Afghan parcel post stamps of 1921 were issued in small sheets of two or four, either in a strip or a block, with perforations on only one or two sides. In the same year the Indian state of Barwani issued its first stamps in small sheets of four, usually imperforate on the outer sides, and stapled together in booklet form.

The first true miniature sheet was issued by Luxembourg on 3 January 1923. A special printing of the new 10fr definitive, in green instead of black, was produced as a single stamp in sheets ranging from 78 × 59 mm to 79 × 61 mm in size. The miniature sheets were sold as a souvenir of the birth of Princess Elisabeth. The definitive itself was not issued until the following March in orthodox sheet form, with a different colour and gauge of perforation. Although Luxembourg did not issue another miniature sheet till 1937 this triggered off a fashion which spread like wildfire in the inter-war period and reached such proportions that Stanley Gibbons announced in 1937 that they would no longer list them in their catalogues. Thirty years later, however, Gibbons were forced to bow to popular opinion and re-instate them. Since then there have even been special catalogues devoted to them.

Belgium (1924) issued a block of four 5 franc stamps in red-brown instead of deep purple in a miniature sheet as a souvenir of the Brussels Philatelic Exhibition. Thereafter variety was injected into these sheets by (*a*) altering colours, (*b*) perforations – often issued imperforate or with facsimile perforations, (*c*) bleeding the colour into the perforations, as distinct from the normal sheet issue with a white margin round each stamp.

The first miniature sheet to combine two or more stamps of different designs or values side by side was issued by Belgium on 15 September 1937 and featured four stamps with premiums for the Queen Elisabeth Music Fund.

The first miniature sheet to project the design into the marginal paper was issued by Israel in 1960, the 25 agorot stamp showing a Prague postal courier of 1741 from an old engraving. The

German military airmail (1942), USA $1 reduced parcel rate for servicemen (1968)

surrounding sheet reproduced the rest of the engraving.

The largest miniature sheet was issued by the German Democratic Republic in 1964 to celebrate the fifteenth anniversary of the republic. It contained fifteen different imperforate stamps superimposed on a map of the country and measured 210 × 285 mm.

Mourning stamps are stamps issued to mark national bereavement. The earliest stamps were printed in black or with a heavy black border, but more recent issues have tended to be less sombre.

Controversy exists over the first mourning stamps. A few Cape Triangular 4d stamps are known in black instead of blue and from the fact that they were later found to have been used in 1861-2 it was thought that they had been issued as a mark of respect for Prince Albert, the Prince Consort, who died in December 1861. However, references to these stamps appeared in the philatelic press before news of the Prince's death could have reached the Cape, so it has since been deduced that the stamps came from proof sheets, pressed into service during a shortage of the normal stamps.

A claim is often advanced for the US 15c grey-black stamp of June 1866 as the world's first mourning stamp. This portrayed Abraham Lincoln, assassinated on 14 April 1865. The gap of 14 months between Lincoln's death and the issue of the stamp, and the fact that it remained in use as a definitive till 1869, preclude it from being regarded as a mourning stamp in the strict sense, although it was undoubtedly intended as a mark of respect for the late president. The British 7d grey-black stamp of 1910 is popularly

Right Hungary 10 ft miniature sheet for the World Cup, 1962

believed to be a mourning stamp but as it was issued on 4 May – 2 days *before* King Edward VII died, and had been planned months earlier, this was purely coincidental.

The first stamps specifically issued for public mourning were released in 1888 by the Courier Stadtbrief Beförderung, a German local postal service. The stamps were printed in black and portrayed the Emperor William I who died that year. When his son, the Emperor Frederick III, died a few months after his accession, the company issued a set

The smallest imperforate miniature sheet (Aitutaki, 1984: actual dimension 45 × 53 mm) and the smallest perforated sheet (Hungary, 1987: actual dimension 50 × 60 mm)

of mourning stamps, with his portrait heavily edged in black. The Imperial German Post ignored both occasions and no official mourning stamps were issued by Germany till 1934 when black-edged stamps mourned the late President Hindenburg.

The first official government issue of mourning stamps was made by the United States in September 1923 when a 2c stamp in black portrayed President Warren G Harding who died suddenly on 2 August. The same design, in brown, was used for a definitive 1½c stamp introduced in 1925. A 17c black stamp was issued in 1925 after the death of ex-President Woodrow Wilson but retained as part of the definitive series till 1938. The second issue of official mourning stamps appeared in Russia within days of Lenin's death on 21 January 1924, printed in red with a heavy black border. These stamps were reprinted and re-issued on the anniversary of Lenin's death each January till 1928.

The first mourning stamps issued outside the home country of the deceased appeared in 1945 in memory of President Franklin D Roosevelt. Mourning stamps were issued on that occasion by Greece, Hungary, Haiti, Honduras and Nicaragua. Other countries, including El Salvador, Guatemala and Brazil, issued memorial stamps over a period of several years thereafter.

The largest number of different mourning stamps for one person was issued on behalf of Sir Winston Churchill, some 287 stamps and 14 miniature sheets being issued by 73 countries within 12 months of his death in January 1965. The runner-up was John F Kennedy, for whom 183 stamps and 32 miniature sheets were issued by 44 countries. Memorial issues for both men have continued to trickle forth in the years since their deaths.

The rarest regularly issued mourning stamp is the 10 rupee value of the Mahatma Gandhi mourning set, issued by India in August 1948, with SERVICE overprinted for the official correspondence of the Governor General – only 100 stamps were issued.

Newspaper stamps, prepaying the postage on newspapers and periodicals, were first issued by Austria on 1 January 1851. They were undenominated but the value was indicated by the colour – blue (0·6kr), yellow (6kr) or rose (30kr). In 1856 the colour of the 6kr was changed to red but as the 'Red Mercury' had a very short life it now ranks as the world's rarest newspaper stamp. These stamps were inscribed ZEITUNGS POST STEMPEL (newspaper postage stamp) to distinguish them from the imperial journal tax stamps which were inscribed ZEITUNGS STEMPEL. A curious feature of Austrian newspaper stamps was that they were all issued imperforate, despite the fact that they continued in use until 1921. Apart from a few issues of 1858-63, all Austrian newspaper stamps portrayed Mercury, winged messenger of the gods, and did not include the name of the country until 1916.

The first newspaper stamp in the British Commonwealth was issued by New Zealand in 1873. The American newspaper stamps, issued in 1865, measured 51 × 95 mm and were, until 1911, the largest stamps in the world. The US $100 newspaper stamp of 1896, depicting Minnehaha, was the highest valued stamp in the world until 1912.

Occupation stamps were first issued by the German Federal Commissioners in the duchy of Holstein on 1 March 1864 following the invasion by Austrian and Prussian forces. By the Convention of Gastein, the administration of Holstein was handed over to Austria in November 1865 and stamps were thereafter issued by the Austrians for use in Holstein. Joint issues of stamps were made by Austria and Prussia in the neighbouring duchy of Schleswig in 1864-5 and by Prussia alone between November 1865 and 1867. Dispute over the administration of the former Danish duchies led to the Seven Weeks' War between Austria and Prussia (1866) and the complete takeover of the duchies by Prussia. On 1 January 1868 the duchies were absorbed into the North German Confederation and used its stamps from then onwards.

Stamps for use in occupied territory were subsequently issued by the North German Confederation for use in Alsace-Lorraine and other parts of France

Mourning stamps from the USA (1923) and USSR (1924)

Newspaper stamps from New Zealand (1873) and Austria (1920)

occupied by German forces during the war of 1870-1. These were inscribed in French language and currency to avoid offending the national sensitivity of the French.

Other occupation issues include:

1878-83 Chilean occupation of Peru.

1895 Turkish occupation of Thessaly.

1898-1900 US occupation of Cuba, Philippines and Porto Rico.

1898 British occupation of Crete.

1899 Russian occupation of Crete.

1900-02 British occupation of the Orange Free State and the Transvaal.

1912 Italian occupation of the Dodecanese; Greek occupation of the Aegean Islands.

1913 Greek occupation of Macedonia and Thrace.

1914-18 German occupation of Belgium, northern France, Poland, Romania, Russia; Austrian occupation of Italy, Serbia, Montenegro and Greek occupation of Northern Epirus; Australian occupation of German New Guinea; New Zealand occupation of Samoa; British and French occupation of Togoland.

1915 British occupation of Bushire, Mafia and Cameroons; French occupation of Cameroons, Rouad.

1916 Bulgarian occupation of the Dobrudja; Belgian occupation of Ruanda-Urundi; Portuguese occupation of Kionga.

1917 British occupation of Iraq, Tanganyika; French occupation of Koritza; German occupation of Romania.

1918 British occupation of Palestine; German occupation of Dorpat.

1919 British occupation of Batum; Allied occupation of Thrace; French occupation of Arad,

Occupation stamps of Thessaly (1895), Crete (1898), Mytilene (1912), Northern Epirus (1914), Eastern Command (Russian Baltic Provinces) (1916), Dobrudja (1916), Romania (1917), Togo (1914), Batum (1919), Venezia Giulia (1918), Aunus (1919), Baghdad (1917), Hungary (Arad) (1919), Vilnius (1941), Ukraine (1942), Eastern Karelia (1941), Ionian Islands (1943)

Cilicia and Syria; Finnish occupation of Aunus; Belgian occupation of Eupen and Malmedy; Italian occupation of Trentino, Venezia, Giulia; Russian occupation of Lithuania; Romanian occupation of the Ukraine and Transylvania; Serbian occupation of Baranya and Temesvar.

1920 Allied occupation of Memel; French occupation of Castellorizo, Memel and Saar; Greek occupation of Thrace; Polish occupation of Central Lithuania.

1922 Italian occupation of Castelrosso.

1923 Italian occupation of Saseno and Corfu; Lithuanian occupation of Memel.

1936 Italian occupation of Ethiopia.

1938 German occupation of the Sudetenland.

1939 German occupation of Bohemia and Moravia, Danzig, Poland; Lithuanian occupation of Vilna; Hungarian occupation of Slovakia and Carpatho-Ukraine.

1940 Greek occupation of Albania.

1941 Italian occupation of Ionian Islands, Montenegro, Fiume and Slovenia; German occupation of Estonia, Latvia, Lithuania, Russia, Luxembourg, and Serbia, Finnish occupation of Eastern Karelia.

1942 British occupation of the Italian colonies; Japanese occupation of Brunei, Burma, Hong Kong, Malaya, Sarawak, Netherlands Indies, Philippines, Andaman and Nicobar Islands.

1943 German occupation of the Ionian Islands, Dalmatia, Montenegro; Allied occupation of Italy; French occupation of Fezzan; Thai occupation of northern Malaya.

1944 German occupation of Macedonia and Slovenia.

1945 Allied occupation of Germany; Yugoslav occupation of Venezia Giulia and Istria.

1946 British Commonwealth occupation of Japan.

1947 Allied occupation of Trieste Zone A.

1948 Yugoslav occupation of Trieste Zone B; British occupation of Eritrea, Somalia and Tripolitania.

1949 French occupation of Ghadames.

1950 North Korean occupation of South Korea.

Official stamps, for use on government correspondence, were first prepared in 1840. They consisted of the Penny Black with the letters VR (*Victoria Regina*) in the upper corners in place of stars. The stamps were printed in April–May 1840 but were never put into use and 3302 out of the 3323 sheets distributed were destroyed on 25 January 1843. Of the balance of 21 sheets 13 were used to distribute specimens with notices to postmasters, and a few of these are known to have been removed from the notices and affixed to letters. Sir Rowland Hill,

himself, used several of these VR Penny Blacks for experiments with various forms of obliteration. Instead government departments used ordinary stamps and postal stationery, though latterly these stamps were perforated with a crown and the initials of the department. Britain did not issue stamps overprinted for departmental use until 1882. This practice continued till March 1904 but since then 'Official Paid' labels and stationery, machine postmarks and meter marks have been used.

The British sixpenny stamp overprinted for the Board of Education was prepared shortly before all official stamps were withdrawn in March 1904. It was never officially issued but six specimens have survived in used condition. Only one is believed to be in private hands making this one of the greatest British rarities.

The first country to issue official stamps for actual use was Spain, in July 1854. The stamps were printed in black on various coloured papers and bore the national coat of arms. No values as such were expressed, only weights (from half ounce to one pound) of correspondence permitted for each stamp. A second series, with an oval frame, was issued in January 1855. Both sets were frequently forged to deceive the authorities and examples have been found postally used. Other early users of official stamps were India (1866), South Australia (1868), the North German Confederation (1870), Denmark (1871), Iceland, Hyderabad and the USA (1873), and British Guiana, Italy and Luxembourg (1875).

Most official stamps bear such words as OFFICIAL or SERVICE in their inscription, but among the less common forms found are: SARKARI (Indian states), DIENSTMARKE (Germany), OFFENTLIG SAK (Norway), TJENESTE (Denmark), TJÄNSTE (Sweden), and RESMI (Turkey). Stamps may also be found overprinted O.S. (Australia), O.H.M.S. or G. (Canada), O.H.E.M.S. (Egypt) or O.H.H.S. (Egypt), the latter abbreviations signifying 'On His Exalted Majesty's Service' (1922) or 'On His Highness's Service' (1907–22), prior to the Khedive assuming the title of King.

The oddest inscription on official stamps is ARMENWET (Poor Law), found on Dutch stamps of 1921. They were intended for use on correspondence from local authorities administering the poor law.

Stamps for computing the volume of official correspondence have been issued by two countries. Germany produced sets of stamps inscribed FREI DÜRCH ABLÖSUNG for use in Prussia (1903) and Baden (1905), each set being used for 12 months in order to assess the amount of revenue owed to the imperial postal service for government mail carried. A similar device was used in Thailand in 1963-4. Stamps inscribed FOR GOVERNMENT SERVICE STAT-

Official stamps from Spain (1854), India (1912) and Norway (1955)

ISTICAL RESEARCH were compulsorily used on official correspondence to determine the amount handled by the various departments.

Parcel stamps, denoting the prepayment of postage on parcels, were produced by freight companies long before government parcel services were organised. The earliest so far recorded is a red oval adhesive label, said to have been used on a parcel from Dublin to Ludlow, Shropshire, about 1821. If authentic, this would make it *the earliest example of an adhesive postage stamp*. Inscribed FROM C & R ELLIOTT'S LONDON & DUBLIN PARCEL OFFICE, 33 SACKVILLE ST OPPOSITE THE GENERAL POST OFFICE DUBLIN, it was rated at 6s 6d. The railway companies were among the earliest users of parcel stamps, both the London & North-Western and the North British railways issuing them by 1846. In addition to stamps for ordinary parcels, these companies issued stamps specifically for sugar samples (Glasgow & South-Western Railway), grain (Great Northern), market basket (Midland Great Western of Ireland), farm produce (South Eastern & Chatham), milk parcels (Furness). Parcel stamps are issued by the railways, freight companies and bus services to this day, since the carriage of parcels does not infringe the postal monopoly.

The first parcel stamps under state auspices were issued by Belgium on 1 May 1879. These stamps, inscribed CHEMINS DE FER, were for use on the service operated by the Belgian state railways and are therefore classed as a government, rather than a private, issue. Although this system continues to this day, the Belgian Post Office has also operated a small parcels service since 1928 and issued distinctive stamps for this purpose. Similar stamps have been issued by SNCF (Société Nationale des Chemins de Fer) in France since 1892.

The first parcel stamp issued by Great Britain was the 9d of the unified postage and revenue series, introduced on 1 August 1883, the day that the Post Office inaugurated its own parcel post. No special stamps were provided for this service, but as no stamp existed which prepaid the 5 lb rate, the 9d

stamp was issued specifically for that reason. At that time the minimum rate was 3d (1 lb) rising by 2 lb stages to a maximum of 7 lb for one shilling. At the same time, however, 9d and 1s stamps were overprinted GOVT. PARCELS for use on official parcels weighing over 3 lb. Parcels below 3 lb were at first sent by letter post to avoid the high charges (55 per cent of the postage) due to the railway companies for conveying the parcels. These government parcel stamps, the only British stamps specifically inscribed for parcel use, were withdrawn in March 1904.

Italy adopted parcel stamps in 1884, and since 1916 these have been issued in bipartite (q.v.) form. The United States did not introduce a government parcel service till 1912. Pictorial stamps from 1c to $1 were then issued, but were discontinued after a few months and used up on ordinary mail. A set of parcel postage due stamps was also issued at the same time.

Parcel stamps may be recognised by such inscriptions as COLIS POSTAUX (France), POSTCOLLO (Belgium), KOLETNI PRATKI (Bulgaria), ZULASSUNGS-MARKE (Germany), PACCHI POSTALI (Italy), ENCOM-ENDAS POSTAIS (Portugal), ENCOMIENDAS (Latin America), BUITOS POSTALES (Mexico), TAXA DE FACTAGIU (Romania) and PORTE DE CONDUCCION (Peru). Uruguay even issued stamps inscribed EN-COMIENDAS DE GRANJA for use on agricultural parcels.

Personal Delivery stamps were issued by Czechoslovakia on 1 March 1937. Blue 50 haleru stamps in a triangular format, with the letter V in each corner, denoted prepayment of an additional fee which ensured personal delivery to the addressee and was affixed by the sender. A similar stamp in red, with the letter D in each corner, represented a fee payable by the addressee who required all his mail to be delivered to him personally. It was affixed to correspondence by the post office delivering the mail. Similar triangular stamps were issued by the German protectorate of Bohemia and Moravia in 1939-40 and by Slovakia in 1940. A 2 crown triangular stamp was issued by Czechoslovakia in 1946 but the service seems to have been discontinued shortly afterwards.

Stamps for computing official correspondence: Germany (1903) and Thailand (1963)

Persia (Iran) parcel post overprint, 1914

Czechoslovakia Personal Delivery 50h, 1937

Pneumatic post stamps were issued by Italy in 1913 to prepay postage on letters and cards conveyed by a pneumatic tube system which operated in Rome, Milan, Naples, Turin and Genoa. France established a system known as the *reseau pneumatique* in 1866 and issued special stamped envelopes and cards for the purpose. Germany (1867) and Austria (1873) introduced a similar service, known as the *Rohrpost,* and issued special stationery.

Britain actually pioneered the pneumatic post, an elaborate system of furnaces, pumps and valves being designed to create a vacuum and increase air pressure in order to propel containers along underground tubes, as long ago as 1826. The Pneumatic Despatch Company was formed in 1859 to convey letters and parcels by pneumatic tube and following a successful trial at Battersea Park in 1861 a pneumatic system was constructed between Euston station and the North-West District Office at Eversholt Street, London. Mailbags were first despatched in this way on 20 February 1863. The service was subsequently extended to Holborn and the General Post Office at St Paul's but was never satisfactory and was abandoned in 1873.

Polar stamps were first issued in 1897 by a German, Captain Wilhelm Bade, for a local service in Spitzbergen. The 10 øre stamps showed a walrus on an ice floe.

The first stamps officially sanctioned for use in polar regions were 1d stamps authorised by New Zealand for use by Sir Ernest Shackleton's Antarctic expedition in 1908. The stamps were overprinted KING EDWARD VII LAND. Three years later New Zealand ½d and 1d stamps were similarly overprinted VICTORIA LAND for use by Captain Scott's expedition to the South Pole. In 1922 the British Post Office authorised the overprinting of British stamps for use by the Shackleton-Rowett expedition to the Antarctic. The expedition was abandoned after Shackleton's death, but a few stamps are known to have been overprinted by hand ENDERBY LAND and TRISTAN DE CUNHA and postally used from that island in May 1922. Norwegian stamps overprinted BOUVET ØYA were used in 1934 during a visit of HMS *Milford* to Bouvet Island, a Norwegian possession in the Antarctic (see also page 186).

Since 1944 stamps have been provided for use by scientific expeditions in the Falkland Islands Dependencies (Graham Land, South Georgia, South Orkneys and South Shetlands). Other polar issues in recent years include Australian Antarctic Territory (since 1957), Ross Dependency (since 1957) and British Antarctic Territory (since 1963). Falkland Island Dependencies stamps were also overprinted in 1955 for use by the Hillary-Fuchs Trans-Antarctic expedition during International Geophysical Year.

Stamps for political propaganda were first issued by Venezuela in 1896. Ostensibly in memory of General Miranda, they depicted a map advancing Venezuela's claim to British Guianese territory west of the Essequibo river. Stamps arguing this claim have continued to the present day, the most recent being a lengthy series of overprints by Guyana

Parcel post stamps from Belgium (1902) and Uruguay (1960)

Left France, pneumatic letter-card

Below The first dispatch of mailbags by pneumatic tube on 20 February 1863 from the North West District Offices in Eversholt Street to Euston Station.

New Zealand stamps overprinted for use in King Edward VII Land (1908) and Victoria Land (1911); Falkland Islands Dependencies overprinted for the Trans-Antarctic Expedition (1955)

ESSEQUIBO IS OURS. Map stamps were also used by Bolivia and Paraguay in their fight over the Gran Chaco (see page 131). Guatemala issued a stamp in 1959 inscribed BELICE ES NUESTRO (Belize is Ours). Map stamps propagating territorial claims have been issued by Bulgaria (1921), Argentina (1947-79), Ecuador (1961), Chile (1947-58), Taiwan (1971), Jordan (1964), Egypt (1949-67).

The first political propaganda issue in Germany was the 2 mark stamp of 1900 depicting an allegory of the union of North and South Germany, and inscribed SEID EINIG, EINIG, EINIG! (Be One, One, One!). This motif remained in use until 1920. During the Nazi period stamps were extensively used for propaganda, from the Saar ownership stamps of 1934 onwards. Notable examples include Hitler's 48th birthday miniature sheet, 1937 (inscribed HE WHO WOULD SAVE A PEOPLE CAN ONLY THINK HEROICALLY), the Austrian plebiscite stamps, 1938 (EIN VOLK, EIN REICH, EIN FÜHRER), the Danzig annexation issue, 1939 (DANZIG IS GERMAN), and the 20th anniversary of Munich *putsch*, 1943 (AND YET YE HAVE TRIUMPHED). On the seizure of the Sudetenland Czechoslovak stamps were overprinted with the swastika emblem and the words *Wir sind Frei* (WE ARE FREE).

The Soviet Union, on the other hand, has made wide use of stamps for more politico-economic reasons. The first of these issues appeared in 1929 to promote the industrial loan (MORE METAL – MORE MACHINES!). Later sets include the anti-war propaganda series (1935), the young pioneers anti-stonethrowing stamp (1936), and the numerous issues connected with Five Year Plans for economic growth. All of the communist countries have made use of propaganda stamps since the 1950s, the most blatant examples being those issued by North Korea caricaturing President Nixon (1969) and condemning American imperialism in Vietnam, Africa and Latin America (1971), and by North Vietnam (1965-76), ranging from the mourning stamp for the Quaker, Norman Morrison who immolated himself (1965) to the numerous issues celebrating the shooting down of American aircraft, and guerrilla attacks on the American embassy in Saigon and other US bases.

Propaganda of a more peaceful nature has been advanced by means of stamps of Italy urging citizens to pay their taxes promptly (1954-5). Venezuela issued a set of twenty in 1974 for the same purpose! Stamps have been issued in recent years by many countries advocating road safety (Cuba, Germany, Turkey), food production (Australia), family planning (USA, India), anti-pollution (Rhodesia), prevention of drug abuse (Austria, UN, Italy, USA), anti-smoking (Ethiopia) and accident prevention (West Germany).

Porte de Mar stamps were issued by Mexico in 1875-9. The inscription means CARRIED BY SEA and denoted mail intended for Europe, carried by French and British steamships who received a fee for the service. A new series was in preparation in 1879, but never issued since Mexico joined the UPU that year and the service was abolished.

Postage Due stamps are used by postal administrations to denote money to be collected from the recipient of unpaid or underpaid mail. They are affixed to mail by postal staff and the amount due collected from the addressee on delivery. Though not on general sale to the public they are usually available in mint condition from philatelic counters and bureaux. They may be recognised by such inscriptions as POSTAGE DUE or TO PAY (English), À PAYER, À PERCEVOIR, TAXE (French), TE BETALEN (Dutch), SEGNATASSE (Italian), PORTEADO, A COBRAR (Portuguese), MULTA, MULTADA, DEFICIT, CORRESPONDENCIA A DEBE, TIMBRE COMPLIMENTARIO DEFICIENTE, DEFICIENCIA (Spanish), DOPLATIT (Czech), or VOM EMPFANGER ZAHLBAR EINZUZIEHEN, PORTO (German), TAXA DA PLATA (Romanian), DOPLATA (Polish), BAJAR PORTO (Indonesian).

They were first issued by France on 1 January 1859. Only one denomination was issued till 1870 (10 centimes), but then a 15c was introduced and the following year the series was extended from 25c to 60c. Baden and Bavaria followed on 1 October 1862. Baden's three stamps were inscribed LAND-POST PORTO-MARKE and denoted postage due on rural

Propaganda stamps of Venezuela (1896), Germany (1900), Sudan anti-Zionist (1974), USA letter-writing (1980), Italy encouragement to taxpayers (1954), West Germany accident prevention (1971), North Korean anti-American, USA beautification (1969), Sudetenland (1938), Germany (1938), Trinidad and Tobago environmental preservation (1981), Vietnam anti-American, Cuba against American use of chemical warfare in Vietnam (1966)

mail. The Bavarian stamp was more explicit and was inscribed *Bayer. Posttaxe vom Empfänger zahlbar* (Bavarian postal charge payable by the recipient). The first American postage due stamp was issued on 9 May 1879 and the first in the British Commonwealth were issued by Victoria (1 November 1890) and New South Wales (1 January 1891). Guadeloupe issued postage due stamps in 1876 – 8 years before ordinary stamps. The Australian Commonwealth issued postage due stamps in July 1902 – 11 years before issuing ordinary stamps. Britain did not adopt postage due stamps until 20 April 1914.

Special categories of postage due stamps:
Parcel postage due – USA 1912.

Postage due stamps of France (1859), St Thomas and Prince Islands (1904), USA (1912), Chile (1898), Danzig (1921), Romania (1932) and the Netherlands (1924)

Obligatory tax due (for failure to use the obligatory charity stamps) – Portugal (1925-8), Yugoslavia (1933-63).

Most postage due stamps are utilitarian in design, but many from the French-speaking countries have adopted pictorial designs. The first pictorial postage dues were issued by French Guinea in 1905, followed by Dahomey, Ivory Coast, Mauretania, New Caledonia, Senegal, Upper Senegal and Niger (1906).

The rarest postage due stamp was a Bavarian 3 pfennig of 1895 surcharged with a '2' in each corner for use as a 2pf stamp. Only six examples, all used at Aichach, have ever been recorded.

Fiscal stamps in lieu of postage due stamps were used by South Africa in 1922. Cigarette tax stamps, in denominations of ¼d and ¾d, were used to denote the amount due on underpaid letters. This irregular and exceptional practice has been recorded on mail handled at Durban on 22 and 23 August 1922 and at Fordsburg the following December.

Postal franks were issued by the British Vice Consul in Antananarivo, Madagascar from 1884 till 1887. These franks were sold to inland residents of the island to facilitate correspondence. They were attached to letters by one corner only and were removed by the consular staff who then forwarded them to Mauritius where the appropriate stamps of Mauritius or Reunion were affixed at Port Louis before onward transmission.

Postal Fiscals are revenue stamps which have been authorised for use as postage stamps. The earliest examples were the British draft and receipt stamps of 1853, but they were not sanctioned for postal use till June 1881. This practice ceased in July 1883. Hong Kong fiscals of 1867 were sanctioned for postage from 1874 till 1902 and for 9 days in 1938 during a

shortage of 5c stamps. Tasmanian fiscals from 1863 onwards were authorised for postage in 1882, while the stamp statute series of Victoria (1871) was authorised in 1884. Other countries permitting this included Western Australia (1893), New Zealand (1882 to the present day).

Postcard stamps are those which have been affixed to postcards prior to sale by post offices. Normally such cards would have the stamp printed direct, but in the Orange Free State postcards were sold between 1889 and 1899 with adhesive stamps affixed and then overprinted with a device showing the national coat of arms. Stamps with this overprint could only have come from postcards.

A similar situation arose in June 1932 when New Zealand stamps (1d and 2d) were diagonally surcharged to reduce their value by half, following a reduction in the rates. These adhesives had previously been added to stamped postcards when the rates were increased and when the tariff was reduced their value had to be diminished accordingly.

Postcard Tax stamps were issued by Persia (Iran) in 1904. They were overprinted *Controle* and denoted a tax on picture postcards then in force. They had to be affixed to the cards in addition to the normal postage.

Printed Matter stamps are those prepared for use on printed matter, circulars and periodicals. The earliest and most prolific issues emanated from the Spanish colonies. Stamps inscribed IMPRESOS were first issued in the Philippines in 1886 and continued at virtually annual intervals till 1896. Cuba followed suit in 1888. The only other country to issue such stamps was Czechoslovakia which issued stamps overprinted O.T. (*Obchodni Tiskopis*) (commercial printed matter) in 1934. In 1940 the 10 haleru newspaper stamp of Bohemia and Moravia was overprinted GD-OT to signify *Geschäfts Drucksache* and *Obchodní Tiskopis*, the German and Czech equivalents of commercial printed matter. Though not specifically inscribed for printed matter, certain denominations of US stamps have been provided for this purpose. They include the ½c stamps of 1922-55, the 1¼c, 1½c and 2½c stamps of 1956-60, the 1¼c of 1967, and the 3·1c, 3·5c, 7·7c, 7·9c and 8·4c stamps of 1976-80, used by non-profit making organisations and other users of bulk-posted printed matter.

Prisoner of War stamps have been printed by the inmates of prison camps in both world wars. During the First World War stamps were produced for use on inter-camp correspondence by British prisoners at Ruhleben (Germany) and by German prisoners at Knockaloe (Isle of Man) and Bando (Japan). During the Second World War numerous stamps were produced by Polish prisoners of war in the German camps of Murnau, Grossborn, Neubrandenburg and Woldenburg. The Swiss Post Office also provided special franks for French prisoners interned during and immediately after the Franco-German War of 1870-1.

Private stamps have been provided by Spain and Portugal for the use of private individuals and organisations on several occasions. The first of these stamps was issued by Spain on 1 January 1869 for the use of Don Diego Castell whose 18-page pamphlet *Cartilla Postal de España* (Spanish Postal Primer) was deemed to be of such great benefit to the public that it should be transmitted by post free of charge. The Spanish Post Office decided that copies should be circulated to all 24 000 schools in the country and Castell was granted free postage for 6 months in order to distribute his booklet. Castell was a professional engraver who designed the frank itself. In 1875 Fernandez Antonio Duro wrote *Reseña Historicò-Descriptiva de los Sellos de Correos de España* (*A history of Spanish stamps*) and was granted free postage on 12 March 1875, although the frank was not issued till July 1881. Inscribed FRANQUICIA

Postcard tax stamp of Persia (Iran), 1922

POSTAL (postal frank) it depicted an open book. Similar stamps, for the use of the Portuguese Geographical and Red Cross Societies and the national rifle club were issued at the turn of the century. The Belgian Red Cross also enjoyed a franking privilege in 1891.

Provisional stamps are those whose value or purpose has been altered after printing, by means of a surcharge or overprint.

The earliest instance of a provisional surcharge occurred in Mauritius in 1854 when undenominated stamps of the Britannia design were overprinted FOUR-PENCE. The following year stamps issued in Cuba and Porto Rico were surcharged with new values. Other early examples are uncommon. In 1863 St Helena's sixpenny stamp was issued in various colours and surcharged for use at different denominations. In 1877 the stamps of Honduras, which had been prepared 11 years earlier but never used, were surcharged in various denominations when the postal service was eventually organised. From 1876 onwards Mauritius had a spate of provisional surcharges and this practice became prevalent elsewhere, particularly in Latin America where many provisionals were produced for sale mainly to collectors.

Mexico, Porte de Mar; Bohemia and Moravia, commercial printed papers; Polish prisoner of war post; Portugal, private stamp for the use of the union of rifle clubs

The first provisional surcharges converting stamps for use in another country were issued in 1867, when stamps of the East India Company were overprinted with a crown and surcharged in Straits currency for use in the Straits Settlements. The following year Straits stamps were themselves overprinted B for use in Bangkok, Thailand. In 1868 also, Portuguese stamps were overprinted for use in Madeira and the Azores.

The first provisional overprints converting stamps for other purposes appeared in 1866 when Indian stamps were overprinted SERVICE for official correspondence. In the same year Indian revenue stamps were overprinted POSTAGE for postal use.

The first stamps provisionally overprinted to denote a political change were issued in 1868 when stamps of Spain, Cuba and Porto Rico were overprinted HABILITADO POR LA NACION (valid for the nation), following the overthrow of the monarchy and the establishment of a revolutionary junta. In 1874 the stamps of Fiji were overprinted with a crowned VR monogram to signify its cession by King Cakobau to the British.

The first overprints for commemorative purposes were made by Hong Kong, to celebrate the colony's jubilee (1891), by Paraguay to commemorate the quatercentenary of the discovery of America by Columbus (1892) and by Shanghai to celebrate the jubilee of the European settlement (1893).

Publicity Envelope stamps were issued by Italy in 1921-3 and consisted of contemporary definitives overprinted B.L.P. (*Buste Lettere Postali*). These stamps were sold at a discount of 5 per cent to an ex-servicemen's society and were affixed to envelopes or letter-cards bearing advertisements, the project being designed to assist disabled veterans.

Railway stamps have been issued by railway companies to denote the prepayment of postage on letters and parcels conveyed by them. The earliest stamps were issued in 1846 by several British railway companies for parcels (q.v.), but in 1891 agreement was reached with the Post Office permitting the carriage of urgent letters by rail at an additional fee of 2d. Between 1891 and 1922 numerous railway letter stamps were issued in the British Isles. In recent years pictorial stamps have been issued by the private light railways of Britain to pay the postage on mail (mainly tourist souvenirs) carried over their lines.

Parcel stamps are issued by many railway companies to this day, those in Belgium and France being produced under the auspices of the state postal services.

In 1933 the Great Western Railway organised an airmail service between Cardiff and Plymouth, 3d

India surcharged for use in the Straits Settlements (1867); Straits Settlements provisionally overprinted 'B' for use in Bangkok (1868)

newspaper parcel stamps being used to prepay the air fee but later a distinctive airmail stamp was issued. The following year the four major rail companies formed the Railway Air Service. No special stamps were issued but distinctive stationery and rubber handstamps were used.

Belgium has issued special stamps for use on railway official correspondence since 1929, either depicting a winged wheel emblem or a 'B' in an oval frame overprinted or incorporated in the design.

Recorded Message stamps were issued by Argentina in 1939 for the prepayment of special fees on messages recorded on discs for transmission by post. The stamps, inscribed CORREOS FONOPOSTAL, featured a bird with a record in its beak (1·18 pesos), the head of Liberty (1·32p) or a record and winged letter (1·50p). Other countries, including the UK, Irish Republic and Taiwan, have operated similar services but never issued special stamps for the purpose.

Registration stamps for use on registered mail, were first issued by Victoria on 1 December 1854, having been authorised by the Post Office Act of November 1853. They were printed from a wood block by S Calvert, the word REGISTERED and the value (1s) being inserted by metal type in a second colour. The Victorian authorities grossly overestimated the need for this stamp, which was withdrawn in 1858. Nevertheless New South Wales followed suit, with an undenominated 6d stamp in 1856, and produced various printings till 1863. Canada issued 2c, 5c and 8c stamps for this purpose from 1875 till 1892.

Other countries issuing registration stamps were Colombia (1865-1932), the Colombian states of Antioquia (1896-1902), Bolivar (1879-1904) and Cundinamarca (1883-1904), Panama (1888-1916), Liberia (1893-1941), El Salvador (1897), Venezuela (1899 to the present day), USA (1911), Dominican Republic (1935 to the present day) and the German Democratic Republic (since 1967). In many cases (e.g., Colombia, Panama and Liberia) the stamps included space for the insertion of the serial number of the letter, and thus did away with the necessity for a separate registration label. The stamps of the German Democratic Republic, in fact, are registra-

Railway letter stamp of GB (1891), Bavarian railway stamp, Queensland railway stamp for newspapers and parcels

tion labels, serially numbered, which are available from slot machines and include the words GEBÜHR BEZAHLT (postage paid).

Registration labels have been used as stamps on two occasions. In Persia (Iran) postmasters had to account for these labels which were valued at a chahi each. For this reason they were sometimes used as chahi stamps, and even blocks of six have been seen in lieu of the 6ch stamps around 1903. Labels used in German New Guinea were overprinted G.R.I. (the British royal monogram) and surcharged with new values in sterling, and used as stamps following the surrender of the German colonial administration to Imperial forces in 1914.

Scout stamps had their origins in the 1d and 3d stamps issued in Mafeking during the siege of 1899-1900. Produced locally, they portrayed Colonel R S S Baden-Powell, founder of the Scout movement and commander of the besieged town, and Cadet Sergeant-Major Warner Goodyear on his bicycle, often described as the first scout to appear on a stamp. The Scout movement was founded in 1907, based on Baden-Powell's experiences working with young people in Mafeking. The Scouts in Prague were responsible for organising the first postal service in Czechoslovakia following independence in

1918. Two stamps inscribed POSTA ČESKYCH SKAUTU (Czech Scout Post) were issued in October 1918.

The first stamp to depict scouts was issued by Hungary in 1925 as part of a sports series. The 1000 korona stamp showed a bugler and camp scene. Hungary was also the first country to issue stamps commemorating a jamboree, at Gödöllö in 1933.

The first slogan postmark publicising scouting was issued by Czechoslovakia for the Prague Slovak Jamboree in June-July 1933.

Shipping company stamps, prepaying the postage on mail conveyed by steamships, were first issued in 1847, David Bryce of Trinidad producing a 5c stamp for mail carried by the *Lady McLeod* between San Fernando and Port of Spain. Before the formation of the Universal Postal Union in 1874 much of the international carriage of mail was in the hands of shipping companies who produced their own stamps. The *Lady McLeod* service seems to have come to an end by 1850, but in the ensuing decade the Pacific Steam Navigation Company operated along the coast of Peru. Its stamps were never used by the company itself, but were handed over to the Peruvian Post Office and thus formed that country's

Registration stamps of Antioquia (1899), Colombia (1889), Canada (1875) and USA (1911)

first stamps (1858-9). Gauthier Frères et Cie, operating between Le Havre, New York and Rio de Janeiro, issued two stamps depicting the SS *Barcelone*, 1856-7.

The other steamship companies which issued their own stamps in the mid-nineteenth century were:

Turkish Admiralty (stamps inscribed in Italian) 1859.
St Thomas and La Guiara, Danish West Indies 1864-9.
ROPiT (Russian Levant) 1865-1914.
Danubian Steamship Company 1866-80.
T B Morton & Co Constantinople and Danube 1866-72.
Tavastehus-Tammerfors, Finland 1867.
Kustendje & Czernavoda, Romania 1867.
Suez Canal Company 1868.
Asia Minor Steamship Company 1868.
Saxe-Boheme Steamship Company 1869.
St Thomas (FAF & ZA Curacao) 1869-70.
St Lucia Steam Conveyance Company 1870-2. The first stamps were blue-edged price labels bearing the company's handstamp.
Helsingfors-Boback Company 1874-9.
Royal Mail Steam Packet Company (Panama-St Thomas) 1875.
Dutch East Indies Steamship Company 1876.
Chimba (Bolivia) Company 1876.
Hamburg-American (HAPAG) 1876.

Special Handling stamps were issued by the United States in 1925, in denominations from 10c to 25c. The purpose of these stamps was to give first class priority to fourth class mail. They were discontinued in 1929.

First Day Cover of the GB 26p stamp celebrating the 75th anniversary of Scouting, with the pictorial postmark of Baden-Powell House

Specimen stamps are, generally speaking, stamps overprinted or perforated for sample purposes (e.g., distribution to member countries of the UPU). Such stamps are thus invalidated for postal purposes.

The first use of a specimen overprint was in 1840, when postal stationery was circulated to postmasters in Britain, overprinted in this way. In 1849 many examples of existing British stamps were thus overprinted for inclusion in official reference collections.

The circulation of specimens to the UPU began in 1879. Since then each member sends sufficient examples of each new issue to headquarters in Berne for three examples to be sent out to each member country – including the member submitting the stamps in the first instance. In Britain, only stamps with a face value over a shilling were overprinted from 1892 onwards. The practice of overprinting stamps SPECIMEN for UPU purposes has gradually died out since 1945. British colonial stamps, supplied by the Crown Agents, were overprinted until about 1930 but thereafter the word was punch-perforated. This practice ceased after the distribution of the Victory stamps in 1946.

The high-value stamps of Australia and its dependent territories were overprinted SPECIMEN for sale to collectors. This practice ceased in 1970. Other countries (notably West Germany, Cyprus, St Vincent and the Grenadines) overprint stamps distributed to philatelic journalists. Mongolia applies a mark across the backs of stamps for the same purpose.

Words indicating specimen usage are: MONSTER (Dutch), MUSTER (Germany), MUESTRA (Spanish),

THE SCOUT ASSOCIATION,
Baden-Powell House,
Queen's Gate, London. SW7 5JS

MALLI Finnish, OBRESTEZ Russian and SAGGIO (Italian).

The only Specimen stamps issued for postage appeared in 1882, when British Guiana perforated 1c and 2c stamps in this manner as a precaution against fraud. Nevertheless, a few examples are known postally used without the specimen perforation.

Strike stamps have been issued by emergency services operating during postal strikes. The first issue of this sort appeared in 1894 for use on a service operating between Fresno and San Francisco by Arthur C Banta. The mail was carried by relays of bicyclists during a strike called by the American Railroad Union. A diamond-shaped 25c stamp was issued to prepay the fee. In May 1909 French postal workers went on strike in sympathy with 54 colleagues sacked by the government because they had demonstrated against the military policy. The Amiens chamber of commerce organised a local service and issued 10c stamps depicting the municipal arms. Normal service was resumed on 19 May. Later strike posts, for which stamps were issued, operated in:

Milan April-May 1920.
Austrian Tyrol December 1923.
Linz-Vienna November 1924.
Orleans-Loiret August 1953.
France (various local chambers of commerce) May 1968.
British Columbia-Port Angeles 1965, 1968.
Albany, NY March 1970.
Dublin 1980

Strike posts have operated in Britain on three occasions. In January 1962, during a postal 'go-slow'

Specimen overprints of Costa Rica (1945) and Sri Lanka (1974)

an urgent mail delivery service was organised by the People's League for the Defence of Freedom. The post was suppressed after two hours because it infringed the Postmaster General's monopoly, but the League were permitted to operate a parcel service to the major cities of the UK and Europe. Stamps from 6d to 5s, including an airmail issue, were used. Similar stamps were used by the League in 1964 during another 'go-slow'. Between 20 January and 8 March 1971 the British Post Office was on strike and the Postmaster General waived his monopoly for the duration. Some 200 private postal services operated during the strike and most of them issued their own stamps.

Submarine stamps were first issued on 9 August 1916 by the Deutsche Versicherungsbank GmbH of Berlin for a registered letter service between Germany and the United States. The mail was carried by the merchant submarines *Deutschland* and *Bremen* with the approval of the imperial German postal administration. Stamps from 5 to 50 marks were printed by Giesecke & Devrient of Leipzig for the service. A second series, omitting the inscription REGISTERED LETTER SERVICE GERMANY–AMERICA was subsequently issued, and 75 and 100mk denominations embossed on paper with a silver or gold metallic surface were added to the series. Letters and packets received in New York by the bank's agent were forwarded to the addressees under plain wrapper. The service was terminated when the United States entered the war in March 1917.

In 1938, during the Spanish Civil War, communications between the Balearic Islands and the mainland were maintained by submarines of the republican navy. Six stamps inscribed CORREO SUBMARINO and featuring submarines were issued in August; three of the stamps were also released in a miniature sheet.

During the Second World War three submarine posts were provided with distinctive stamps: the Italian *Base Atlantica* at Bordeaux (1944), German fieldpost in Crete, Vukovar, Rhodes and Leros – airmail stamps overprinted INSELPOST (island post) for transmission by air or submarine (1944-5), and the German garrison on the Hela peninsula, Danzig (March-May 1945).

Sunday Delivery stamps were issued by Bulgaria in 1925-39 and 1941-2. They had to be affixed to mail intended for delivery on Sundays and public holidays in addition to the normal postage. The revenue from the Sunday delivery fees was used for the maintenance of a sanatorium and rest homes for postal employees and their families. The stamps actually depicted the sanatorium.

Thematic stamps are stamps issued in sets with a

Emergency stamps used during postal strikes: Rickshaw, Juan de Fuca Despatch (Canada, 1965) TDR and London (GB, 1971), and Austrian Tyrol (1923)

common theme or subject and on sale for a limited period only. The first set of this type was issued by San Marino in April 1953 and depicted different sports. Earlier sets (such as Hungary's sports series of 1925) were issued for a specific purpose – either with a charity premium, or to commemorate an event or personality. The San Marino issue had no other motive than to provide collectors with a series whose designs explored a single theme. In December 1953 San Marino issued a set of nine stamps depicting flowers. A similar series featuring different breeds of dog appeared in 1956 and other purely thematic sets followed at regular intervals thereafter. Hitherto several countries had issued definitive sets with a single theme – e.g., USA, Presidential series (1938), Austria, provincial costumes (1934, 1948) scenery (1945), Bulgaria, historical scenes (1942), Canada, war effort (1942), Colombia, products (1932), Czechoslovakia, landmarks (1936), Liechtenstein,

birds (1939 airmails), pioneers of aviation (1948 airmails), German Democratic Republic, politicians, artists and scientists (1948) and Italy, medieval republics (1946) and provincial occupations (1950). Another contender, however, is the Famous Americans series (1940). Between 29 January and 28 October seven sets of five stamps were issued, one or two stamps at a time, portraying famous authors, poets, educationalists, scientists, composers, artists and inventors. In 1943-4 the United States also issued a set of thirteen stamps depicting the flags of the oppressed nations. In both cases the issue was spread over a lengthy period and the stamps were substituted for definitive stamps during their period of issue.

The longest thematic set was issued by Turkey in 1958 and comprised 5 and 20 kuruş values depicting all the major towns from Adana to Zonguldak, a total of 134 stamps.

The first stamps depicting the most popular themes (confined to government issues):

Aircraft: USA (1912).
Animals: Canada (1851). The St Louis postmaster stamps (1846) depicting bears.
Arms and armour: Alwar (1877).
Birds: Basle (1845), USA (1851), W Australia (1854).
Coins: New South Wales (1861)
Flags: Costa Rica (1863), USA (1869).
Flora: New Brunswick (1851), Nova Scotia (1853), Newfoundland (1857).
Landmarks: Egypt (1867).
Locomotives: New Brunswick (1860).
Maps: New South Wales (1888), Venezuela (1894).
Motor vehicles: USA (1901).
Mythology: France (1849), Austria (1851).
Religion: Portugal (1895).
Scenery: New South Wales (1850), Nicaragua (1862).
Ships: Buenos Aires (1858), New Brunswick (1860).
Sport: Greece (1896).
Stamps: Sirmoor (1892).

Trimmed stamps are those which have had part of their design removed before issue. The first example was in 1866 when Indian revenue stamps were re-issued for postal use, after the revenue inscriptions had been cut off at top and bottom and a POSTAGE overprint applied to the remainder. Macao adopted a similar procedure in October 1887 when fiscal stamps had their upper or lower revenue counterfoils removed, prior to overprinting for use as postage stamps. In 1892 Ecuador converted stamps, which had been overprinted for official or telegraphic use, back to ordinary postage stamps by trimming off the upper portion bearing the overprints. The French Indian Settlements issued fiscal stamps in 1903 cut in half. The upper halves were then overprinted for postal use.

Bulgaria, Sunday Delivery stamp, 1925

Unified postage and revenue stamps were first issued in the UK on 12 July 1881. Previously separate issues were made for postage and revenue purposes, but the Penny Lilac was inscribed POSTAGE AND INLAND REVENUE. The word 'Inland' was omitted from subsequent stamps but appeared in the penny denomination till 1902. Only stamps up to the 2s 6d denomination indicated that they could be used for postage and revenue, though higher values were often used fiscally.

Stamps used abroad, in overseas post offices, agencies and consular bureaux, were a feature of international mail before the establishment of the UPU in 1874, and for some years thereafter. The first overseas post offices were the *bureaux étranger* established by France in neighbouring countries, the first being opened in Venice on 24 March 1561 and suppressed on 3 November 1675. A French post office was opened in Rome about 1580 and functioned till 1793, being re-opened in 1801 and continuing till 1871. The first of these offices to have

Cover from the Cook Islands to England during the British postal strike of 1971, bearing the Special Mail Service 30+20c stamp which facilitated handling via the Netherlands and thence by courier to England

Early examples of today's most popular themes: arms (Alwar, 1877), flora (Newfoundland, 1857), motor vehicles (USA, 1901), locomotives (New Brunswick, 1861), ships (Buenos Aires, 1858), sport (Greece, 1896)

a postmark was in Geneva (DE GENÈVE) by 1695 and from the same year date the namestamps used by French military forces at Courtrai and Suze (Piedmont) during campaigns in the War of the League of Augsburg.

Permanent post offices and postal agencies were established by France and Britain in many countries during the nineteenth century to expedite the handling of overseas mail. Austria, Italy, Russia and India were among the other countries which operated post offices outside their own frontiers and used their own stamps, distinguished only by the postal markings.

British offices abroad were established from 1814 onwards, following the re-establishment of British packet routes at the end of the Napoleonic Wars. On the introduction of Uniform Penny Postage in 1840 prepayment was gradually introduced in many of these offices, using crowned Paid handstamps. Adhesive stamps of Great Britain were employed in overseas offices in the following foreign countries: Argentina (1860–73), Bolivia (1865–78), Brazil (1866–74), Chile (1865–81), Colombia (1865–81), Cuba (1865–77), Danish West Indies (1865–79), Dominican Republic (1869–81), Ecuador (1865–80), Egypt (1860–82), Fernando Poo (1874–7), Haiti (1865–81), Mexico (1865–76), Nicaragua (1865–82), Peru (1865–79), Porto Rico (1865–77), Uruguay (1864–73) and Venezuela (1865–80). They were first used in Argentina (1860) and last used in Egypt and Nicaragua (1882). In the colonies British stamps were used till 31 December 1884 (Malta) and 31 December 1885 (Gibraltar). British stamps were used in Ascension Island from 1867 till 1922, the island being administered directly by the Admiralty and children born there being registered in the parish of Wapping! Unofficially, however, British stamps were used in Tristan da Cunha till 1952. No provision was made for the supply of stamps to the island but unstamped mail arriving in Britain was only surcharged at the single rate and not the customary double deficiency. Mail franked by British stamps and cancelled by one of the unofficial cachets of the island was accepted as fully paid by the British Post Office.

Ordinary French stamps were used in the following countries, and can only be distinguished by the numeral cancellations used:
China (1862–1922), Crete (1897–1913), Egypt (1852–1931), Japan (1865–80), Libya (1880–1912), Madagascar (1880–96), Monaco (1860–85), Morocco (1862–1913), Romania (1857–75), Tunisia (1852–88), Turkey (1852–1914) and Zanzibar – now part of Tanzania – (1889–1904).

Austria-Hungary operated post offices in various parts of the Turkish Empire. The stamps of Lombardo-Venetia were used there from 1863 till 1867, and Hungarian stamps were used in Romania 1867–9.

Ordinary Russian stamps were used in China (1870–99), while German stamps were used in China (1886–98), Morocco (1893–9), Turkey (1870–84), New Guinea (1888–98), East Africa (1888–91), Zanzibar–Tanzania (1890–1), South West Africa (1888–97), Cameroun (1887–97), the Marshall Islands (1889–1901), Samoa (1886–1901) and Togo (1888–1901). American stamps were used in China (1900–19) while Japanese stamps were used there from 1876 till 1900. Australian stamps were used in Papua-New Guinea (1945–52) and the Cocos-Keeling Islands (1955–63 and 1966–9), while New Zealand stamps were used by Pitcairn Island (1922–40). Conversely Christmas Island has used the stamps of the Straits Settlements (1900–41), Japan (1942–5), Australia (1945–6), Malaya under British Military Administration (1945–8), Singapore (1948–58) before issuing its own stamps.

War Tax stamps, raising money for the prosecution of a war, were first issued by Spain in 1874–7. Inscribed IMPUESTO DE GUERRA (war tax) they were

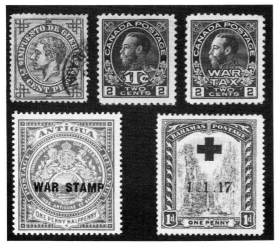

Zemstvo stamps from Starorusk and Stavropol

War tax stamps from Spain (1874), Canada (1916), Antigua (1916) and Bahamas (1917)

obligatory on all correspondence, the money being used for the conduct of the Carlist Wars. War tax stamps were again issued in 1898 during the Spanish American War. In several cases these stamps were continued long after the war and some were in use as late as 1920.

The idea was revived in the British Commonwealth in 1915. In February that year Canada issued three postage stamps overprinted WAR TAX. Though intended for fiscal purposes there was some ambiguity in the circular announcing their issue and they were, in fact, postally used. Later in 1916 1c and 2c stamps inscribed WAR TAX were issued for compulsory use on correspondence in addition to the normal postage. In 1916 stamps combining postage and the war tax were issued.

Stamps overprinted WAR TAX or WAR STAMP were issued by a number of British colonies: Fiji, Dominica, St Helena, St Lucia, Grenada, St Vincent, Antigua, Jamaica and British Honduras (1916), Montserrat, Virgin Islands, Trinidad and Tobago, Turks and Caicos and the Cayman Islands (1917),

and the Falkland Islands, Gibraltar, Bahamas, Bermuda, British Guiana, Gold Coast and Malta (1918). Surprisingly, the mother country never issued any war tax stamps, but the postal rates were raised by a halfpenny in February 1918, allegedly as a temporary wartime measure. Outside the Commonwealth, the only war tax stamps were issued by Liberia in 1918. No stamps for this purpose were issued during the Second World War.

Zemstvo stamps were issued in many parts of Tsarist Russia, the word meaning 'rural'. The Russian imperial post only served the cities and major towns but in 1864 local authorities were permitted to establish networks of postal services in the rural areas and to connect them with the imperial posts. The first zemstvo post was established at Vetlonga in 1864 but no stamps were issued. The first stamps were issued at Schlüsselburg in 1865. By a decree of 3 September 1870 the zemstvo posts were allowed greater freedom in their choice of design and from then until the Bolshevik Revolution (when the last surviving services were suppressed) several thousand zemstvo stamps were produced. They include the world's rarest stamp (Kotelnich) and some of the oddest shapes – ovals (Vessiegonsk and Luga), diamonds (Dmitrov and Pskov) and circulars (Kasimov and Maloarchangelsk). The zemstvo services gradually died out between 1900 and 1917.

The technology of stamps

STAMP DESIGN

The greatest number of people involved in the design of a single stamp was in 1839-40, when the world's first stamps were being planned. Apart from the 2600 entrants in the Treasury Design Competition the actual stamps were based on an idea by Rowland Hill, using a profile of Queen Victoria sculpted by William Wyon and adapted by Henry Corbould for engraving by Charles and Frederick Heath on a background engine-turned by Jacob Perkins. The Canadian Christmas stamp of 1898, often credited to the Postmaster General, William Mulock (who conceived it) was actually designed by R Weir Crouch, Gustave Hahn, A H Howard and R Holmes.

Unusual stamp designers

The Prince of Wales (later King George V) and J A Tilleard, Secretary of the Royal Philatelic Society, London designed the Canadian definitive series of 1903-12. Franklin D Roosevelt, President of the United States, designed the 16c Airmail Special Delivery stamp of 1934. Jean Cocteau, the French artist, writer and philosopher designed the Marianne 20 centime definitive of France, 1961. A nun, Sister Frances Randal, designed the stamps for the Papal Visit to Kenya, 1980, and a priest, Father Francis Welch, designed the Sierra Leone centenary series of 1933. Sir Daryl Lindsay designed Australia's 3½d UPU stamp, 1949, Sir Harry Johnston designed the armorial series of British Central Africa, 1895, Sir Leslie Probyn, Governor of Jamaica, designed the 10s stamp of 1920, General Sir James Willcocks, Governor of Bermuda, designed the Tercentenary stamps of 1920, and Sir Sandford Fleming, Chief Engineer, designed Canada's 3d beaver stamp of 1851. Lady Carter, wife of the Governor of Barbados, designed the *Orange Blossom* commemorative of 1906. Born Gertrude Codman Parker of Boston, Massachusetts, she was also the first American lady to design a stamp. Freya Stark, authoress and traveller, designed the pictorial stamps for the Kathiri State of Seiyun, 1954. The Hon Sir George Bellew, Garter King of Arms, designed the British high values (1939-48) and the UPU 1s stamp (1949). Charles P Rang, Editor of *Gibbons Stamp Monthly*,

Stamps designed by King George V (Canada, 1903), Jean Cocteau (France, 1961), General Sir James Willcocks (Bermuda, 1920), Lady Carter (Barbados, 1906) and a prisoner of war, W. E. Jones (Hong Kong, 1946)

Above left, the obverse of the Wyon City Medal of 1837. It was this profile of Queen Victoria which was used on the first and on subsequent stamps produced in her reign. Above right, Henry Courbould, the artist who adapted the 'Wyon' profile and produced a line drawing to guide Charles Heath, below left, who, with his son Frederick, engraved the master die for the world's first adhesive postage stamp, the Penny Black, below right. Printed by Perkins, Bacon and Petch it was issued on 6 May 1840

designed two of Sierra Leone's Royal Visit stamps, 1961.

Military men have found time from soldiering to design stamps. Sergeant Triquérat designed the 10c of New Caledonia – the second French colonial issue – picking out the design on a stone with a pin (1860). Sergeant W F Lait designed the Christmas concessionary stamps of the British Forces in Egypt (1932-5) and Sergeant T A Griffiths the Gibraltar £1 stamp of 1954. Captain H L Thuillier designed India's first stamps, the ½, 1 and 4 annas of 1854, Captain E A Stanton designed the Camel Postman stamps of the Sudan (1898) and more than half a century later, as Colonel Stanton, designed the 50p stamp of 1951. Captain H St C Garrod designed Gibraltar's 1931-3 and 1938-51 pictorials. Captain H Greener designed the 3d stamp of Mafeking, 1900. Lieut-Colonel C Fraser designed the Forces letter seal of Egypt, 1932-3 and Colonel W L Atkinson designed two of the 1950 airmails and the low values of the 1951 series of the Sudan. Lieut-Commander Harry C Luke designed the abortive stamps for Mount Athos (1916) and, as Sir Harry Luke, Western Pacific High Commissioner, designed the Fiji pictorials of 1938. Lieut-Commander Harry Pirie-Gordon designed and printed the Long Island stamps of May 1916. A Japanese prisoner of war, W E Jones, designed the Victory pair of Hong Kong (1946) while in captivity. The design shows a phoenix rising from the ashes of defeat.

The youngest stamp designer is Samantha Brown of Rhoose, South Glamorgan, who was aged 5 when she designed the 11½p Christmas stamp of 1981, showing Santa Claus. This was one of the winning designs in a competition organised by BBC TV's *Blue Peter* programme. Children's drawings and paintings were first used for stamp designs in October 1958, when three were utilised in stamps from Czechoslovakia celebrating the inauguration of the UNESCO Building in Paris.

The youngest stamp designer: Samantha Brown was 5 when she designed the 11½p British Christmas stamp in 1981

The oldest stamp designer was the Rev W Keble-Martin, aged 91 when he designed four flower stamps for Britain in 1967. Runner-up was Professor Max Svabinsky whose career as a stamp designer had run from 1920 till 1962. In 1963 he designed a 1·60 koruna stamp for Czechoslovakia honouring his own 85th birthday.

The longest career as a stamp designer was that of Ferenc Bökrös who made his début in 1919 with the stamps of Bela Kun's Soviet republic in Hungary, and whose swan song was the Anti-fascist Martyrs series of December 1974 – a career spanning 55 years.

The most prolific stamp designer is Gyula Vasarhelyi who has designed about 5000 stamps for

Block of four flower stamps designed by Rev W Keble Martin

When he designed his flower stamps in 1967 for Britain, the Rev W Keble Martin at 91 years of age was the oldest stamp designer

The first woman to design stamps was a Miss Devine who produced the 2d and 8d stamps in the New South Wales centenary series, 1888.

Two husband and wife design teams were Michael and Sylvia Goaman and David Gentleman and Rosalind Dease (since divorced). Both couples have designed stamps together or individually since 1953.

The first designer to have his name on any stamps was Louis Yon whose name appears in the grapes forming the head-dress of Ceres on the Bordeaux lithographed series of 1870. Six years later both J A Sage (designer) and Eugène Mouchon (engraver) had their names prominently inscribed in the margin of the Peace and Commerce definitives of France, while Sr de la Pena had his name on the Benito Juarez definitives of Mexico, 1879.

The first designer to have his name on British stamps was Clive Abbott, whose two stamps marked the inauguration of the Post Office Tower in October 1965.

Coincidence in design has occurred on only one occasion. The city of Alexandria, Virginia had its own 5c stamps, issued in 1846 by postmaster Daniel Bryan. The design was circular, typeset, with the

110 countries since 1962. Exact details of his designs are lacking as his stamps are not always accredited to him in official catalogues. Runners up were Gordon Drummond (1227) and Victor Whiteley (1033). The most prolific lady designer is Jennifer Toombs who has designed 1043 stamps for Commonwealth countries since 1965.

The most prolific American is Bradbury Thompson who has produced 96 designs since 1958. Chuck Ripper has designed 59 stamps since 1980. C R Pickering produced 53 designs between 1947 and 1962.

David Gentleman has produced the most designs for British stamps – 91 since 1962; but John Nicholson has produced the greatest number of designs for any part of the British Isles – 207 designs for the Isle of Man since 1958.

In the USSR Viktor V Zavialov (flourished 1925–73) was responsible for no fewer than 577 designs, while his sons A V and L V Zavialov, individually or together, accounted for a further 118 between 1952 and 1974. All three Zavialovs collaborated on the Russian Navy series of September 1973.

The only other example of a family designing stamps together occurred in 1921 when Frank Cundall had overall responsibility for the Jamaican pictorial series, the 1d and 5s were designed by his daughter and the 3d by his wife, while the frames for all thirteen stamps were drawn by Miss Cundall and Miss Wood.

Souvenir card honouring Max Svabinsky on his 85th birthday

inscription ALEXANDRIA POST OFFICE within a framework of 39 or 40 rosettes and with PAID 5 in the centre. Only a handful of these stamps in buff are known, and two on blue paper. The first example of these stamps was not discovered till 1872.

Incredibly, two years earlier, in 1870, the Russian town of Alexandria in Kherson province issued a 10 kopek stamp typeset in black on pale brown paper. The inscription in Cyrillic signified 'Zemstvo Post Alexandria', with P.Z.M. across the centre and a framework of rosettes. This was almost an exact copy of the American stamp of 1846 but no one knows how the postmaster of an obscure town in Russia could have seen a copy of it, especially since the existence of the American stamp was not known to philatelists at the time!

Plagiarism in design has occurred on many occasions. The British stamps of 1840-80 served as models for the first issues of Mauritius (1847-59) and the profile issues of New South Wales (1851-3), while the frames of the Penny Black were copied in the 'Sydney Views' (1850-1) and the early stamps of Nevis which also plagiarised the frames of the 4d, 6d and 1s British stamps for its corresponding values of 1861-78.

These colonial examples may be regarded as forms of flattery, but other cases are less innocent. The Ceres stamps of France (1849-71) were faithfully

Alexandria, USA and Alexandria, USSR local stamps in almost identical designs

Crete, postage due series, 1901, inspired by Norway's 'Posthorn' design

Spanish postcard of 1870 modelled on a Belgian stamp of 1869

The only instance of double plagiarism: US postage due of 1879 copied by Mexico (1882), New South Wales (1891) and Australia (1902)

copied by the Argentinian state of Corrientes (1876), Newfoundland's 3c Queen Victoria stamp of 1890 was blatantly copied by Uruguay for the Liberty 5 milesimas stamp of 1898. Newfoundland's 10c brigantine stamp of 1887 was faithfully reproduced by a Lübeck local post the following year. The frame of Britain's 2d of 1880 was used on two stamps issued by the Leipzig Courier service in May 1893 and the frame of the ½d vermilion of 1887 was reproduced in an entire series of the Mühlheim-Deutz-Köln service in 1888. The 1900 zemstvo stamps of Sapozhok copied Switzerland's 'Seated Helvetia' design of 1862, while Norway's 'Posthorn and Numeral' design was cribbed by Crete for its postage due series of 1901.

Probably the worst example of plagiarism, however, was the 10 centavo express delivery stamp of the Dominican Republic (1925) which was copied from the US special delivery 10c of 1922. The placing of the inscriptions was ingeniously copied, but it is in the detail of the vignette, showing a special delivery messenger, foot on doorstep, with his motor cycle at the kerb, that every detail was faithfully duplicated. The stamp printed on the Spanish postcard of 1870 is an almost exact replica of the Belgian low value stamps of 1869, with only minor changes in the details and, of course, the inscriptions. Catalan nationalist labels of 1900 used the framework of the contemporary British half-penny stamp. The entire series of local stamps issued by Griazovetz in 1899 copied the most notable contemporary designs – an amusing example of imitation being the sincerest form of flattery. The US postage due stamps of 1879 were plagiarised by Mexico (1882), New South Wales (1891) and on three occasions between 1902 and 1909 by Australia.

The only stamps so far to have been designed by computer were issued by the Netherlands on 7 April 1970 and comprised a set of five summer charity stamps with complex geometric motifs produced entirely by a computer.

Errors in design have been perpetrated since 1852 when the British Guiana 1c and 4c stamps got the colony's motto wrong. The Latin should have signified 'We give and ask in return' but the word PATIMUS was inscribed instead of PETIMUS, and the meaning became 'We suffer in return'. Errors of spelling are the commonest aberration, but errors of grammar, word usage, the wrong subject, inaccuracy in detail, reversed portraits, wrong captions and errors of omission have also been noted. Among the mistakes to be found on stamps are:

Spelling
Colombia, 1877, 20c: REPULICA instead of REPUBLICA – corrected 1889.
New Zealand, 1898, 2½d: LAKE WAKITIPU – corrected to WAKATIPU.
Newfoundland, 1910, 4c: Z in COLONIZATION reversed.
Belgium, 1919, 25 centime: LIÉGE instead of LIÈGE.
Portugal, 1935, 10 and 15 centavos: with or without accent on PORTUGUÉSA.
Panama, 1942, 2c: CARRERO, corrected to CARREO (1948).
Canada, 1946, 17c: special delivery EXPRÊS corrected to EXPRÈS (1947).
North Borneo, 1950, 50c: JESSLETON, corrected to JESSELTON (1952).
Ceylon, 1952, 35c: Tamil inscription – dot omitted over character (corrected 1954).
Pakistan, 1955, 2½ anna: Arabic fraction on left instead of right (corrected 1956).

Three of the five stamps designed by computer and issued by the Netherlands, 1970

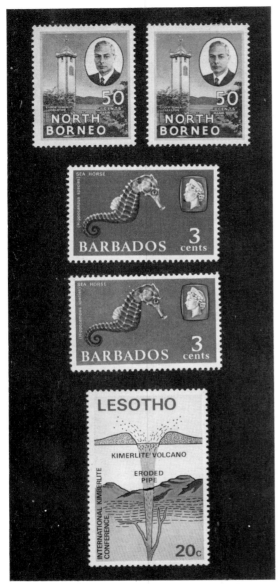

India (ONE AND HALF ANNA); Pakistan (crescent right and wrong way); India (Bodhisattva mirror image)

Spelling errors: North Borneo (JESSLETON and JESSELTON); Barbados (*Hippocanpus* and *Hippocampus*); Lesotho (KIMERLITE and KIMBERLITE on same stamp)

Pakistan, 1961, 1, 2, 5 paisa: SHAKISTAN in Bengali.
Ecuador, 1965, National Anthem set: composer's name spelled MERAN instead of MERA.
Barbados, 1965, 3c: HIPPOCANPUS, corrected to HIPPOCAMPUS (1967).
Gambia, 1966, 10s: MUSAPHUGA instead of MUSOPHAGA.
Portugal, 1969: MUSCHIA for MUSSCHIA.

St Kitts-Nevis, 1970, 15c: HISPANIANUM instead of HISPANIARUM (corrected September 1970).
Oman Imamate, 1970 series: ARAB GOLF instead of GULF.
Cook Islands, 1967, 4c: WALTER LILY instead of WATER LILY (corrected soon afterwards).
Lesotho, 1973, 20c: KIMERLITE instead of KIMBER-LITE. This stamp was unique in having the word twice in the same design – one correct and the other misspelled!
Antigua, 1974, ½c: ENLISH and FOSTAL for ENGLISH and POSTAL.
Grammar
Bulgaria, 1885, 1 stotinki: EDIN STOTINK instead of EDNA STOTINKA; 2s: DVA STOTINKI instead of DVE STOTINKI, both used masculine instead of feminine forms of the numerals.
Greece, 1933, 1dr: DRACHMAI (plural) instead of singular.
India, 1919: 1½a ONE AND HALF ANNA – corrected to 1½as ONE AND A HALF ANNAS (1921).
Usage
Newfoundland, 1910 6c; LORD BACON (should have been SIR FRANCIS BACON or LORD VERULAM).
Greece, 1927, 5 drachma: SIR CODRINGTON – later corrected to SIR EDWARD CODRINGTON.
France, 1937, 90 centime: Descartes' title DISCOURS SUR LA METHODE instead of DE LA METHODE, the form originally used (later corrected).

Errors and corrections from Czechoslovakia (1918), Newfoundland (1928), Jamaica (1921), East Africa (1935), Ceylon (1935) and Guernsey (1967)

Wrong Subject

Newfoundland, 1897, 2c: portrait of Sebastian Cabot substituted for that of his father John Cabot.

Belgium, 1930, airmails: Dornier monoplane with Italian instead of Belgian markings.

Philippines, 1932, 18c: Vernal Falls, Yosemite, California instead of the Pagsanjan Falls as captioned.

Australia, 1947, 2½d: Lieut John Shortland – father portrayed instead of his son.

German Democratic Republic, 1956, 10 pfennige: Robert Schumann with Schubert's *Wanderers Nacht-lied* later corrected.

Italy, 1961, 205 lire rose: Presidential visit to South America – wrong map of Peru. Redrawn and colour changed to avoid confusion.

South Korea, 1951: Italian flag with Cross of Savoy – later corrected to the republican flag now in use.

China (mainland), 1964: Centenary of the First International – St Martin-in-the-Fields (Anglican church) depicted instead of St Martin's Hall, Endell Street where the Communist International met.

Inaccuracies

Newfoundland, 1865, 5c: seal with fore-paws; corrected to flippers, 1880.

Wrong person depicted (Newfoundland, 1897 and Australia, 1947); Columbus using a telescope a century before its invention (St Kitts-Nevis, 1903); wrong dates and title (Nicaragua, 1957)

Brazil, 1890: Southern Cross constellation leaning to right instead of left (corrected 1936).

St Kitts-Nevis, 1903: Columbus using a telescope, more than a century before it was invented.

Czechoslovakia, 1918: Hradcany Castle with sun in background (sunset) – later omitted as a bad omen for the dawn of the new republic.

Jamaica, 1921, 2½d: Union Jack upside down (later corrected).

Falkland Islands, 1929: whale spouting while afloat – whales can only spout when almost totally submerged.

Cook Islands, 1932, ½d: HMS *Endeavour* anchored under full sail.

Ceylon, 1935, 2c (rubber-tapping) and 9c (tea-plucking): many inaccuracies in both designs (corrected 1938).

Pakistan, 1948: crescent pointing right instead of left (corrected 1950-1).

India, 1949: Bodhisattva mirror image (corrected 1950).

Monaco, 1956, Monte Carlo Rally: Scottish piper holding bag in front, drone missing.

Nicaragua, 1957: Scout set 3c, wrong handclasp. 25c and 1 cordoba wrongly captioned 'Lord Robert Baden-Powell' and date of birth given as 1856 instead of 1857.

Reversed Portraits

USA: George Washington's portrait by Stuart is shown facing left (New York, 1845), right (1847), left (1851), right and left (1861), right (1869), left (1902, 1903, 1932), right (1954).

Portugal: Queen Maria II facing right instead of left (1953).

Great Britain: Droeshout portrait of Shakespeare right instead of left (1964).

Great Britain: Nasmyth portrait of Burns facing right instead of left (1966). Both instances of artistic licence were explained at the time as avoiding disrespect to the Queen – yet the Skirving portrait of Burns is facing left, away from the Queen.

Wrong caption

USA, 1898, $1: 'Western Cattle in Storm' is actually John McWhirter's painting of Scottish Highland cattle entitled *The Vanguard*.

Guatemala, 1902, 10c: Lake Atitlan wrongly captioned Amatitlan.

Newfoundland, 1928, 1c: Cape Bauld and Cape Norman captions transposed on map (later corrected).

Panama, 1915, 1c: postage due inscribed Castilla de San Lorenzo, Chagres, actually shows San Geronimo Castle gate, Portobello.

Samoa, 1952, 3d: Malifa Falls, incorrectly captioned Aleisa Falls.

Great Britain, 1968, 4d: Tarr Steps, captioned as Prehistoric (actually Medieval).

Guernsey, 1967, 1d and 1s6d: latitude given as 40°30′N, later corrected to 49°30′N.

Errors of Omission

Kenya, Uganda and Tanganyika, 1935: 5c and 50c sail rope not joined to mast – corrected 1936 (5c) and 1938 (50c). 30c Jinja Road Bridge omitted under railway bridge, corrected 1938.

Fiji, 1938, 2d and 6d: 180° meridian (international date-line) omitted; inserted 1940.

Fiji, 1938, 1½d: outrigger canoe unmanned under sail; canoeist added 1940.

Strangely enough Newfoundland does not hold the record for the greatest number of errors on its stamps. This doubtful honour is held by Afghanistan, which has chalked up at least twenty stamps

Whale spouting on surface (Falkland Islands, 1928); ship anchored under full sail (Cook Islands, 1932)

with *faux pas* in 40 years (1927-67) mainly errors in the spelling of French words by local designers unfamiliar with that language. Only occasionally were the more glaring errors rectified, as, for example, in 1953 when the 125p stamp contrived to be wrong on three counts: Roman numerals XXIII instead of XXII, ANNIVERAIRE and MADECINE instead of ANNIVERSAIRE and MÉDECINE. All three mistakes were subsequently corrected. In 1964 stamps celebrating the 46th anniversary of independence had the erroneous caption 33rd blocked out by an overprint before issue.

PRODUCTION

The most expensive stamps ever produced, relative to their actual value, were the 1d and 2d 'Post Office' stamps of Mauritius, 1847. According to the accounts (preserved in the British Library), J Barnard was paid ten guineas (£10·50) for engraving the die and printing 500 of each denomination. As the total face value amounted to £6·25 the cost of production far outweighed the revenue from sales, let alone the cost of the postal service which these stamps were intended to defray.

The most costly stamp in terms of intrinsic value was the 1200fr denomination in the 1972 series from Guinea, celebrating President Nixon's visit to Peking. The stamp, measuring 46 × 37mm, was printed on 22 carat gold foil with rubies inset. This jewelled stamp was produced by Société Pierre Mariotte of Paris.

The first stamps to be printed for use in another country were the Basle Dove 2½ rappen stamps issued on 1 July 1845. They were produced for the Swiss authorities by the firm of Krebs of Frankfurt-am-Main, Germany. They were also the first stamps printed in multicolour – carmine, black and blue – and combining two processes – embossing and letterpress.

Stamps partially printed in one country, finished in a second, and issued in a third appeared in Ethiopia in March 1942, following the liberation from the Italians. The stamps, portraying the Emperor Haile Selassie, in his coronation robes, were lithographed at the Security Press, Nasik, India, and the values were added by letterpress at the McCorquodale Press, Khartoum in the Sudan. Later, the stamps were produced entirely by lithography at Nasik.

Stamps produced in three countries by three different processes were issued in the Anglo-American zones of Germany in 1945, inscribed AM (Allied Military) POST DEUTSCHLAND. The first series was letterpress printed by the US Bureau of

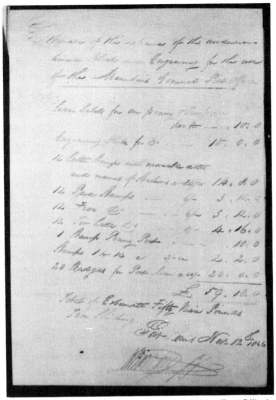

Original estimate for the production of the Mauritius 'Post Office' stamps, 1846

Engraving and Printing in Washington and issued between 19 March and 1 July as the Allies advanced. The second issue was produced by photogravure by Harrison and Sons of High Wycombe, England and released between 28 August and 19 September. Final production was entrusted to Westermann of Brunswick who printed the stamps lithographically between late July 1945 and January 1946. Apart from the different printing processes, the stamps can be distinguished by their shades, perforations and minute details in the spandrel ornaments.

The police have produced stamps on two occasions. In January 1907 the police at Reefton, New Zealand endorsed various stamps of the 1906 series, from ½d to 2s, 'Official' in red ink and marked them 'GREYMOUTH – PAID – 3' inside a circular postmark. The so-called Reefton Provisionals were short-lived and examples, especially in used condition, are very rare.

In February 1908 a shortage of 2½d stamps in the Cayman Islands, required for the postage on mail to Cuba, was met by Inspector J H O'Sullivan of the

Ethiopia, Haile Selassie series, 1942

Canadian 10c of 1935 showing the date of production concealed in the bottom corner of the design

local police, who surcharged four sheets of 4d stamps by hand with the new value.

Stamps have been produced aboard ships on several occasions. Stamps of the French Levant were overprinted aboard a warship in 1915 for use on Rouad island, off the Syrian coast, when it was seized by French marines. In 1928 French stamps were provisionally surcharged aboard the liner *Ile de France* for use on mail flown ashore by catapult aircraft. In 1934 Norwegian stamps were overprinted aboard HMS *Milford* for use during a visit to Bouvet Island in the Antarctic. On both occasions permission was given by the French and Norwegian consuls (in New York and Capetown respectively), giving validity to these issues.

The only instance of stamps wholly produced aboard a ship in wartime occurred in 1916 when stamps for use by a projected Allied expedition to Mount Athos were printed by a photographic process aboard the aircraft carrier HMS *Ark Royal* in the Aegean Sea. The stamps were inscribed in English, Greek and Russian, valued in pence, lepta and kopeks and contained a curious blunder – a picture of the Madonna (everything female is banned by the monks of Mount Athos). The expedition was cancelled but a few of these unique stamps were subsequently used at the British field post office in Salonika.

The first stamps to bear the date of their production were the 'Tigers' of Afghanistan, which bore Moslem dates, changed each year. Since 1935 Canadian stamps have had the date of their production concealed in tiny numerals in the design.

The marginal dating of stamps was first used by

the People's Republic of China in 1952. Previously, from 1950, stamps were given serial numbers which appeared in the lower left-hand margin of the stamp below the design. The first numeral signified the number of the set in the order of issue each year, the second numeral denoted the number of stamps in the set and the third numeral the number of that stamp within the set. The date in the Christian calendar was added in 1952. The serial numbers were abolished in 1967. When they were revived at the end of 1970 they were simplified and merely give the running sequence for each year. Marginal dates were adopted by Italy (1955), and Austria, Hungary and West Germany (1969). Belgium adopted this in 1962 but has since tended to incorporate the date in the design, as have France, Andorra and Monaco since 1963. Britain did not adopt marginal dates till 1987.

Since the beginning of 1973 all Brazilian stamps (other than .definitives and obligatory tax stamps) have featured the last two digits of the year prominently after the country name. Since 1980 American stamps have had the copyright symbol © and the date in the sheet margin.

The longest-established stamp manufacturers are the Spanish Government Printing Works in Madrid, which has produced most Spanish stamps since January 1850. The only exceptions were some Republican issues during the Civil War (printed in Barcelona) and some Nationalist issues (printed at Burgos, Vigo, Vitoria and Zaragoza, and by Enschede of Holland and Orell Füssli of Zürich). The

Germany Allied Military Government issue, 1945; New Zealand, Reefton provisional, Greymouth, 1907

China, (1952) and Brazil (1973) showing methods of dating

Austrian State Printing Works in Vienna has produced all Austrian stamps since June 1850, with the exception of the provisionally overprinted German stamps in 1945 and an Allied occupation issue produced in Washington.

The oldest private stamp company still active is De La Rue of London and Basingstoke, founded in 1819 by a Guernseyman, Thomas De La Rue, for the manufacture of straw hats. In 1824 he began embossed book-binding and began manufacturing playing cards in 1828 and general stationery in 1830. In the 1840s the firm developed a machine for making envelopes and secured their first stamp contract in 1853, for the British draft and receipt stamps. The first postal contract came in July 1855, for 4d stamps, and the first overseas contract was awarded the same year by the East India Company.

This company has had the distinction of printing the only French stamps outside France (1945) and the only American stamps outside the USA (the 1c and 5c Confederate stamps of 1862). In almost 130 years De La Rue have printed stamps and postal stationery for some 200 countries.

The American Bank Note Company of New York was founded on 1 May 1858 as a consortium of seven printing firms including Messrs Rawdon, Wright, Hatch and Edson who had been printing stamps for the USA (since 1845) and Canada (since 1851) and can therefore claim the longest association with stamp production, though not under the same name.

The first private company to print stamps was Perkins, Bacon and Petch of London, who were

The stall of Messrs De La Rue and Co. at the Great Exhibition of 1851, with an envelope-making machine in the foreground

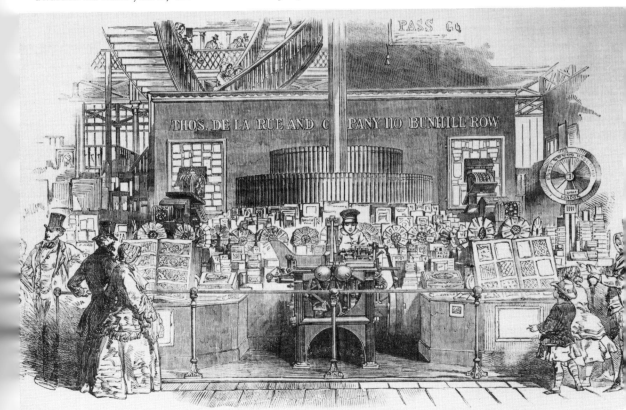

De La Rue stamps for the Confederate States (1861) and France (1945)

awarded the contract to print British stamps in 1840. The company lost its British contract in 1880 and most of its colonial contracts in 1863. It continued to print stamps for a few countries, notably Newfoundland, as late as 1941. In 1968 the security firm of Sprague (who had taken over Perkins, Bacon many years earlier) was awarded several colonial contracts and revived the name of Perkins, Bacon for this operation. From this short-lived revival belong the Olympic set of the Cayman Islands (October 1968), the Development series of Montserrat (July 1969) and the Tourism set of the British Virgin Islands (October 1969).

The only British stamps printed by a foreign company were the 8p definitives of 1979. Demand for this value, then prepaying the first class letter rate, was so high that it was necessary to farm out

part of the contract held by Harrison and Sons to Johan Enschede en Zonen of Haarlem. Individual stamps are hard to distinguish, but corner blocks can easily be identified. Enschede stamps have large cylinder numbers in the margin, while Harrison stamps have small cylinder numbers, and also horizontal colour bars in the bottom margin.

The countries using the fewest printers are Austria and Hungary. Since 1850 all Austrian stamps have been printed at the State Printing Works in Vienna, with the exception of German Hitler Head stamps in 1945 (originally printed in Berlin and provisionally overprinted by Hohler of Vienna or the Steyermuhl Press of Vienna) and a series of June-November 1945 lithographed at the US Bureau of Engraving and Printing, Washington.

With the exception of imperial journal tax stamps of 1867-73, printed in Vienna, all Hungarian stamps since 1871 have been produced by the State Printing Works in Budapest. A floral series of 1950 had the vignettes typographed at the State Printing Works but the frames were intaglio-printed by the National Enterprise Bank Note Company.

Prior to 1894, when the US Bureau of Engraving and Printing took over stamp production, American stamps were produced by private companies, including the American Bank Note Co, the Continental Bank Note Co, the National Bank Note Co and

GB 8p stamps printed by Enschede en Zonen, Haarlem (*left*) and Harrison & Sons of High Wycombe (*right*)

Toppan Carpenter Casilear & Co of Philadelphia. British stamps have been printed by Perkins Bacon (1840-80), De La Rue (1855-1962), Somerset House (1911-34), Harrison and Sons (1911-), Waterlow Brothers & Layton (1913-15), Waterlow and Sons (1934-57), Bradbury Wilkinson (1918-73), Enschede en Zonen (1979), John Waddington (1980-) and the House of Questa (1980-).

The country using the most printers is Colombia which has employed 31 since 1859: J & C Martinez. D Ayala & I Medrano, D Paredes, F Valiente of Barranquilla, J L Arango of Medellin, the National Printing Works, Bogota, the American Bank Note Co, Perkins Bacon, Villaveces of Bogota, Waterlow & Sons, the Salesian College of Pope Leo XIII, Bogota, the Government Printing Works, Berlin, De La Rue, Columbian Bank Note Co, the Institut de Gravure, Paris, Courvoisier of La Chaux de Fonds, Switzerland, the Wright Bank Note Co of Philadelphia, the Manhattan Bank Note Co of New York, R Ronderos of Bogota, Talleres Banco de la Republica, Bogota, the Austrian State Printing Works, Vienna, Enschede en Zonen, Editorial Retina of Bogota, Litografia Colombia, the Japanese State Printing Works, Tokyo, the State Printing Works, Madrid, Carvajal y Cia of Bogota, the Curtis Co, C Valiente M of Bogota, Meisenbach Riffart & Co of Munich and A Garcia-Bergen of Barranquilla.

A close runner-up is Ecuador which has used 30 printers since 1865. As well as seven Ecuadorean printers (including the Military Geographical Institute in Quito which has produced all the stamps since 1974) Ecuador used all the British security printing firms between 1897 and 1957 and five American firms, as well as the government printers of France, Italy, Austria, Germany, Portugal, Spain and Finland and the leading companies in the Netherlands and Switzerland.

Unusual printers of stamps include:
The Diamond Soap Works, Kishangarh: Kishangarh, 1913-16.
The Jail Press, Jaipur: Jaipur, 1911-28.
The Capuchin Fathers, Beirut: Syria (1921-4), Lebanon airmails (1924), Alaouites (1924-9).
Greek Orthodox Convent, Jerusalem: Palestine, 1920.
Salesian College of Pope Leo XIII, Bogota: Colombia airmails (1932).
Several newspapers have printed stamps:
Royal Gazette, Georgetown: British Guiana 1850-1, 1862.
Official Gazette, Georgetown: British Guiana 1856.
Zanzibar Gazette: British East Africa 1895.
Fiji Times, Levuka: Fiji 1870-1.
Polynesian Gazette, Levuka: Fiji 1874.
Times of India: Bundi 1947.

Daily News, St John's, Newfoundland: Hawker airmail, 1919.
Royal Gazette, St John's, Newfoundland: Alcock and Brown airmail, 1919.
Bulawayo Chronicle, Rhodesia: Matabele provisionals, 1896.
Samoanische Zeitung, Samoa: NZ occupation, 1914.
The Star, Auckland: Tonga 1894-5.
De Zoutpansberg Wachter: Pietersburg, 1901.

The earliest stamps of Charkari (1884-97) were printed one at a time from a steel die which the Maharaja kept himself.

Stamps printed from the same plates by several printers were issued by Hong Kong in 1945. The plates were manufactured by De La Rue who printed the initial consignments in 1938-41. Following the destruction of De La Rue's premises in London by an air raid, the plates were farmed out to Bradbury Wilkinson, Harrison and Sons of High Wycombe and Williams & Lea of London who printed the stamps issued in Hong Kong following its liberation from the Japanese in 1945. There are many instances of plates used by one printer being subsequently employed by another. The most notable examples occurred in 1863 when Penrose Julyan, the Crown Agent, ordered Perkins Bacon to hand over their plates to De La Rue. De La Rue also took over the British and colonial contracts from Waterlow and Sons in January 1958 and used their plates for several years.

Errors in production are legion, scarcely any issue escaping without its quota of missing colours or partial imperforation. Below are listed the various things which can go wrong during production:

Colour. The earliest examples of the wrong colour arose when a cliché of one value was inadvertently inserted in a forme of another during letterpress printing. Examples include the unique Swedish 3 skilling-banco yellow (instead of green), 1855 and the Cape of Good Hope 1d and 4d 'Woodblocks' in blue and vermilion instead of vice versa.

Charkari, ½a, 1884

Substituted cliché. Even worse than the above was the case of the Cape Verde 40 reis stamps of 1877 which contained a 40 reis stamp of Mozambique by mistake.

Inversion of part of the design. This usually occurs when two or more colours are used, requiring the paper to pass through the presses at more than one operation. The Western Australia 4d of 1854, however, has the frame inverted – all the more remarkable since the stamp was printed in one colour at a single operation. This error arose during the composition of the transfers used in the lithographic process.

The first examples of stamps with inverted centres were the 4 annas indigo and red of India (1854) and the two-coloured stamps of the US series of 1869. The 1 dinero stamp of Peru (1861) is known with the centre sideways.

Corner figures and inscriptions doubly impressed, one inverted, occur on several values of the Helvetia series of Switzerland, 1862-81.

The wrong vignette occurred on 6d stamps of the Falkland Islands battle jubilee series of 1964. A sheet which first received the black printing, showing HMS *Glasgow*, was inadvertently included with a batch showing HMS *Kent* and subsequently received the framework of the 6d instead of the 2½d value. Only fifteen examples of this error out of a possible 60 have so far been found.

The wrong value has occurred in cases where the denomination was inserted into the plate by means of a movable slug. This happened in 1922 when the 12c stamp of Indochina was discovered with the value 11c. This was corrected by running the sheet through the press with the value amended, the result producing stamps with *two* values, right and wrong.

The wrong frame also occurred in 1922, when sheets of 6a stamps of Lithuania were found to contain eight examples of the frame of the 8a denomination. This produced pairs of 6 and 8a stamps side by side, the 8a stamps being in the wrong colour and wrong portrait in the centre.

Value omitted, like the wrong value, occurs in cases where keyplates were used with movable value slugs. The 50r Don Carlos stamp of Portugal, 1895 and the Indochina postage due 4c of 1922 are good examples. In recent years missing colours in multi-colour stamps have produced a similar effect, notably Great Britain Geographical Congress 4d, 1964 and the Paintings series of 1968.

Vignette omitted, a possibility where two or more colours are involved in the printing process. The earliest and most spectacular example occurred in 1867 when 1s stamps of the Virgin Islands appeared without St Ursula in the centre – the famous 'Missing Virgin' error. Again modern British multi-coloured stamps provide numerous examples, the best-known being the Red Cross 3d (1962) – Queen's portrait omitted; and the Post Office Tower 3d (1965) – Tower omitted.

Provisional overprints and surcharges have produced numerous errors, the commonest form being the double overprint. Almost as common are stamps with the overprint inverted, and rather more elusive are those with double overprint in which one is inverted. Spelling errors in overprints are all too common, but the oddest of these occurred in the independence overprints of Burundi (1962). The stamps were overprinted ROUYAUME DU BURUNDI but examples of the 50 centime and 6.50 franc are known overprinted ROYAUME DU ROYAUME.

Overprints with an error of date occurred in 1929 when Guatemalan stamps were erroneously overprinted 1930, and in 1930 when Finnish airmails were erroneously overprinted 1830.

Genuine errors have been deliberately mass-produced on two occasions, to defeat philatelic speculation. Greece, 1937: After a few examples of the 50 lepta Red Cross stamp were discovered with the overprint inverted, the postal administration prevented philatelic speculation in the errors by ordering a large quantity of the inverts to be printed and put on sale at the main post offices.

When a sheet of the Dag Hammarskjold 4c stamp of 23 October 1962 leaked out with the yellow background inverted, the US Post Office authorised an unlimited printing on 16 November to prevent the error attaining the status of a rarity. The Hammarskjold inverts are actually more plentiful than the normal version. An attempt to repeat this practice, when Canal Zone 4c stamps commemorating the Thatcher Ferry Bridge (12 October 1962) were found with the bridge omitted, failed when the possessor of the sheet of errors obtained an injunction in the US Supreme Court. Consequently this misprint is currently catalogued at £4,250, compared with a mere 15p for the normal version.

Western Australia 4d, 1854 – frame inverted

Burundi, 6.50fr, 1962 'Royaume du Royaume' instead of 'Burundi' (*centre stamp*)

Errors have also been perpetrated clandestinely on two occasions. The map stamps of the Dominican Republic, 1900 may be found with the words DOMINICA and HAITI transposed, with ATLANTICO and MAR CARIBE transposed, and with the 50c stamp inscribed CINCO (five) instead of CINCUENTA (fifty). These errors were deliberately perpetrated by staff of the printers, the Hamilton Bank Note Company of New York, for sale to collectors.

The definitive series of Georgia (1921) showing the medieval heroine, Queen Tamara, may be found with all manner of freak varieties, caused by distortion of the lithographic transfers. It is said that these freaks were created for the purpose of paying in kind the engineer who repaired and maintained the printing presses.

The only instance of an overprint on alternate stamps throughout the sheet occurred in Denmark in September 1938. Alternate 5 øre stamps were overprinted D.F.U. FRIM. UDST. 1938 in red (Danish Philatelic Union Stamp Exhibition). These sheets were not available from post offices, but could only be purchased at the Exhibition, and from a 'ring' of local dealers who offered the stamps at a substantial premium over face value.

PRINTING PROCESSES

Collotype or collotypy, known in America as photogelatin, has only been used in the production of one stamp – the 1 kopek zemstvo stamp issued by

Canal Zone, centre inverted (1906); Greece 50L Red Cross upright and inverted, 1937

Denmark, Philatelic Exhibition overprint, 1938

Poltava, Russia in July 1912. This process, involving a thick glass plate bearing gelatin images of photographs, is used extensively in book illustration and has often been used in the forgery of stamps (simulating both intaglio and lithography), the favourite method used by Jean de Sperati. The only other philatelic application was the souvenir sheet of the London International Stamp Exhibition, 1950, reproducing some of the great classic rarities.

Cyclostyled stamps were first issued by Reuters Telegraph Service in Matabeleland in March 1894. 2s 6d, 5s and 10s stamps were run off on a form of duplicator, the designs being hand drawn on a stencil.

Thomas Alva Edison invented a similar process known as mimeography which could be used with a typewriter. This was used in printing the 7 sen stamp issued at Kume Shima (Ryukyu Islands) on 1 October 1945.

Die-cut stamps are produced from a die which incorporates a cutting edge so that each stamp is individually severed from the surrounding paper at the time the impression is made. The first examples of this were the Scout Post stamps of Czechoslovakia, 1918 (see p. 59). Pairs, strips and other multiples are, of course, impossible. This process was first widely used by Sierra Leone in 1963, rapidly followed by Tonga and Norfolk Island, in conjunction with self-adhesive gum and backing paper.

Die-stamping or embossing is a method of stamping in relief, the raised impression being obtained by placing the paper between male (relief) and female (recess) dies. This process has been widely used for fiscal stamps on cheques and legal documents since the late seventeenth century. Postally, it was first used in 1838 for the stamped letter sheets of Sydney, New South Wales and the 1d and 2d stamped envelopes of Britain from 1841 onwards. It was used till recently for registered envelopes in the British Isles. The Sydney letter sheets were embossed albino (in colourless relief), whereas most examples have the relief colourless against a coloured ground. Adhesive stamps in colourless relief were issued by Sardinia (1853) and Natal (1857), while stamps with coloured backgrounds and embossed relief were first issued by Basle (1845) and Scinde (1852). The British 10d and 1s (1847) and 6d stamps (1854) were embossed at Somerset House. Portugal, Russia, Bavaria, Heligoland, several of the minor German states and the Gambia used embossing extensively in the nineteenth century. In the twentieth century it has been rarely used for adhesives, Iceland (1911-12) and West Germany (1953-5, 1957, 1963-4, 1969 and 1974) being isolated examples. Embossing has occasionally been used for overprints, the Czechoslovak Olympic Congress set of 1925 being a notable example. Coloured embossing was adopted by Britain in 1968 for the Queen's profile. This was printed in gold and then embossed on various commemorative and special issues until 1973.

Engine-turning is a form of ornamentation applied mainly to the background of stamp designs in a bid to defeat forgery. Jacob Perkins (of Perkins, Bacon and Petch – see p. 75), invented the rose engine in 1819 for printing patterns on calico and later adapted it to produce intricate *guilloché* patterns on banknotes. It was first used in producing the Penny Black and Twopence Blue, 1840 and remained a feature of the British low values (½d–2d) till 1880. It was a major characteristic of the colonial stamps printed by Perkins Bacon from 1848 onwards and, to a lesser extent, was used on stamps printed by the American Bank Note Co.

Halftone is a photo-mechanical process in which the tones are represented by varied dots ranging in size and density. Although widely used since the 1890s for newspaper and periodical illustration, it has seldom been applied to stamps. The first stamps using the halftone process appeared in 1908 when Uruguay's independence series had halftone vig-

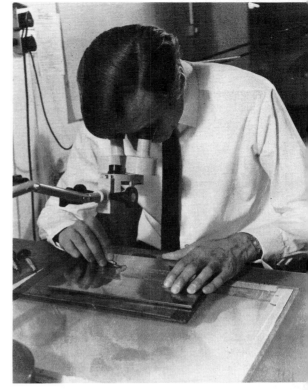

1 The approved design is engraved by hand onto the die made of ³⁄₁₆ inch thick mild steel.

2 Background designs and patterns are added by a machine engraver.

3 Once the steel die has been hardened by treating it chemically at a high temperature, the image can be transferred to a mild steel roll.

4 The image is transferred from the hardened roll on a hand operated transfer press. The roll is rolled back and forth under a pressure of some 5 to 10 tons per square inch and the image can be replicated as many times as necessary on the steel printing plate.

5 The printing plate is shaped, so as to fit the impression and plate cylinders of the printing press.

6 The plate is then hardened, polished and chrome faced for longer wear when printing.

7 The plate, fixed to the plate cylinder of the printing press, is inked and then wiped by a combination of steel blade and soft material or paper, to remove the ink from the surface but leave it in the engraved areas of the plate. The paper is fed between the plate and the impression cylinder under great pressure which forces it into the engraved areas and pulls out the ink from them. The resulting print then stands up in relief and the tactile effect of this when dry is the major feature of intaglio printing, and gives it its unique quality.

nettes, the frames being letterpress printed. The entire stamp was produced by halftone in the 1913 series of Kishangarh. The halftone process has also been used for the Latvian monuments series (1937),

2

3

4

5

6

7

the Orchha definitives (1935) and the Thuringia provincial issue (1945). It has also been widely used in photolithography (q.v.) in more recent years.

Handstruck stamps were common in the more backward countries in the nineteenth century, and include such issues as Afghanistan (1882-90), the Bermuda postmasters' issues – by William Perot at Hamilton and J H Thies at St Georges (1848-61), the Falkland Island 'franks' (1861-77), Bhor (1879), Charkari (1912-22), Faridkot (1879-86), Jammu and Kashmir (1866-77) and Soruth (1864). The stamps of Dhar (1897-1900) and Duttia (1893-1920) were impressed with a control mark prior to issue. The stamps of the New Republic in southern Africa (1886-8) were produced by rubber stamps applied to ready-gummed and perforated paper sent out from Europe. Two different metal handstamps, plus typewriting, were used to produce the 1913 series of Albania. Three different handstamps were used to print the independence anniversary stamps of November 1913. Two different rubber stamps were ordered from Athens for printing stamps of Long Island (Gulf of Smyrna, 1916) but never used, although a few essays are known in red and violet ink. The first handstruck adhesive stamp was a 3c local issued by the Philadelphia Despatch Post in December 1842. The Philadelphia carriers' stamps of 1852-6 were also handstamped, as were several issues of the Confederate States during the American Civil War: Bridgeville (Alabama), Emory (Virginia), Greenwood (Virginia), Grove Hill (Alabama), Hallettsville (Texas), Hamburgh (South Carolina), Hillsboro (North Carolina), Independence (Texas), Lenoir (North Carolina), Marion (Virginia), New Smyrna (Florida), Rutherfordton (North Carolina), Spartanburg (South Carolina) and Unionville (South Carolina).

Intaglio or recess printing is a process using plates in which the lines have been cut in recess. Ink is applied to these recesses and the paper is forced under great pressure into the recesses where it takes up the ink. This produces a tell-tale ridge on the surface of the paper. This process was (and still is) widely used in the manufacture of banknotes and share certificates and was used for British stamps from 1840 till 1880, for the high value stamps from 1913 till 1977, and for occasional commemoratives (1924-5, 1929, 1964, 1966, 1973 and 1980). It is the process used for the majority of US stamps and has also been extensively employed by France, Czechoslovakia and Sweden.

Letterpress, sometimes though inaccurately referred to by collectors as surface-printing or typography, is a process in which the paper is pressed into contact with the inked printing surface of the block,

plate or cylinder, the lines of the image being raised in relief – and thus the opposite process to recess or intaglio printing. The master die would be engraved in wood or metal and then duplicated in electrotyped or stereotyped clichés, assembled in a forme to produce the sheet size. The first stamps produced by this method were the Ceres 20c and 1fr stamps of France (January 1849), followed by Bavaria's *Schwarzer Einser* (November 1849) and the Zürich 2½ rappen (March 1850). This was the process perfected by De La Rue as a cheap alternative to Perkins Bacon intaglio, and was first used for British fiscal stamps in 1853 and postage stamps from 1855 till 1934 and for postage due stamps from 1914 till 1971. It has also been widely used by France (low values, precancelled stamps and postage dues), West Germany (definitives), the German Democratic Republic (1961-71 definitives), Ireland (1922-68) and India (1854-1951).

Lithography takes its name from the Greek words *lithos* (stone) and *graphein* (to write) and is a process perfected by Alois Senefelder about 1795, using polished limestone plates on which designs were laid down from transfers or drawn by hand in grease pencil. Limestone was used in the production of the earliest lithographed stamps, the cantonal stamps of Zürich and Geneva (1843) and the first issue of India (1854), as well as many of the mid-nineteenth century issues of the German states. Later thin metal plates were utilised and this is the method used in photozincography and other modern versions of lithography. Another variant, now widely used in stamp production, involves the transfer of the image from the original plate to a rubber cylinder and thence to the paper. This method, known as offset-lithography, permits the use of poorer quality paper with a rougher surface. Another variant, patented by De La Rue, is Delacryl, used in the production of multicoloured stamps since 1967.

1, 2 From her original photograph, her portrait was incorporated in the stamps design.

3, 4, 5 The design is repeated photographically on film which is then placed in contact with a photosensitive litho plate. When exposed to light and processed chemically the image is etched on the plate. The printing area of the image absorbs ink but repels water whereas the non-printing area absorbs water and repels ink.
On the litho printing machine this plate is wrapped round a cylinder. It is both dampened with water and inked so that a clear inked image is produced and which, as the cylinder rotates, is transferred to a rubber roller in contact with it. The paper passes over the latter and so the image finally appears on the paper.

6, 7 A full colour image is produced usually from four basic colours, blue, red, yellow and black. Each colour is printed separately just as described, each from its own film and plate. Proofs, as the ones in this illustration, are made of these four basic colours and when they are approved, the four colours are printed one on top of the other to give the finished result.

1

On 13 February 1982, a young philatelist, Carol Tully, appeared on the BBC TV programme *Jim'll Fix It* following her visit to the stamp printers Harrison and Sons, High Wycombe, Buckinghamshire. During her visit, Harrisons printed her own stamps for her by offset lithography some of which were subsequently sold in aid of charity.

2

3

4

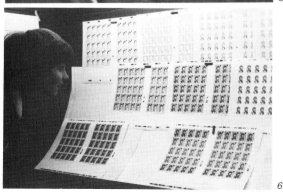

5

6

7

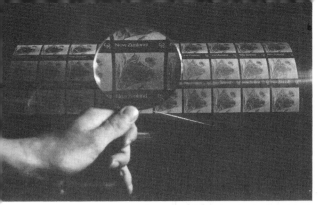

Photogravure printing cylinders, each showing the design etched on the surface as a pattern of recessed dots

Lithography was not used for the printing of British stamps until 1973 when it was combined with letterpress in the Inigo Jones set. Definitive stamps have been lithographed by John Waddington and Questa since 1980.

Photography was first used in the manufacture of stamps in 1900, the 1d and 3d stamps issued at Mafeking under siege being printed by the ferroprussiate process used in reproducing draftsman's technical drawings. A rare error of the 3d was caused by printing the photographic negative in reverse, producing a mirror image. A 3 satang local stamp was printed at Dusitanos, Thailand in 1910, using small sepia photographs which were subsequently perforated and gummed. Black or brown photographs were the basis for the Regensburg semi-official air stamps of 1912 and the Chilean airmail portraying Clodomiro Figueroa in 1919. The Mount Athos stamps printed aboard HMS *Ark Royal* (1916) were also produced photographically.

Photogravure, sometimes known alternatively as heliogravure or rotogravure, was developed in Germany in the 1890s as a process for book and magazine illustration. It was first used for the Bavarian definitive series of 1914, printed by F A Bruckmann of Munich. In this process the design is first photographed to produce a master negative, then duplicated by the 'step and repeat' process to produce the multipositive which is then transferred to the printing cylinder. The design is etched into the surface of the cylinder in a pattern of dots varying in size and density. The process is akin to intaglio, in that the ink lies in the recessed dots. Other pioneers of photogravure for stamp production were Harrison and Sons, whose first stamps by this method were issued by Egypt in 1923, Vaugirard of Paris (responsible for many French colonial issues of the inter-war years) and Courvoisier of La Chaux de Fonds, Switzerland, who pioneered modern multicolour photogravure. Harrisons printed their first colonial photogravure stamps for the Gold Coast (1928) and have printed British definitives by this method since 1934. South Africa pioneered a variant known as grainless photogravure or rotogravure (with plain lines instead of a dotted screen) in 1930. The first two-colour photogravure stamp was the Egyptian £1 stamp issued 5 January 1924. Britain, however, did not issue a two-colour photogravure stamp until September 1960 (Europa pair).

Photolithography or photographic lithography was developed in the late nineteenth century for printing multicoloured labels. It was first used philatelically in 1911 when Oskar Consee of Munich produced the sets commemorating the 90th birthday of Prince Regent Luitpold and the 25th anniversary of his regency. Both line and multicolour halftone photolithography were used in the printing of West Germany's *Mona Lisa* stamp of 1952.

Thermography or thermoplastics is a technique which produces a pattern in raised relief and involves the heating of a resinous compound. Although widely used in commercial trade printing it has seldom been used in stamps. It was first employed, in the form of an overprint, on stamps issued by Sierra Leone in May 1965 in memory of Sir Milton Margai and Sir Winston Churchill. It was combined with lithography to produce raised plastic relief on stamps issued by Turkey, the first being a set of three in May 1966 featuring Turkish faience pottery and subsequently for the Sultan Suleiman set (1966), the International Tourism Year issue (1967) and the Independence medal pair (1968).

Three-dimensional stamps have been attempted on several occasions, using various processes. The first essay in 3-D stamps was made by Italy in

December 1956 when two stamps, celebrating the first anniversary of Italian membership of the United Nations, were lithographed with red and green images slightly out of alignment. When viewed through appropriately coloured spectacles an ana-glyphic or three-dimensional image was created. Laminated prismatic ribbed plastic surfacing was used for stamps issued by Bhutan in October 1967 celebrating space achievements. Subsequently stamps using this technique featured butterflies (1968), fish and birds (1969), animals and the conquest of space (1970), moon vehicles and motor cars (1971) and the Apollo 11 moon landing (1973). Bhutan also experimented with plastic surfacing simulating the rough texture of oil paintings (1970) and plastic-moulded surfaces simulating the relief in sculpture (1971).

Typeset stamps, printed from movable type, predate the introduction of Uniform Penny Postage. The Dundee bookseller and stationer, James Chalmers, produced essays for adhesive stamps, letter-press-printed in movable type, with a border of printers' ornament. Although his son Patrick Chalmers claimed that these stamps were produced in 1834, James Chalmers himself claimed 1838, and used examples bear postmarks of February 1838. Many of the essays submitted in the Treasury Competition of 1839 were typeset, but the first actual stamps to use this method were issued by British Guiana, whose 'Cottonreels' of 1850-1 were typeset by the *Royal Gazette* in a circular format. Later Guianese typeset stamps included the unique 1c black on magenta (1856) and others issued as late as

Typeset stamps of Antioquia, Colombia, Persia and Spremberg (German Democratic Republic)

1882. Among other typeset stamps may be mentioned various issues of the Confederate States (1861), the Hawaiian 'Missionaries' (1851-2) and inter-island issues (1859-65), Reunion (1852), Guadeloupe (1878-84), Mexico (1867), various Colombian states (1883-1902), Guatemala (1902), Venezuela (1902), Uganda (1896), Fiji (1870-1), Bamra (1888-95), Dhar (1897-1900), Duttia (1893-1920), Nawanagar (1877-80) and Soruth (1867-8). Several of the local issues of Germany (1945-6) were typeset, including those of Bad Nauheim, Freudenstadt, Grossräschen, Lauterbach, Lohne, Lütjenburg, Spremberg, Strausberg and Unna. Postage due stamps in typeset designs were issued by Baden (1862), Malta (1925) and St Lucia (1930).

Typewritten stamps were first issued at Mengo in Uganda between March 1895 and November 1896 and were produced by the Rev Ernest Miller on a Barlock machine. They are popularly known as the 'Cowries', from the fact that their values were given in cowrie shells (200 = 1 Indian rupee). A typewritten 3c stamp was issued by Cuthbert Brothers of British Honduras for their Caye Service in September 1895. Tongan stamps were provisionally surcharged HALF-PENNY by typewriter in 1896. A Yost machine was used to overprint stamps of the Transvaal and Orange Free State during the Boer War (July 1900). Typewritten stamps, for a Boer service between Ermelo and Carolina, were also produced during the war. Later typewritten stamps include the Battambang provisionals, Thailand (1902), Albania (1913-15), Long Island (1916), Colombian airmails (1920), Nicaraguan airmails (1929), German emergency issues of Bad Saarow and

Bhutan, laminated prismatic ribbing for the Fishes series, 1969

Typewritten stamps of Uganda (1896), Tonga (1896), Thailand (1902), Long Island (1916) and Eckartsberga (1945)

Eckartsberga (1945) and Pakistan overprints on Indian stamps (1947).

COLOUR

The first two-coloured stamps were issued by Zürich in March 1843 (black and red).

The first three-coloured stamps were issued by Basle in 1845 (red, black and blue).

The first four-coloured stamps were issued by the Soroka zemstvo post of Bessarabia, Russia in 1879 (red, yellow, blue and black).

The first four-coloured stamps, issued by a government postal administration, were the pair issued by El Salvador in March 1897 to commemorate the Federation of the Greater Republic of Central America (blue, rose, gold and green). In June 1911 Bavaria issued two stamps in four-colour combinations for the 25th anniversary of the Regency.

Stamps in more than four-colour combinations were first issued by the USSR in October 1940, a set of seventeen depicting the pavilions at the All-Union Agricultural Fair, in full colour.

The earliest stamps of Kashmir and Afghanistan were all printed in the same colour, regardless of denomination, because they tended to be printed side by side in the same sheet. The 1866-77 issues of Jammu and Kashmir, and the issues for the combined states (1878-94) were mostly printed by handstamping in watercolours on various kinds of paper of local manufacture. The Afghan stamps of 1871-7 were lithographed in sheets made of various denominations. Between 1876 and 1880, moreover, sets were issued in different colours for each of the main towns. Thus those used at Kabul were all in greyish-green, those at Peshawar in slate or grey, those at Tashkurghan in violet and those at Jalalabad in brown.

Conversely, the only country to issue all its stamps in the same colours was Heligoland. All 33 stamps issued between 1867 and 1890, when the island was ceded by Britain to Germany, were printed in green, white and red – the Heligoland national colours, from the green grass, white sand and red cliffs. The only additions were yellow (border of the shield) on the 3 pfennige and 20 pfennige of 1876, and black (value) on the 1 mark and 5 mark stamps of 1879.

The first attempt to standardise the colours of stamps was made in 1850, as part of the German-Austrian Postal Convention. Certain colours were prescribed for certain basic postal tariffs, and to some extent this influenced the colours of the stamps issued by the countries subscribing to the Convention: Austria, Prussia, Baden, Württemberg, the Thurn and Taxis postal system and the north Italian duchies under Austrian influence. Attempts to standardise the colour used for mail passing from one state to another soon broke down. The idea was not revived by the UPU till the Congress at Washington in 1898. Thereafter it was decreed that stamps were to be coloured green (international printed matter), red (postcards) and blue (letters). Thus British stamps prepaying these rates – ½d, 1d and 2½d, were printed in green, red and blue from 1902 till 1951 (by which time inflation had made the colours meaningless), French 5c, 10c and 25c; German 5pf, 10pf and 25pf, Swiss 5c, 10c and 25c; and American 1c, 2c and 5c stamps were among those to conform to the so-called Universal Colours. Britain changed the colours of her low-value stamps in 1951 to conform to the colour-scheme (1½d green, 2½d red and 4d blue) but the project was officially abandoned by the Brussels Congress, and took effect on 1 July 1953.

The colour of a stamp was changed because of a commemorative issue. On 24 January 1893 the US Special Delivery 10c stamp was changed from blue to orange because of confusion with the 1c and 4c double-sized Columbus commemoratives. The blue colour was resumed on 5 January 1894, when the Columbus series was about to be withdrawn.

Metallic ink was first used by Switzerland for the 60c (copper-bronze) and 1fr (bronze-gold), issued in May 1867. The 1fr was printed in gold from 1867 till 1882. The Netherlands 50c stamp was printed in gold ink from October 1867 till November 1871.

The first stamps to be printed entirely in metallic ink were the Greek drachmae values of 1901, the 2dr being in bronze, the 3dr in silver and the 5dr in gold ink. Essays for a British £5 stamp in gold ink were prepared in 1882 but in the end ordinary vermilion ink was used instead. Before the advent of multi-colour photogravure stamps in the 1960s metallic ink was used by El Salvador in March 1897 for the Federation of Greater Republic of Central America commemoratives. It was also used by New South Wales for the 2½d (2s 6d) Consumptives Home charity stamp issued on 28 June 1897. On both occasions gold ink was combined with three and two other colours respectively. Metallic inks were used for the borders of the Persian coronation series (1915) and the South African 2d showing the Rand goldfield (1938), while silver ink was used in the production of the South African stamps celebrating the Royal Silver Wedding (1948).

PAPER

The first stamps were printed on a fine-quality, hand-made rag paper by Stacey Wise of Rush Mills, Hardingstone, near Northampton. The sheets varied considerably in thickness and were issued with a ragged or deckle edge on all four sides. A blueing agent is added to the pulp during manufacture to whiten the paper. It is said that this process was discovered accidentally in 1746 by Mrs Button-shaw, wife of a papermaker, who was preparing to wash linen when she inadvertently dropped her bag

of blueing into a tub of pulp. She kept quiet, hoping that it would not be noticed, but when her husband became ecstatic over the fine white colour of the paper from this batch of pulp she blurted the truth.

The rag paper used for British colonial stamps in the 1930s was specially made for Bradbury Wilkinson who maintained an agent in the Midlands to buy up worn-out linen shirts worn by Irish navvies from the scrap merchants, these being deemed to produce the finest quality of paper.

The thickest paper ever used for stamps, generally issued for postage, was a type of cardboard known as carton, used for the 5 centavos of Argentina (March 1867) and the 5c of Chile (1879–99). In November 1915 10, 15 and 20 kopek stamps were issued by Russia printed on cardboard, with an inscription on the reverse to signify their use in lieu of silver coins. Nevertheless, a few are known to have been used postally.

The thinnest paper used for stamps was a form of tissue known as pelure, used for a very rare printing of New Zealand stamps (1862) and the stamps of the Transvaal (1876).

The unusual kinds of paper used in stamp production include: unfinished Bolshevist and anti-Bolshevist banknotes, the backs of German war maps, cigarette paper and lined paper from school exercise books (Latvia, 1918–19), ruled exercise-book paper (Ecuador, 1872 and Mexico, 1884–7), paper with post office forms printed on one side (Oaxaca, 1915), blue sugar-bag paper (British Guiana, 1856), ribbed paper with corrugations on one side (USA 1c, 1873, Philippines 5 cuartos, 1859), rice paper (El Salvador 1c, 1889), blue French banknote paper (Guernsey, 1942), woodpulp news-print paper (Jersey, 1944), newsprint, cigarette cartons, wood-shavings and toilet paper (Polish POW camp posts, 1941–4).

The only time that the selvedge was pressed into service as postage stamps occurred in the French Post Office in Zanzibar on 20 July 1897. The margins of sheets of stamps and the gutters between the panes were overprinted POSTE FRANCE/ZANZIBAR with values in French and Indian currency, during a shortage of 2½ anna (25 centime) and 5a (50c) stamps.

Other unusual materials used for producing stamps: Goldbeaters' skin was used for the high value stamps of the German Empire, 1886, intended for parcels. This oddly named substance, primarily employed in gold-blocking on book-bindings and illuminated manuscripts, consists of a tough, thin, transparent resin-impregnated paper. The stamps were printed on the collodion surface of the reverse and gum was applied on top of the ink.

The idea was that affixing the stamps to the parcels would effectively destroy them and render them incapable of re-use. These stamps were not sold to the public but were affixed to the parcels by the counter clerks on cash payment of the parcel postage.

Stamps printed on cloth were first issued by Hungary in September 1958 when a miniature sheet containing four triangular floral stamps was printed on waxed cloth to commemorate the International Philatelic Congress in Brussels. Silk rayon was used as the medium for a set of stamps issued by Bhutan in 1969 and depicting prayer banners.

Aluminium foil was used as the basis of a 5 forints air stamp issued by Hungary on 5 October 1955 to celebrate the Light Metal Industries International Congress in Budapest. The Soviet Union produced a 1 rouble stamp on foil on 17 October 1961 to commemorate the space flights of that year. It was re-issued six days later with an overprint to mark the 22nd Communist Party Congress. These stamps had orthodox printing on them, but in June 1963 Tonga

Latvian stamps printed on incomplete banknotes

issued its first circular stamps embossed on metal foil, a gimmick which was subsequently adopted by Sierra Leone, Burundi, Jordan, Sharjah, Umm al Qiwain and Bhutan as well as several countries of the French Community (notably Guinea, Benin, Cameroun, the Central African Empire, Chad, Congo, Gabon, Ivory Coast, Mali, Mauritania, Niger, Togo and Upper Volta). Embossing on metal foil was the speciality of Walsall Security Printers (England) and the French companies of Boccard and Pierre Marrotte. Most of these experiments were short-lived, reaching their zenith about 1969-70.

The record for using the unlikeliest materials is held by Bhutan which issued circular metal foil embossed stamps (1966, 1975), laminated prismatic-ribbed plastic stamps (1967-73), plastic relief surfaced stamps (1968-70), plastic-moulded stamps (1971). As well as silk rayon, for the prayer banner set of 1969, Bhutan issued stamps printed on steel plates, celebrating the 5000th anniversary of the steel industry (1969), while scent-impregnated paper was used for the roses set (1973). The ultimate in stamps, however, was the set of seven released in 1973 in the form of miniature gramophone records which played the national anthem and provided a commentary on the history of the country! This essay in talking stamps has not been repeated anywhere else.

GUM

The gum used on the backs of the Penny Black was composed of potato-starch, wheat-starch and acacia gum. The Post Office called it cement and early stamps bore instructions printed in the sheet margins 'In Wetting the Back be careful not to remove the Cement'. This created a panic that the gum was injurious to health, and led to a Select Committee on Postage Label Stamps being convened in 1852 to enquire into its composition. Charles Dickens wrote an article entitled 'The Great British Gum Secret' in the May 1852 issue of *Household Words*. Some American stamps used British gum, while others used an extract of tapioca.

Green-tinted gum was first used for the British 6d stamp of 1854 so that the operator of the embossing machine could distinguish the right side of the paper for printing while red gum was used in the stamps of Hanover (1850-9). Nevertheless, there are several instances of British stamps printed on the gummed side. By the 1860s an improved dextrine gum was in use, and this continued till 1968 when invisible non-curl PVA (polyvinyl alcohol) gum was substituted. Again there was an outcry at the time, that the alcoholic gum would intoxicate anyone licking it!

China is the only country regularly to issue stamps ungummed, a glue-pot being provided on post office counters for this purpose.

Bhutanese stamps on silk
rayon, steel plate and plastic
simulating painted canvas

The Republican anniversary series of Czecho-slovakia (1923) had the gum applied in a pattern showing the initials of the republic (CSP). Many of the provincial issues of Germany immediately after the Second World War had *Spargummi* (economy gum), applied in blobs to reduce by 50 per cent the amount of gum required to cover the surface. A pattern of wavy lines appeared in the gum of German stamps (1921) and a geometric pattern in the stamps of Germany (1934), Switzerland and Liechtenstein (1936-9).

The first self-adhesive stamps, with peelable backing paper were issued by Sierra Leone on 10 February 1964.

PERFORATION

The earliest stamps were issued imperforate and had to be torn apart or cut with scissors. The printers, Perkins Bacon, actually had a small perforating machine in 1840 if not earlier, and used it to perforate cheque-book counterfoils, but they re-garded the perforation of sheets of stamps as impracticable, owing to the closeness of the stamps and the unevenness of the layout, caused by paper shrinkage after printing. An Irishman named Henry Archer is said to have got the idea of perforating stamps from seeing a perforated metal sunblind while working as a railway clerk. More probably, however, he would have seen perforations on ticket counterfoils. His contribution was to adapt the principles of perforation to something so intricate as a sheet of stamps. He allegedly spent £2,500 on the construction and perfection of stamp perforating machines and received £4,000 from the British government for his patent rights and expenses.

Archer submitted his proposal to the Postmaster General on 1 October 1847 and after consideration by Post Office technicians it was recommended to the Commissioners of Stamps and Taxes for acceptance. Two machines were constructed. The first had two rotary cutters for horizontal and vertical perforations consisting of short cuts. The second had lancet blades piercing the paper with a series of cuts.

Penny stamps from plates 70 and 71 are known with a trial roulette (row of piercing cuts) gauging 11½ (see below). A third machine, tested at the Perkins Bacon factory in December 1848, had a comb perforator gauging 16, fitted with a line of pinheads. Though unsuccessful (because the gum clogged the slots into which the pinheads fitted) it was the prototype for later comb machines. Archer quarrelled with Perkins Bacon who criticised his machine. De La Rue (Perkins Bacon's great rival) said that the machine should not clog if the gum were properly dried.

After further modifications, the machine was transferred to Somerset House in January 1850, approved by the Commissioners of Stamps and Taxes in August 1850, and then considered by a Select Committee who approved its purchase on 21 May 1852. New machines to Archer's specifications were constructed by David Napier & Sons and installed at Somerset House. During 1853 further trials took place using penny stamps from Alphabet II (perforated 16) and Alphabet I (perforated 14). Both are very rare. The trials perf 16 can only be distinguished from the later general issue if they are on actual covers dated before 28 January 1854 when perforated stamps were officially introduced.

The first country to issue perforated stamps for general use was Britain, followed by Sweden (July 1855). The Swedish Post Office also perforated stamps for Norway in November 1856. The first perforated stamps in the USA were produced by Toppan, Carpenter & Co using a treadle machine supplied by Bemrose of Derby, England, in February 1857. The first British colonial stamps to be perforated were those of Canada (by the American Bank Note Co, December 1858), followed by stamps of Natal, despatched by Perkins Bacon in April 1859.

Illustrations showing a perforating cylinder being prepared (left), and in position on the perforating machine for stamp production.

Perforations led to reduction in the size of British stamps on two occasions in four months. From 1840 till 1934 the size of the image on the majority of British stamps was standardised at 0·8875 × 0·7375 in, allowing for a gutter between images of 0·0625 in. This was very restrictive, since the diameter of the perforating pins was 0·035 in. With 2340 pins in a triple comb, considerable accuracy in the setting of the perforator was required to prevent the perforations cutting into the stamp image. In November 1934, after Harrison and Sons had experienced difficulties with the initial consignment of 1d and 1½d stamps (printed in August–September 1934), the image of the definitive stamps was reduced to 0·875 × 0·725 in, giving a wider gutter of 0·075 in. This was further reduced at the beginning of 1935 to an image of 0·8 × 0·7 in, with a gutter of 0·095 in.

Modern multiple comb perforators have 3380 pins, but are gradually being ousted by rotary perforators. Those used at the US Bureau of Engraving and Printing can perforate 7500 sheets of 400 units per hour. The Jumelle presses used in the printing of British stamps have a rotary perforator capable of perforating 30 000 000 stamps an hour.

The perforation gauge was invented by Dr Jacques Amable Legrand of Paris in 1866. This simple device, measuring the number of holes in a line 2 cm long, is universally used to this day, and enables philatelists to describe variations in perforations with great precision. Thus a stamp described as 'perf 14' would have a gauge of 14 holes per 2 cm *0·787 in* on all four sides. Stamps perf 15 × 14 would have a gauge of 15 holes per 2 cm *0·787 in* on the top and bottom, and 14 at the sides.

The largest holes to separate stamps are to be found on American 1 and 2c stamps of the December 1908 issue. These stamps were provided imperforate in sheets of 400 for use in private mailing machines. They were subsequently cut up into coil strips, with

no perforations at top and bottom, and various rudimentary forms of separation vertically. Stamps with so-called Attleboro or Schermack perforations have two elongated rectangular 'slots' or two to five large holes on each side. New Zealand 1d 'Universal' stamps (1905-6) may also be found with two large holes at the sides and imperforate horizontally, from slot-machine coils. The largest holes covering the entire side of a stamp gauge 5½, on Brazilian stamps issued in 1899. There was an unofficial gauge 7 applied by Messrs Susse Frères of Paris for the convenience of their customers in 1861. The same gauge was used on stamps of the Indian state of Bussahir, June 1895. The perforation, which varied irregularly from 7 to 11½, was effected by a sewing machine. Bosnian stamps (1901-7) are known gauging 12½ × 6 or 12½ × 6½.

The highest gauge of perforation was used for the definitive sets printed by De La Rue for the Malay States in 1949-55 – 17½ × 18. In practice any gauge over 15 is impractical, since the closeness of the holes tends to make the stamps come apart too easily for convenient handling in sheets. An unofficial experimental gauge of 18½ is known on Austrian stamps of 1854.

The stamps with the greatest variation in perforation were issued by Poland for use in Upper Silesia, 1922. The 5 mark yellow-brown, for example, has been recorded with no fewer than 64 different gauges and compounds of perforations. Only the most specialised catalogues trouble to distinguish them. Stanley Gibbons dismisses them as 'perf 9 to 14½ and compound'. The stamps of Bosnia and Herzegovina (1879-1900) had fifteen different gauges of perforation. The 1872-91 issue of the Netherlands had twelve gauges of perforation.

Unusual perforations
Queensland, 1867, 1d, 2d, and 6d; perf 12½ square holes × 13 round holes.
Bulgaria, 1884-5, Postage Due 5, 25, 50 stotinki: Lozenge-shaped perforations 5-7½.
Australia, 1943, coil stamps: small holes at sides, getting larger towards the centre.
Mexico, 1939, National Census set: perf 12 × 13, with alternating large and small holes.
Netherlands, 1925-33: interrupted perforations at corners. Danzig, 1932-5 also used this.

Johore, Malaya, 1949, perf 17½×18

Most stamps are perforated in a more or less straight line but the following are exceptions:
Bahamas, 1968, Gold Coin set: kidney shaped with curving perforations.
Gibraltar, 1969, New Constitution: perforated in the outline of the rock of Gibraltar.
Malaysia, 1971, Circular stamps: perforated all round.

The Blitz perforations are those found on British colonial stamps of 1940-1. When De La Rue's London premises were destroyed by German bombing the stamps were handed over to Waterlow and Sons for perforating, the gauge being different from that normally used by De La Rue.

Mixed perforations can be found on the 1901 stamps of New Zealand. Some sheets of this issue were found to be defectively perforated. The original perforations were patched on the back with narrow strips of paper and the stamps then re-perforated using a different gauge.

Other forms of separation are known as rouletting and differ from true perforation primarily in the fact that no paper is actually punched out, merely pierced or cut. Thus Henry Archer's first experiments were with a rouletting device (1848). The terms used to describe the kind of roulette are French, like the word itself (meaning a toothed disc for perforating paper). The normal roulette is in a straight line of short dashes (*percé en lignes*).
Arc roulette (*percé en arc*) – scalloped edge (Brunswick, 1864-5).
Cross roulette (*percé en croix*) – Madeira, 1868.
Oblique roulette (*percé en lignes obliques*) – Tasmania, 1866-7.
Pin roulette (*percé en points*) – Mexico, 1872-4.
Coloured roulette (*percé en lignes de couleur*) – Queensland, 1899; Thurn and Taxis, 1866-7.
Saw-tooth roulette (*percé en scie*) – La Guiara.
Serpentine roulette (*percé en serpentine*) – Finland, 1860.
Serrated roulette (small semi-circular cuts) – Tasmania, 1868-9.
Zigzag roulette (*percé en zigzag*) similar to saw-tooth but shorter cuts with square tops – Greece, 1911-23; Germany, 1923.

Stamps with perforations and rouletting combined include South Africa 'bantam' series (1942), Duttia ¼ anna (*c* 1912), Queensland (1899) and Papua New Guinea, Elema art set (1969), Gibraltar Christmas (1969).

SECURITY DEVICES

The earliest devices to defeat forgery were watermarks, distinguishing marks or patterns visible when the stamp is held up to the light. The first watermark was a small crown, one of which appeared on each Penny Black and Twopence Blue of 1840. All British stamps from 1840 till 1967 bore a watermark. Usually a single watermark appeared on each stamp, the exceptions being stamps of 1856–67 with heraldic emblems in each corner, the halfpenny of 1870 (the word 'halfpenny' spread over three stamps) and the large-sized pound values of 1882–1913 which had two or three anchors or orbs. Multiple watermarks were adopted in 1912 and used for the low-value definitive and commemorative stamps till 1967, and the high-value stamps from 1951 onwards.

Normally watermarks are caused by a slight thinning of the paper, but rare examples of a thickening of the paper are to be found on stamps of Russia (1858) and Tannu Tuva (1926–7). Watermarks combining thicker and thinner areas of paper are found on German stamps (1933–40).

Imitation watermarks, security devices simulating a watermark, include embossed or impressed devices – Switzerland (1862) and Romania (1889–90), printed devices simulating watermarks, on the backs of stamps – New Zealand (1925), Argentina (1922) and El Salvador (1935). A burélé band appears on the back of Queensland stamps (1879, 1896). See also security underprints (below).

Errors in watermarks. The commonest error is reversed, inverted or sideways watermark caused by misplacement of the sheet of paper in the printing press, but many stamps may be found with the watermark deliberately inverted or sideways – from

Denmark Stamp Day, 1964: watermarks, perforations and varieties found on Danish stamps

booklets and coils respectively. Errors caused by mistakes in the composition of the metal bits on the dandy roller over which the paper pulp is spread during manufacture include:

Great Britain – rose instead of thistle in the Emblems watermark (1856–67).

British colonies – missing crown (1950–2) and wrong crown substituted (1957–8).

Errors of watermark caused by using the wrong paper. New South Wales, 2d (watermarked '5'), 1862; 3d (watermarked '6'), 1872.

Transvaal, 1d (1905–9) on anchor-watermarked paper of the Cape of Good Hope, instead of multiple crown CA paper.

British Virgin Islands, 1974, 5c, printed on the Basotho Hat watermarked paper of Lesotho.

A silk thread enmeshed in the paper, analogous to the metal strip in banknotes, has been used as a security device in the stamps of three countries. It was patented by John Dickinson between 1809 and 1839 and first used in Britain for the Mulready

Papua New Guinea, Elema art series, perforated and rouletted

Work in progress on a dandy roll. This roll, covered in wire cloth, carries the watermark design. It rolls freely on top of the wet web of paper as it is being formed on the paper machine and so leaves a repeated watermark in the web

wrappers and envelopes and a trial printing of 1d stamps. Later it was used in the embossed envelopes and the 10d and 1s embossed adhesive stamps printed at Somerset House.

A similar device was used on stamps issued by Bavaria (1849-68) and Switzerland (1854-62).

Burélage as a security underprint was first used on the Danish stamps of 1851-4 and consisted of an intricate network of wavy lines on which the design of the stamps was then superimposed. Burélage also appeared on the stamps of Hanover (1855-6), Wenden (1863-6) and the Dominican Republic (1881), while in the stamps of Alsace and Lorraine (1870-1) it formed the main feature of the design, the network covering the entire face of the stamps. Colourless ink (carbonate of lead) was used to apply a burélé pattern to stamps of Prussia and the North German Confederation and certain early issues of Italy. The purpose of this invisible ink was to show up any attempt to wash off the postmark, since immersion in water rendered the ink visible. Phenolphthalein was used in the printing of a security pattern on Imperial German stamps in the 1890s. This device only came to light when a consignment of stamps, aboard the SS *Eider*, wrecked off the Isle of Wight on 31 January 1892, was salvaged and the network was apparent on the stamps which had been immersed in sea water.

The latter incident may have given the Colonial Office the idea of protecting stamps with a moiré (watered silk effect) pattern. Stamps despatched to British Honduras in 1915, when the U-boat campaign was at its height, were first overprinted in this way to distinguish them from prewar consignments, should they fall into enemy hands. They arrived safely and were issued in the usual manner.

Paper with a greyish-blue surface imprint of overlapping circles and the words WINCHESTER SECURITY PAPER was used in the printing of the Venezuelan series of 1932-8. Plain white paper was substituted in 1939.

Burélage on the first stamp of Denmark (1851) and the 1915 issue of British Honduras

The cleaning and re-use of stamps has been prevented by the United States (1868-71) by embossing a grilled pattern of tiny squares. This broke the fibres on the surface of the paper, enabling the postmark ink to penetrate more thoroughly and rendering cleaning more difficult. Eleven types of grille are classified by philatelists.

Varnish lines were applied diagonally across the surface of Austrian stamps, 1901-7, to hinder cleaning and re-use. Three different widths of bar were applied. Russian stamps of 1909 and 1917 used a lozenge pattern.

Fugitive ink, which ran if any attempt was made to clean the stamp, was patented by De Le Rue and used in the printing of fiscal stamps (from 1853) and postage stamps (from 1855). In the 1880s double fugitive inks (lilac and green) were used as an extra precaution.

Stamps overprinted as a security measure prior to distribution were issued by Mexico from 1856 till 1883. The country was divided into 56 districts, each with its head post office, and the majority with subordinate post offices. To prevent the use of stamps stolen by highway robbers in transit from Mexico City, postmasters were provided with handstamps of the district name which they applied to stamps before issue. In 1864 the system was changed, stamps being overprinted at Mexico City with the consignment invoice number and date, and then handstamped with the district name. Most districts subsequently overprinted the stamps with sub-consignment numbers (sometimes the year as well) before sending them on to their sub offices. In 1868 the system was simplified, stamps being merely overprinted in Mexico City with a serial number identifying the district and with the last two digits of the year. They were then handstamped locally with the district name. The district serials eventually ran from 1 (Zamora) to 61 (Cordoba). In 1878 a new system of numbers was adopted, from 1 (Zamora) to 55 (Colima). As railway communications developed the need for this system evaporated. It came to an end by 1883, although stamps after that date occasionally bore the handstruck district overprint.

France, 50fr airmail, 1936 with burélé pattern as a security underprint

Austria, varnish lines (1901); Mexico, district overprint (1875), East Germany, currency reform overprint (1948)

Stamps were overprinted to prevent looted stocks being used in Ecuador, July 1902, following a fire at the head post office in Guyaquil. American stamps were experimentally overprinted KANS. and NEBR. in May 1929, primarily for use in Kansas and Nebraska, following the theft of stamps there.

The drastic revaluation of the currency used in the Soviet zone of Germany in June 1948 necessitated the provisional overprint of the Allied occupation stamps then in use, to distinguish those of the Anglo-American zones from those of the Soviet zone. The stamps were overprinted with the postal district names and the number of the *Oberpostdirektion*. Over 1900 different handstamps were used in this operation, covering some 1100 postal districts. These stamps were superseded by the Allied definitives overprinted SOWJETISCHE BESATZUNGS ZONE (Soviet Occupation Zone) on 3 July 1948.

Fluorescent security markings were first used by the Cook Islands in October 1968 and consist of tiny coats of arms printed in an overall pattern over the surface of the stamps. These marks are visible to the naked eye, if the stamp is tilted to the light.

Ecuador adopted a similar system in 1969. The Ecuadorean markings are invisible to the naked eye but can be clearly seen with an ultraviolet lamp. Four different inscriptions have been used. Other stamps, without these inscriptions on the front, have light green control marks on the reverse under the gum, in the form of a coat of arms in a double-lined circle inscribed GOBIERNO DEL ECUADOR.

PRINTING MISCELLANY

Stamps derived from other media:
Blue-edged jampot or price labels – St Lucia Steam Navigation Company, 1870.

Lithographed labels, intended as cigarette cards – Compania Colombiana de Navegacion Aerea, 1920.
Coils of tickets – Lundy Island airmails, 1935.
Cigar box tax labels – Ecuador, 1924-40.
Matchbox labels – Isle of Man (strike post), 1971.
Bookbinder's labels – Gonzales, Texas, 1861.

The record for minuscule printing on stamps is held by Cuba which has issued stamps on several occasions with microscopic printing. In January 1961 a set of three stamps was issued portraying the patriot José Marti. The background consisted of the text of Castro's Declaration of Havana, spread across the three denominations. The text was printed in English, French and Spanish, making nine stamps in all. Two stamps were issued in July 1964, marking the eleventh anniversary of the outbreak of the revolution, portraying Raul Gomez Garcia and Fidel Castro. Extracts from their writings were printed in the background. The publication of Castro's Second Declaration of Havana was honoured in December 1964 by a set of two values, each printed in strips of five, with the complete text of the declaration imposed on a map of Latin America – an estimated total of 25 000 words. Offset lithography was used to achieve this.

The first stamps with printing on the back were issued by Greece in 1861. From then until 1880 most stamps had double-lined numerals, indicating the value, printed on the back under the gum. Later examples include:
1867-82: British stamps with names or initials of the Oxford Union Society and four other organisations or firms, as a security measure.
1886-91: Sweden, definitives, with a blue posthorn.
1887: Britain, PEARS SOAP experiment, ½d and 1d.
1893: New Zealand, commercial advertisements.
1895: Portugal, St Anthony's prayer on reverse of stamps for the saint's 700th anniversary.
1901-32: Spain control numbers on definitives and commemoratives. Extended to the Spanish colonies

Colombia: cigarette card converted for use as an airmail stamp, 1920

Complete text of Castro's Second Declaration of Havana on a strip of stamps, 1964

(1902) and Andorra (1926).

1919: Fiume POSTA DI FIUME three times on each stamp.

1920: Fiume, snake and stars emblem of the Arditi.

1925: Hungary Sports set, explanation of 100 per cent premium.

1966: France coil stamps serially numbered each tenth stamp.

1969: Gibraltar, military uniforms set – description printed *over* the gum, disappeared when licked. Later

sets (till 1976) had inscriptions under the gum.

1968-71: Portugal commemoratives.

1971: Mauritius, tourist series.

1972: Portugal definitive series CTT and date in continuous print.

1973: USA, Postal Service Employees set.

1982-6: GB, various definitives with a star or letter D on the back to denote issue in special booklets sold at a discount.

Tibet is the only country whose stamps were entirely hand-made: the paper, the pigments and inks, the hand-carved wooden blocks, struck by hand to make the impressions, and finally the datestamps and obliterators which were individually carved by hand. The stamps were issued imperforate and had to be cut or torn apart by hand. These primitive issues were in use from 1912 till 1959.

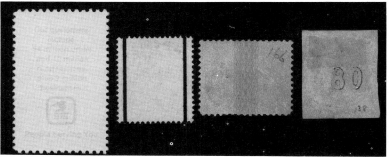

Printing on the back of stamps: from right to left, numerals (Greece, 1861), burélé band (Queensland), graphite lines (GB, 1957) and explanatory inscription (USA, 1973)

Postal stationery and ancillary labels

The first letter-sheets, pre-stamped and sold to the public for postal transmission, originated in the kingdom of Sardinia by decree of 12 August 1818. Sheets were sold at state post offices and tobacconists (a royal monopoly) from 7 November. Known as *Carta Postale Bollata* (stamped postal sheets), they were sold in three denominations with stamps of different shapes – 15c (circular), 25c (oval) and 50c (octagonal). All showed a horn-blowing putto on a galloping horse, hence the philatelists' nickname *Cavallini* (little horsemen). All letter sheets had to be stamped, whether despatched by post or not, and the Cavallini represented a tax. As taxed letters were transmitted by post at no further charge these stamps are regarded as postal rather than fiscal in Italy, but this definition has been challenged by postal historians in other countries.

The first pre-stamped letter sheets intended purely for prepayment of postage were issued by New South Wales in 1838. Sheets bearing the

Sardinia, 50c *Cavallino*, on a letter of 1829

embossed seal of the colony were sold for a penny and prepaid correspondence in the Sydney area. Although unpaid letters were charged twopence, the letter sheets were not popular and are scarce in used condition, even though they remained in use till 1850 when adhesive stamps were introduced.

Other countries put more faith in postal stationery than adhesive stamps. Prepaid stationery was issued by the following countries, the date of their first adhesive stamps being shown in parentheses:
1845 Russia (1858);
1845 Finland (1856)
1846 Thurn and Taxis (1852)
1849 Hanover (1850)
1858 Poland (1860)

Britain's first postal stationery for public use consisted of envelopes and letter sheets printed in black (1d) and blue (2d), bearing a florid pictorial design by William Mulready, RA. The motif, showing Britannia despatching letters to the far flung outposts of Empire, was ridiculed by the public and satirised in verse by Thomas Hood:

> Britannia is sending her messengers forth
> To the east, to the west, to the south, to the north;
> At her feet is a lion wot's taking a nap,
> And a dish-cover rests on her legs and her lap.

Rowland Hill placed more faith in the Mulready stationery than in the adhesive stamps and was surprised when the latter outstripped the former in popularity. The Mulready stationery was withdrawn in 1841 and replaced by plain envelopes and letter sheets bearing embossed stamps.

The first stationery for official correspondence was issued in Britain on 16 January 1840 for the use of members of parliament. Three types were issued, inscribed 'Houses of Parliament', 'House of Lords' and 'House of Commons'. The Parliament and Commons envelopes were printed in black and the Lords envelopes in red. This stationery became necessary on the introduction of Uniform Penny

William Mulready RA, 1786-1863, designer of decorated postal stationery for Rowland Hill in 1840

Postage in 1840, when members of parliament lost the franking privilege which they had enjoyed since the seventeenth century.

The first postal stationery for use by a government department was issued by Britain in 1866 and consisted of stamped letter sheets for the use of the Board of Trade.

The longest–lived postal stationery was the British penny pink envelope, introduced in January 1841. It remained in use, with minor variations in die, until January 1902 – a life of 61 years.

The first newspaper wrapper with impressed stamp was issued by the United States, at the end of 1857. The first British newspaper wrappers were issued in October 1870.

The first postcard was issued by Austria in October 1869. It was invented by Dr Emmanuel Herrmann of the Military Institute of Vienna. The Austrian Post Office was doubtful whether the public would permit such lack of privacy in their correspondence, even though it was half the cost of a letter, and the earliest cards bore an inscription signifying: 'The Post Office undertakes no responsibility for the contents of the communication'. Other countries, including Britain, adopted postcards in 1870.

The first reply cards were issued by Bavaria and the German Empire in 1872. These comprised two cards joined together, one for the message sent originally and the other for a reply from the recipient. Britain adopted reply cards in October 1882 and discontinued them in 1970.

Registered envelopes were pioneered by Britain, the first being issued on 1 January 1878. Adhesive stamps covering the postage had to be affixed to the front of the envelope but a special twopenny registration stamp was embossed on the flap.

Stamped receipts for registered mail were first issued by Finland in 1871 and bore impressed 10 pennia stamps. **Stamped receipts as certificates of posting** were issued by Britain experimentally in 1877-8 (London and Liverpool) and 1881 (Glasgow), but subsequent receipts required adhesive stamps.

The first letter cards were issued by Belgium in 1882. Britain did not issue any for sale to the general public till 11 February 1892. Letter cards stamped to order of private individuals, however, were printed at Somerset House in 1887 – five years before the Post Office issue.

Reply letter cards were pioneered by Newfoundland (1912) and consisted of a letter card with a smaller one inside, for use by the recipient.

The first airmail stationery, consisting of postcards and letter sheets with printed inscriptions and an armorial device, was produced in Paris for carriage by balloon during the siege of 1870-1. These items were privately printed, but received official sanction. Envelopes with an impressed stamp and the inscription POSTE AERIENNE were issued by Belgium in 1913.

2c postcards and 3c envelopes of Newfoundland overprinted in five lines 1ST ATLANTIC AIR POST, MARTINSYDE, RAYNHAM, MORGAN were produced on the initiative of Edwin Cleary, a reporter of the *Daily Express* (London) covering the Trans-Atlantic attempts in 1919 and were never sanctioned by the Newfoundland Post Office, nor flown by the Martinsyde aircraft although examples postmarked by favour are known. Printed envelopes were used on a pioneer airmail flight from Lethbridge to Ottawa on 21 June 1922. Stamped envelopes for airmail were issued by Colombia (Sociedad Colombo-Alemaña des Trasportes Aviacion – SCADTA) in 1921-3 and by Germany from 1923, Mexico from 1927 and Austria from 1929.

The first air letter sheets were issued by Colombia (SCADTA) and Germany in 1923, followed by Mexico in 1930. Lightweight airmail stationery, inscribed 'Air-o-Gram', was devised by R B Jackson and used in Thailand in 1932-3. Again, these sheets had no franking validity and required adhesive stamps to be affixed.

The first stamped air-letter sheets, in the modern form, were designed by Douglas Gumley and issued by Iraq on 15 July 1933. These sheets bore the inscription AIR MAIL LETTER CARD, but were otherwise in the same format as the air letter sheets introduced by Britain in 1941. The first British sheets were for mail sent to prisoners of war and were inscribed in English, French and German. Aerogrammes for general use by the public followed on 18 June 1943. The rate remained at sixpence until 1966.

Privilege envelopes, giving preferential treatment to a charitable organisation, were first issued by Prussia in 1867 for the use of the *Victoria National Invaliden Stiftung*, a charity under the patronage of Crown-Princess Victoria for wounded soldiers after the Austro-Prussian 'Seven Weeks' War. Packets in these envelopes were transmitted for a flat rate of 4 pfennige, regardless of weight or size, and envelopes up to 2 ft *61 cm* in length have been recorded.

The first commemorative postal stationery was issued by the United States in July 1876 and consisted of 3c green or vermilion embossed envelopes celebrating the Philadelphia Centennial Exposition. New South Wales produced commemorative stationery in 1888 for the centenary of the colony and the 50th anniversary of the postal stationery of 1838,

The world's first postcard, Austria, 1869

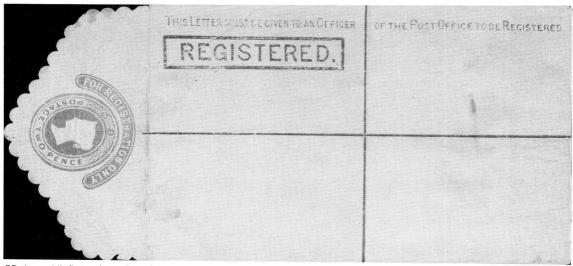

GB, the world's first registered envelope, 1878

and Britain issued commemorative envelopes and postcards in 1890 for the jubilee of Penny Postage, the latter carrying a heavy premium in aid of Post Office widows and orphans. The first commemorative aerogrammes were issued by Britain in 1948 in honour of the Olympic Games, Wembley.

Fieldpost cards and envelopes, for the use of troops on active service, were first issued by the North German Confederation in 1870, for use during the Franco-German War. Stamped envelopes for use by soldiers and seamen were issued by India in 1879.

ANCILLARY LABELS

Adhesive labels for commemorative purposes, but without franking validity, were first issued in Austria (1845) and consisted of medallic impressions in black and gold, portraying the Emperor Ferdinand I and commemorating the national industrial exhibition in Vienna. A rectangular 'stamp' impressed on envelopes was used by officials of the Great Exhibition in London (1851). Most of the early labels were connected with exhibitions. The first label to depart from this convention was issued in France in 1855 as propaganda for the Congrégation du Sacré-Cœur.

The first fund-raising label was issued in Italy in 1860. Inscribed SOCCORSO A GARIBALDI, it portrayed the Italian patriot and raised money for his campaign against Sicily.

The first label commemorating a historic event was issued in England in 1864 to mark the tercentenary of the birth of William Shakespeare and was sold for 1d to raise funds for the Shakespeare memorial. It was also **the first label to be perforated.**

The first Christmas charity seals were issued by Denmark in December 1904 and were devised by Einar Holboell, a Danish postal official. The idea spread to Sweden and Norway and was adopted by the United States in 1907. Since 1929 they have been sold through the South African Post Office, which issued a postage stamp in 1979 to commemorate the 50th anniversary. Einar Holboell was portrayed on a Belgian stamp of 1955 (see page 139).

Labels for officially sealing registered mail were first issued by Colombia in 1865. Known as *Cubiertas* (from the Spanish word meaning 'covered') they depicted the national flag in full colour and were inscribed *sin contenido* or *con contenido* (without or with a declaration of value). Large perforated labels

GB, Shakespeare Penny Memorial label, 1864

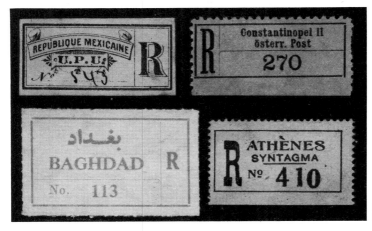

Early registration labels of Mexico, Austrian
PO in Constantinople, Baghdad, and Athens

inscribed REGISTERED were issued by the United States in 1872 for the same purpose. Later labels were issued for officially sealing packets damaged in transit (January 1877) and have since been adopted by other countries.

Registration labels, bearing the serial number of the packet, were first issued in Germany in 1870 and

Sweden in 1874. By the 1880s the system was well established in Europe and the UPU Congress in 1882 decided to standardise the design, a prominent R being featured in a panel at one side. The United States adopted labels of this type in 1883, but France did not issue them till 1900 and Britain till 18 February 1907.

Airmail labels, bearing an inscription denoting transmission by air, were first used on 26 February 1912. Inscribed FLUGPOST (airmail), they were affixed to items flown by Grade between Bork and Brück. They showed a winged envelope at the top and scenery at the sides, with a rectangular space in the centre inscribed *Platz für Freimarke* (place for stamp), the adhesive postage stamp being affixed on top in the space provided.

The words PAR AVION (literally 'by bird') first appeared in a violet rubber-stamped cachet on mail flown by Lieutenant Rouin from Villacoublay to Bordeaux on 15 October 1913. French flights used small labels (etiquettes) thus inscribed from 17 August 1918 onwards. The UPU decreed that airmail labels should be inscribed in French and the language of the issuing country. The first British label was issued in 1920, the same year as Denmark, the Netherlands and Sweden.

Parcel post labels were first issued in the British Isles on 1 August 1883. Distinctive labels were provided for every post office in the United Kingdom. This practice was gradually phased out during the First World War, when blank labels were adopted, but a few of the smaller sub offices were still using named labels as late as 1946.

In connection with the parcel post, pink labels inscribed FRAGILE – WITH CARE were introduced on 8 March 1887 and 'Egg' labels in April 1904.

A selection of airmail labels of the world

Philately

The first stamp collector was John Bourke, Receiver-General of Stamp Duties in Ireland, who in 1774 formed a collection of fiscal stamps in an album which he annotated as *A Collection of the Impressions to be made on every Skin, or piece of Vellum or Parchment or every sheet of Paper, in manner and form as hereinafter expressed.*

The first collector of adhesive postage stamps was Dr John Edward Gray of the British Museum, who purchased a block of Penny Blacks on 1 May 1840 and preserved it as a memento of the introduction of Uniform Penny Postage, a matter in which he had taken a keen interest. Gray added to his collection as other stamps were issued and later published one of the earliest stamp catalogues (1863) and the first set of gummed album titles.

The term philately (*philatélie*) was coined by Georges Herpin of Paris as a more suitable alternative to the original pseudo-scientific word *timbromanie* (stamp madness) used in the 1860s. Herpin eschewed such a derogatory hybrid, and selected a word that was wholly Greek in derivation. Unfortunately, his knowledge of Greek was not as faultless as his logic. He wished to convey a love (*philos*) of things which signified that no (*a*) tax (*telos*) had to be paid, e.g., a stamp denoting prepayment. Strictly speaking, therefore, the word should have been atelophily. Significantly, the Greeks, who presumably know their own language best, ignored the negative element altogether and use the word *philoteleia* (a lover of taxation).

Other pseudo-scientific terms for branches of philately:

Decalcomania – a study of stickers and labels.
Deltiology – a study of (picture) postcards.
Erinnophily – the study of commemorative labels.
Marcophily – the study of postal markings.
Maximaphily – the study of maximum cards (i.e. postcards whose picture coincides with the motif on the stamp and the postmark).

Philometry – the study of metered mail.

The largest collections of stamps were formed by Count Philipp la Rénotière von Ferrary (1848-1917), Thomas Keay Tapling (1856-93) and Frederick Breitfuss (1851-1911). These three collectors were generally acknowledged in the nineteenth century as possessors of the greatest accumulations of stamps, both in terms of size and value. Ferrary bequeathed his collection to the Reichspost Museum in Berlin but it was sequestrated by the French government and sold towards the German war reparations account between 23 July 1921 and 26 November 1925, yielding a total (at the then rates of exchange) of £402 965. The collection formed by Tapling was bequeathed to the British Museum and is on permanent display in the Kings Library. The Breitfuss collection was originally intended for purchase on behalf of the Russian people by Grand-Duke Alexis Michaelovich in 1895 but the deal fell through when the grand-duke died. The bulk of the vast collection was sold to Charles Phillips of Stanley Gibbons Ltd in 1907, Breitfuss retaining a mere 70 albums of Russian stamps, sold after his death.

It would be impossible for any collector today to emulate the prodigious collections of the nineteenth century. The last of the great whole-world collections where those formed by Alfred Caspary (sold for $2 750 000 in 1958), Maurice Burrus (sold by Robson Lowe for £1 272 699 in 1962-5) and Josiah K Lilly (sold in 1968 for over $3 000 000).

The world's greatest philatelists were honoured by Liechtenstein which issued sets of stamps (1968-72) portraying Sir Rowland Hill, Count Ferrary, Maurice Burrus, Carl Lindenberg, Theodore Champion, Emilio Diena, André de Cock and Theodore Steinway.

Heads of state who were philatelists include, in Britain, King George V, whose magnificent collection is preserved at Buckingham Palace. King

Edward VIII, when Prince of Wales, was a keen collector. King George VI, who inherited the royal collection, took some interest in it. The Queen collected stamps as a girl, and also maintains the royal collection, now the largest assemblage of British and Commonwealth stamps in existence. Other collectors included Kings Fuad and Farouk of Egypt, King Carol of Romania, King Alfonso XIII of Spain, Prince Rainier III of Monaco and President Franklin D Roosevelt of the United States. Stamps portraying Roosevelt with his stamp albums have been issued by Monaco, Nicaragua and Samoa.

The first stamp dealer was Jean-Baptiste Moens (1833-1908) in Brussels, 1852, as a side-line to his bookshop in the Galerie Bortier, Marché de la Madeleine. He became one of the outstanding authorities on philately and published handbooks and catalogues. The earliest full-time dealer in Britain was William S Lincoln, who traded in Holborn, London about 1853. Joseph W Palmer, who traded in the Strand in the 1880s, claimed to have been established in 1852, but he was not actually born till 1853.

The firm of Stanley Gibbons, in the Strand, London, has chalked up more records than any other dealers. **The oldest philatelic firm in the world still in existence**, it was founded in 1856 by Edward Stanley Gibbons. Born in the same year as the Penny Black, he traded from his father's chemist shop in Plymouth before setting up a separate stamp business in 1864. The company celebrated its 125th anniversary in 1981 by opening **the largest retail premises in the world** at 399 Strand. The Gibbons catalogues, first published in 1865, are **the oldest in the world in continuous publication**. The Gibbons *Stamps of the World* catalogue (1982 edition) was **the largest single-volume catalogue in the world**, listing over 216 000 stamps with over 47 900 illustrations, had 1890 large pages and weighed 3·25 kg *7·2 lb*. Stanley Gibbons Ltd was **the first philatelic company to go public** (April 1968), its 950 000 5s shares starting at 20s a share and rising within a month to 31s 9d. Gibbons **made the largest single purchase in philatelic history** (1979) paying $10 000 000 for the Marc Haas collection. Gibbons is **the only philatelic company to have had stamps issued in its honour**, a set of eight being released by Ajman in May 1965 to celebrate the centenary of the Gibbons catalogues, two of which were illustrated alongside famous rarities.

The oldest philatelic bureau in the world is the Crown Agents for Overseas Governments, founded in 1833 to act on behalf of thirteen British colonies. The Crown Agents got their first stamp commission in 1848 (Mauritius Britannia design). The first

supply of distinctive paper to the printers was the Crown CC watermarked paper (1863). Paper with the Crown CA watermark was introduced in 1882. The Crown Agents have supervised the production of stamps for 122 Commonwealth countries, associated states and dependencies since 1848, and handled the publicity, marketing and distribution of stamps for a wide range of foreign countries including, at one time or another, Australia, Egypt, Nicaragua, USSR, United Nations, Ethiopia and the Faeroe Islands.

The Crown Agents first supplied stamps direct to the philatelic trade in 1906. The Crown Agents Stamp Bureau, as a separate branch of the Security Printing Division, was established in 1944. Its activities were severely restricted because of wartime regulations. These were relaxed in 1950 and a full world-wide service was inaugurated in 1960.

The first album printed specifically for stamps was published by Lallier of Paris in 1862, in French,

Below, Edward Stanley Gibbons

Right, the original Stanley Gibbons shop at 391 Strand, London

Far right, Stanley Gibbons' premises at 399 Strand, London – the world's largest stamp shop

English and German editions. Edward A Oppen published the first stamp album in England shortly afterwards. The first Gibbons album was the *VR Illustrated Postage Stamp Album*, published at Plymouth in 1870. It pioneered a layout, with a catalogue on the left-hand pages and spaces for the stamps on the right, which has continued to this day in the 'one-country' albums.

Stamp hinges or mounts were invented in 1869. The 1 January 1869 issue of *The Stamp Collector's Magazine* gave as a useful tip to collectors (who had hitherto glued their stamps to the album page): 'cut up the margin of a sheet of stamps into little strips' and gave a diagram of how the hinges should be folded.

The first stamp catalogue was auto-lithographed by Oscar Berger-Levrault of Strasbourg and circulated privately in 1861. This slim volume, entitled simply *Timbres-Poste*, did not give valuations.

The first catalogue commercially published was compiled by Alfred Potiquet and published jointly by Edouard de Laplante and Eugène Lacroix in December 1861. The first British catalogue (also unpriced) was compiled by F W Booty and entitled *Aids to Stamp Collectors* (April 1862), closely followed

by the catalogues of W Mount Brown (1862-4) and Dr John Gray (1862-75).

The first priced catalogue was published by the German dealers, Messrs Zschiesche & Köder of Leipzig (July 1863), originally serialised in their house journal. The first priced catalogue as a separate work was published by Arthur Maury of Paris later the same year. The first British priced catalogue was published by Stanley Gibbons in November 1865.

The first one-country catalogue was H L'Estrange Ewen's Great Britain catalogue, published in 1893.

The first subject catalogue was devoted to revenue stamps and was published by F Trifet of Boston, Mass in 1879.

The first airmail catalogue was published by Théodore Champion of Paris in 1921: *Catalogue Historique et Descriptif des Timbres de la Poste Aérienne*.

The oldest catalogue in continuous publication has been produced by Stanley Gibbons since 1865. The runner-up is the Scott catalogue, which evolved out of J Walter Scott's monthly price lists (1867) and was first published in book form in 1868.

The largest catalogue is the German *Michel Cata-*

Above and left, views of the new Stanley Gibbons shop officially opened in November 1981

Right, the Stanley Gibbons catalogue published in December 1878

logue, now published in 8 volumes totalling 9500 pages.

The first philatelic periodical was the *Monthly Intelligencer* which included a section for stamp collectors and was first published in September 1862. *The Monthly Advertiser*, launched 15 December 1862, was the first exclusive to philatelists. It ceased publication in June 1864. *The Stamp Collector's Magazine*, first published in February 1863, lasted 12 years.

The first English newspaper to run a philatelic column was the *Daily Telegraph*, whose weekly feature was written by Fred J Melville from 1910 till his death in 1940.

The first club catering to stamp collectors was the Omnibus Club of New York, founded in 1856, which also dealt with coins, medals, crests, seals and autographs.

The first club exclusively for stamp collectors was founded by Georges Herpin in Paris in 1865, but only flourished for a few months. More successful was the Excelsior Stamp Association, formed in St John, New Brunswick, Canada in 1866. About the same time informal meetings of collectors were held at the Rectory, All Hallows Staining, on Saturday afternoons under the chairmanship of the Rev F J Stainforth.

The oldest society still in existence is the Royal Philatelic Society of London, founded in 1869.

The world's first stamp auction took place at the Hôtel Drouot in Paris on 29 December 1865 and consisted of the stock of the deceased dealer, J W Elb. The sale realised 800 francs, the best prices being paid by M Riester for Egyptian essays and proofs. The second sale – first in America – took place in the Clinton Hall Book Sale Rooms and Art Galleries, New York in May 1870. The sale,

organised by J Walter Scott and conducted by Leavitt, Strebeigh & Co, realised $500.

The largest stamp auction ever staged was held by Peter Rapp at the Hotel International in Zürich on 7-15 November 1980. Some 11 300 lots were offered in 21 sessions and all were sold, with bidding continuing till 10 pm each evening. More than 86 000 bids were received. The pre-sale estimate of £2 683 000 was surpassed by the actual total – a staggering £8 287 000.

A sale by David Feldman in Zürich on 18-26 September 1981 contained over 14 000 lots but the total realised was much lower – a mere £5 million.

The highest price paid at auction for a single item was $1 million, paid at a Feldman sale in Geneva in May 1981, for the only known example of the Alexandria *Blue Boy* on cover. The vendor had purchased it at a Feldman sale for £82 000 in 1975.

The highest price paid at a British auction was £105 000 for a block of 39 of Norway's first stamp, the 4 skilling blue of 1855 (estimate £50 000). This item was auctioned by Phillips of London in May 1981. The previous British record was £75 000, at a Robson Lowe sale in March 1970, for a pair of British Guiana 2c Cottonreels.

The largest sale devoted to a single series comprised the Rhodesia 'Doubleheads' (1910-13) formed by Robert M Gibbs, sold at Sotheby's on 23-4 October 1987 for £725 000.

The first exhibition to include stamps was the Exhibition of Arts and Crafts, held in Brussels in 1852.

The first exhibition devoted exclusively to stamps was held in Dresden in 1870.

The first international philatelic exhibition was held at Frankfurt am Main in 1887 and coincided with the tenth anniversary of the local philatelic society. The Frankfurt Circular Post (a local service) issued a 1 pfennig stamp in five different colours to mark the event, and five labels portraying Crown Prince Frederick William were also produced.

The first international exhibition in Britain was staged at the Portman Rooms, Baker Street, London as part of the celebrations marking the Jubilee of Penny Postage, 1890. The only souvenir of the occasion consisted of Mauritius Britannia remainders overprinted L.P.E. 1890 (London Philatelic Exhibition).

POSTAL MUSEUMS

The earliest nucleus of a postal museum was a small collection of stamps and postal stationery formed by Dr William Vaux of the British Museum, about 1865. In 1871 the Ipswich stamp dealer, Whitfield King, offered the Museum a collection containing over 10 000 stamps, but no money was available for its purchase. Nothing was done with the Vaux collection till 1891 when it was added to the Tapling collection, bequeathed to the Museum that year. Portions of the Tapling bequest were first exhibited in 1893, but the whole collection was not put on display till 1904.

The first postal museum, housed separately from other exhibits, was the Reichspost Museum, Berlin, founded by Heinrich von Stephan in 1872. The Museum was partially destroyed by Allied bombardment in the closing stages of the Second World War and looted by the Red Army in May 1945.

The largest museum collections in the world are held by the Smithsonian Institution, Washington, DC and the British Library, London. Both claim to be the largest but as neither has produced exact figures of the astronomical number of stamps in their care the controversy continues. Undoubtedly, however, the British Library collection is the more important, in view of the scope and value of the rarities it contains.

If all the institutional collections in London were brought together, however, it would be indisputably the largest in the world. In addition to the British Library, vast collections are housed in the National Postal Museum (maintained by the Post Office), Bruce Castle Museum (Borough of Harringey), the Science Museum, the Victoria and Albert Museum (Cole papers relating to the 1839–40 Treasury Competition) and the Imperial War Museum. The Royal Collection at Buckingham Palace, the collections of the Royal Philatelic Society and the National

The world's oldest stamp catalogue in continuous publication, and the latest *Elizabethan* catalogue, honoured by Ajman, 1965

Philatelic Society and the incomparable reference collection of Stanley Gibbons Ltd are also housed in London.

STAMPS IN LITERATURE AND THE ARTS

The first fictional reference to stamps was a short story entitled 'My Nephew's Collection', published in *All the Year Round*, 19 July 1862. Novels about stamps were *Antigua Penny Puce* by Robert Graves (1936) and *Solomon's Seal* by Hammond Innes (1980). Technical minutiae of stamps feature largely in Anthony Trollope's novel *John Caldigate* (1879), while an insight into the psychology of stamp-collecting is given by Nicholas Monsarrat in *The Tribe that Lost its Head*. Other novels with a philatelic theme include *The Wrecker* (R L Stevenson and Lloyd Osborne), *The Robe of Lucifer* (F M White), *The Spider's Web* by Agatha Christie and *The Bearer Plot* by Owen Sela (1972). French novels about stamps or postal services include *Le Roi du Timbre-poste* by G de Beauregard and H de Gorsse (Paris, 1898), later serialised as *The Stamp King* in Gibbons Weekly Journal; *Le Facteur des Postes* by D Delvin (Lessines, 1921); *Ces Dames de P.T.T.* by Jacques des Roches (Paris, 1930); *La Poste aux Chevaux* by Henri de Lacretelle (Paris, 1860); *Histoire d'un timbre-poste* by Marie Laubet (Paris, undated); *Monsieur Maubenoit* by Frédéric Lefevre (Paris, 1941); *Le Timbre-poste de Sabine* by Bénédict Quincay (Paris, 1912); and *La Directrice de Poste* by Marie-Ange de Tréverdy (Tours, 1894). Philately has even invaded the realms of science fiction, in *La Philatélie Interplanétaire* by J Suizalley (Méricourt, 1904).

Stamps have been the subject of poetry since the street-ballads of Paris, 1653 extolled the Petite Poste of Renouard de Villayer. Nearer the present time (1842) the first poetic reference to stamp collecting was published by Colonel Sibthorpe in *Punch*:

When was a folly so pestilent hit upon,
As folks running mad to collect every spit upon
Post-office stamp that's been soil'd and been writ upon?
Oh for Swift! such a subject his spleen to emit upon.

Thomas Hood's epic extravaganza, *Miss Kilmansegg and her Precious Leg* contains a satirical description of the Mulready pictorial envelope of 1840.

The earliest full-length poem on the postal service was composed by M de Cubières-Plamezeaux and entitled *Chamousset ou La Poste aux Lettres*, a poem in four cantos, published in Paris, 1816. Volumes of philatelic poetry include *Les Vieux Timbres* by R P Delaporte (Paris, 1891), *Philatélie* by Thomas Braun (Paris, 1910) and *Philatélie 47* by Jacques Broussier (Paris, 1947). Other poems include *The Overland Mail* by Rudyard Kipling, *The Pony Rider* by Driggs and *The Postman* by Sheard.

Philately has been the subject of two stage plays (other than dramatic adaptations of novels listed above). The first was a situation comedy entitled *La Famille Benoiton*, staged in Paris, 1864. One of the principal characters is a precocious 7-year-old called Fanfan who speculates in Confederate stamps in the open-air Bourse. Fred J Melville wrote *The Lady Forger* acted by the Junior Philatelic Society about 1908.

Philately has also featured prominently in motion pictures. The first photoplay dealing with the postal services was called *The Mailman* and was released by the Film Booking Office, New York on 14 December 1923. Rare stamps were central to the plots of *Barbados Lady*, starring Tom Conway, *Charade*, starring Cary Grant and *The Saint in Palm Springs* starring George Sanders.

Postal services are referred to in popular music, the best-known example being the Elvis Presley hit of 1962 *Return to Sender*. Late-Victorian music provides numerous examples, of which *Postman's Knock* and the *Stamp Gallop* were the favourites. The sheet music of the time was suitably embellished with philatelic motifs. Other songs include *Ich bin die Christel von der Post* from the operetta *Der Vögelhändler* by Carl Zeller (1891) and *The Yellow Mailcoach* by Dutch composer Jos Cléber, a hit for Caterina Valente in the 1960s.

INDEX